T0326550

Risk-Adjusted Performance and Bank Governance Structures

Corporate Finance and Governance
Herausgegeben von Dirk Schiereck

Band 12

Christoph Böhm

Risk-Adjusted Performance and Bank Governance Structures

Bibliographic Information published by the Deutsche Nationalbibliothek
The Deutsche Nationalbibliothek lists this publication in the Deutsche Nationalbibliografie; detailed bibliographic data is available in the internet at http://dnb.d-nb.de.

Zugl.: Darmstadt, Techn. Univ., Diss., 2012

Cover Design:
Olaf Glöckler, Atelier Platen, Friedberg

D 17
ISSN 1869-537X
ISBN 978-3-631-63916-0
© Peter Lang GmbH
Internationaler Verlag der Wissenschaften
Frankfurt am Main 2013
All rights reserved.
PL Academic Research is an imprint of Peter Lang GmbH

www.peterlang.de

Acknowledgements

Completing a dissertation is the result of a long process, starting with idea generation and data collection, followed by data analysis and assessment, and finally putting all the threads together in a compelling thesis. Reaching and completing the final stage of such a process is hardly feasible without the support of others.

I received considerable support throughout the dissertation process and I would like to express my sincere thanks. Firstly, I owe a special thanks to my supervisor, Prof. Dr. Dirk Schiereck. His ongoing guidance, questions, and suggestions provided invaluable input for this work.

In addition, I would like to express my gratitude to all the friends who supported me in various areas such as discussing the content and methodology as well as proofreading the dissertation. In particular, I would like to thank Florian Wieser for many, sometimes seemingly endless, discussions with valuable insights that significantly contributed to the quality of this work.

Finally, I thank my family for supporting me during this time. Special thanks go to my father for his insightful comments on local and regional politics based upon his practical experiences, especially at the very beginning of my research project.

Christoph Böhm

Foreword

In the second quarter of 2012, the continuing impact of the financial crisis on major German savings banks is still evident. Besides the operational clean up in banking institutions initiated by bank supervisors, an intense discussion on the quality of controlling bodies within banks has begun; furthermore, the influence of political decision makers on supervisory boards of savings banks is highly debated. Political decision makers get specific incentives for taking over supervisory board mandates at savings banks. While mayors typically have to pass on almost their entire income from general supervisory board mandates to the public authorities they work for, they are allowed to retain the income from supervisory board mandates at savings banks. This regulation indicates the importance accorded by the personnel laws to the duties of supervisory board members in savings banks.

Banking supervision authorities make considerable efforts to evaluate the professional competence of the members of supervisory bodies in banks and savings banks. This suggests a relationship between the supervisory quality and performance in the German financial industry. But does this first impression reflect the reality of German savings banks? The literature on the success of corporate governance and on the quality of supervisory board members in the German banking industry is still inadequate. Additionally, research on the impact of supervisory quality on savings and cooperative banks is even more limited, and the results of international studies on listed banks cannot simply be applied to German savings banks.

The present thesis has addressed this significant research question in detail, with the primary aim of explaining the influence of supervisory board composition on the risk behaviour and performance of German savings banks, based on the accounting data and specific indicators calculated by the German Bundesbank. The thesis also offers policy recommendations for supervisory practices. Furthermore, these findings are useful for economic policy makers to understand and assess corporate governance in the German banking industry, particularly public sector financial institutions, and the influence of politics on the banking industry.

Mr. Böhm has explored his thesis topic extensively, and he fully achieves his objectives. The highly interesting findings and his effective writing will certainly hold the readers' interest.

Professor Dr. Dirk Schiereck

Table of Contents

List of Tables XI

List of Abbreviations XIII

List of Symbols XV

I   Main Introduction 1

II   The Evident Banking Expertise of Supervisory Board Members of
      German Cooperative and Savings Banks 7

    II.1   Introduction 7

    II.2   German Banking Sector and Legal Background 11

    II.3   Methodology 14

    II.4   Data 18

    II.5   Empirical Results 19

    II.6   Conclusion 24

    II.7   Appendix 27

III   Financial Expertise in Supervisory Boards, Bank Performance and
      Risk-Taking: Evidence from German Savings Banks 47

    III.1   Introduction 47

    III.2   Related Literature 50

    III.3   Data and Methodology 53

        III.3.1   Sample and Data 53

        III.3.2   Hypotheses and Model 54

        III.3.3   Financial Expertise 55

        III.3.4   Measurement of Performance and Risk 56

        III.3.5   Control Variables 57

    III.4   Results 58

        III.4.1   Summary Statistics 58

        III.4.2   Regression Results 62

        III.4.3   Robustness Checks 64

    III.5   Conclusion 65

    III.6   Appendix 68

IV   Financial Expertise of Supervisory Board Members,
      Overconfidence, and Bank Risk-Taking 85

    IV.1   Introduction 85

    IV.2   Related Literature 88

    IV.3   Data and Methodology 90

        IV.3.1   Sample and Data 90

        IV.3.2   Hypotheses and Model 92

        IV.3.3   Financial Expertise 93

IV.3.4   Measurement of Risk and Performance 94
IV.3.5   Control Variables 94
IV.4   Results 96
IV.4.1   Summary Statistics 96
IV.4.2   Regression Results 101
IV.4.3   Robustness Checks 106
IV.5   Conclusion 107
IV.6   Appendix 109

V   Bank Performance and Risk: Contest of the Risk Advocate
Hypothesis 133
V.1   Introduction 133
V.2   Related Literature 137
V.3   Data and Methodology 139
V.3.1   Sample and Data 139
V.3.2   Ownership Concentration 140
V.3.3   Risk-Adjusted Performance and Risk 140
V.3.4   Control Variables 141
V.3.5   Model 143
V.4   Results 143
V.4.1   Summary Statistics 143
V.4.2   Regression Results 147
V.4.3   Regulation, Bank Size, and Ownership 152
V.5   Conclusion 154
V.6   Appendix 156

VI   Main Conclusion 181
References 185

List of Tables

Table II.1:   Classification of occupations 15

Table II.2:   Assignment of financial expertise 17

Table II.3:   Supervisory board composition (mean values 2004-2009). 20

Table II.4:   Financial expertise (mean values 2004-2009). 22

Table II.5:   Comparison of mean values (mean values 2004-2009) 23

Table II.6:   Financial expertise clustered by bank and board size (largest banks in bank and board size in Cluster 1, smallest banks in Cluster 4). 24

Table II.7:   Distribution of banks across expertise clusters (based on mean values 2004-2009). 24

Table III.1:   Professional backgrounds with assumed financial expertise 55

Table III.2:   Definition of control variables and sources. 58

Table III.3:   Supervisory board composition, Top 200 savings banks. 59

Table III.4:   Summary statistics, Top 200 savings banks. 60

Table III.5:   Bank level variables, clustered by financial expertise, Top 200 savings banks. 61

Table III.6:   Pairwise test of the significance between expertise clusters, Top 200 savings banks. 61

Table III.7:   Random-effect regressions with dependent variables RORWA and ROE, Top 200 savings banks. 63

Table III.8:   Random-effect regressions with dependent variables z-score and NPL ratio, Top 200 savings banks. 64

Table IV.1:   Professional backgrounds with assumed financial expertise 93

Table IV.2:   Definition of control variables and sources. 95

Table IV.3:   Supervisory board composition, Top 200. 96

Table IV.4:   Summary statistics, Top 200. 98

Table IV.5:   Summary statistics, clustered by financial expertise, Top 200. 100

Table IV.6:   Pairwise test of significance between expertise clusters, Top 200. 100

Table IV.7:   Random-effect regressions with dependent variables z-score and NPL ratio, Top 200. 103

Table IV.8:   Coefficient comparison, random-effect regressions with dependent variables z-score and NPL ratio, Top 200. 104

Table IV.9:   Random-effect regressions with dependent variables RORWA and ROE, Top 200. 105

Table IV.10:   Coefficient comparison, random-effect regressions with
               dependent variables RORWA and ROE, Top 200. 106
Table V.1:   Definition of control variables and sources. 142
Table V.2:   Summary statistics. 144
Table V.3:   Development over time from 2004-2008 (mean values). 145
Table V.4:   Banks clustered by size. 146
Table V.5:   Banks clustered by regulation. 147
Table V.6:   Random-effect and fixed-effect regressions with dependent
               variable RORWA. 149
Table V.7:   Random-effect and fixed-effect regressions with dependent
               variable ROA. 150
Table V.8:   Random-effect and fixed-effect regressions with dependent
               variable beta. 151
Table V.9:   Random-effect and fixed-effect regressions with dependent
               variable z-score. 152

List of Abbreviations

AktG	Aktiengesetz
AO	Abgabenordnung
BaFin	Bundesanstalt für Finanzdienstleistungsaufsicht
Bn	Billion
CAR	Capital Assets Ratio
CEO	Chief Executive Officer
Cf.	Compare
CIR	Cost-Income Ratio
Coeff.	Coefficient
Df	Degrees of freedom
E.g.	For example (exempli gratia)
EAEG	Einlagensicherungs- und Anlegerentschädigungsgesetz
EUR	Euro
FE	Fixed-Effect Regression
GDP	Gross Domestic Product
GenG	Genossenschaftsgesetz
GwG	Geldwäschegesetz
HASPA	Hamburger Sparkasse
HGB	Handelsgesetzbuch
KWG	Kreditwesengesetz
Ln	Logarithm
Market Cap	Market Capitalization
MFI	Monetary Financial Institution
No	Number
Non-MFI	Non-Monetary Financial Institution
NPL	Non-Performing Loan
Prob.	Probability
RE	Random-Effect Regression
ROA	Return on Assets
ROE	Return on Equity
RORWA	Return on risk-weighted Assets
R-sq	R squared
SOX	Sarbanes-Oxley Act
Std. dev.	Standard deviation
SE	Standard error
SpG	Sparkassengesetz
t	Test statistic

USD	US-Dollar
Vol.	Volume
Vs.	Versus
WpHG	Wertpapierhandelsgesetz

List of Symbols

α	Regression intercept Alpha
β	Regression coefficient Beta
γ	Regression coefficient Gamma
δ	Regression coefficient Delta
ε	Error term of the regression
θ	Regression coefficient Theta
Σ	Sum
σ	Standard deviation
τ	Regression coefficient Tau
$\S$	Paragraph
$\%$	Percent
B	Bank level variables
$CR\ 3$	Concentration ratio 3
C	Country level variables
c	Subscript denoting cooperative banks
DV	Dependent variable
FE	Financial expertise
H_0	Null hypothesis
i	Subscript denoting individual banks
j	Subscript denoting individual shareholders
M	Macroeconomic variables
OC	Ownership concentration
OS	Ownership share
S	Sector level variables
s	Subscript denoting savings banks
SD	Savings banks dummy variable
t	Subscript denoting time (year)
v	Subscript denoting variable
z	constant for time fixed effects

I   Main Introduction

Banks' Janus-headed importance for economic prosperity and growth is one of the reasons corporate governance of banks has been in debate for long and has attracted considerable research. On the one hand, banks lay the foundation for economic development (Kroszner, Laeven, and Klingebiel, 2007; Levine, 1997, 2006); they provide external funding as they collect savings and channel capital to wealth-increasing projects. Not least because of this, countries with well-developed financial systems outperform countries with less developed systems (Rajan and Zingales, 1998). On the other hand, banks pose a major threat to the financial systems which they actually should support. They are inherently fragile due to the nature of their business; among other reasons, any bank would collapse if all its customers demand their deposits at the same time (Bhattacharya, Boot, and Thakor, 1998; Diamond and Rajan, 2001). In this respect, bank size is not the only consideration. While large banks might be "too big to fail", smaller, weaker banks could be "too many to fail"; in either case, the failure of one can result in the collapse of the entire financial system (Acharya, 2009; Acharya and Yorulmazer, 2007; De Vries, 2005; Kaufman, 2002).

Moreover, bank governance is different from other industries. While traditional principal agency theory views the manager-owner antagonism with diverging interests of the two parties as the core of the problem, the mere alignment of the owners' and managers' interests, suggested as the traditional solution, is inadequate in the banking scenario (Jensen and Meckling, 1976; Mullineux, 2006). Furthermore, in the banking industry, stakeholders' interests are not only divergent, but also mutually exclusive. For example, the shareholders' appetite for risk comes at the expense of depositors' safety since more risk-taking shifts the risk directly to them (Galai and Masulis, 1976). Other stakeholders like regulatory bodies, deposit insurance agencies, and taxpayers are also affected when banks face bankruptcy.

Insufficient bank governance structures in general and inadequate industry expertise of directors in particular are frequently discussed as causes of that near-meltdown of the financial system which resulted in an estimated USD 2.3 trillion cumulative bank write-downs in the hardest hit economies for the years 2007-2010 (Ard and Berg, 2010; Choundhry, 2011; International Monetary Fund, 2010; Kirkpatrick, 2009). As a consequence, new regulations have been released and institutions have been created to improve bank monitoring and foster governance structures (Moshirian, 2011). However, there are still calls, explicitly demanding more expertise in internal bank governance (Ard and Berg, 2010; Walker, 2009).

Bank supervision is anything but easy as the business has become more complex and therefore requires superior expertise to manage and supervise bank risks (Mehran, Morrison, and Shapiro, 2011). Apart from the competence to supervise bank risks adequately, it is also the question who or what drives bank risk-taking. On one hand, bank owners have an interest in high-performing banks to ensure high returns. On the other hand, they should also have an interest in stable banks and in safeguarding the prosperous development and continuance of the institution. With increasing stakes, shareholders can better influence banks' decisions, for example, on bank activities, asset mix, or the matching of assets and liabilities. Theoretical evidence is not clear on whether large shareholders advocate more risk or whether they exert a risk-decreasing effect (e.g., Berle and Means, 1933; Galai and Masulis, 1976). In line with diverging theoretical evidence, empirical studies are not clear as well (e.g., Laeven and Levine, 2009; Magalhaes, Gutiérrez, and Tribó, 2008; Shehzad, de Haan, and Scholtens, 2010). The majority of previous studies leave room for further research in three specific areas: the risk-adjustment of banks' performance based on their risk profile, the simultaneous use of accounting-based and market-based risk indicators, and the analysis over time.

The first three studies of this thesis deal with financial expertise of the supervisory boards and its impact on performance and risk. The analyses target three specific objectives: first, they address the question on how the supervisory boards are composed and how financially literate its members are; second, they answer the question whether financial expertise influences banks' risk-return profiles; third, they examine whether financial expertise in internal bank governance contributes to more stability and less risk in banking.

Research has shown that the German banking system with its three sectors is a prime object of investigation. Despite different legal characteristics and ownership types, two of the sectors – cooperative and savings banks – lend themselves for an apt comparison as they have similar business models and have organizational structures which allow comparative analyses. For the purpose of the first three analyses in this thesis, the database comprises supervisory board members of 257 cooperative and 209 savings banks with 39,365 data points at the individual level. In line with the calls for more expertise, Germany took up the issue of adequate qualification of board members. New legal requirements concerning the financial competence of bank supervisory board members have been released (BaFin and Deutsche Bundesbank, 2010).

From a governance perspective, the legal change is of high importance for cooperative and savings banks in particular. Both are not tied to capital markets for equity funding and therefore do not have the same "market for corporate control" as exchange-listed banks do (Manne, 1965). While exchange-listed commercial banks have equity investors with a limited investment horizon as one important element in their overall governance structure, cooperative and savings banks lack this kind of investor control. Consequently, the supervisory board takes over a very important role in the governance system.

The answers to the leading questions of these analyses are deemed to be useful for various parties. First, the results are of high importance to regulators. The analyses provide evidence on the effectiveness of some regulatory measures and highlight the regulations that miss their goals. The results shed light on how banks' supervisory boards are staffed and how the members' assumed competences are related to risk and return. In this respect, the examination provides helpful insight in whether the calls for more expertise in internal bank governance are justified. Second, the findings provide useful insights for public discussions. The 2008 banking crisis proved the need to stabilize the banking system. However, not all measures brought up in public discussions and which appear helpful at first sight are still useful after a thorough analysis. In this respect, these analyses provide the stimulus and input for further public and political discussions. Furthermore, the results help to evaluate potential regulatory measures. Third, it also may be of interest to bank managements and the owners. In particular, bank owners might want to receive evidence whether and how the supervisory board members' competence is associated with performance, risk, and stability.

The analyses are structured thus: the board composition is analysed in the first study. Supervisory board members are classified according to their employment into the categories: self-employed, employed, and retired. Subsequently, within each category, individuals are classified according to their explicit occupation. Finally, on the basis of their occupation, individuals are assigned financial expertise.

The second study builds on the examination of the supervisory board composition and extends it to the impact of financial expertise on performance and risk of 200 of the largest German savings banks. The impact of the financial expertise of the total supervisory board and of outsiders – people who are not employed at the respective savings banks – on the risk-return profile is analysed in detail.

The third study completes the research strand by analysing whether financial expertise contributes to bank stability. For this purpose, the dataset is extended to 400 banks, comprising cooperative and savings banks. Because of their characteristics, cooperative banks act as an ideal control group to savings banks and can confirm the robustness of the results. Both banking groups have similar business models as both focus on typical lending and deposit taking activities, operate regionally and have local and regional enterprises as well as private households as primary customers (Hackethal, 2004; Schmidt, 2009).

Results show that, on average, 48% of German cooperative banks' supervisory board members and 65% of savings banks' have financial expertise. Compared to private banks, these numbers indicate relatively high expertise levels. For a small sample of German private banks, Hau and Thum (2008) find values of 31%-40%. Further analyses show that financial expertise of the supervisory board members does influence the risk-return profile of German savings banks. Although financial experts can impact the profile, they cannot suspend the trade-off. Overall, they seem to benefit and the positive impact on performance appear to be predominant. According to this trade-off, higher returns are associated with higher risk. Less stability and higher risk is consistent across ownership types. Hence, with regard to the question whether financial expertise in supervisory boards makes the banking system more stable, the third study provides negative news.

Apart from the question on how bank risks can be better supervised and managed, the focus is also on who advocates risk in banks. One approach is based on banks' ownership structure. The fourth study analyses the impact of ownership concentration on risk-adjusted performance and risk from 2004 to 2008. The results of this examination are of high importance to two addressees: regulatory bodies at the national and international level and the financial institutions themselves. Regulatory bodies need to know whether certain ownership structures impose a significant risk factor, which risk measures display risk more adequately and in a timely manner, and whether regulatory measures achieve their goals under different ownership settings. For banks themselves, it is important to know how different ownership structures impact performance and risk. The question on whether anchor shareholders are in the managements' interest or whether a diversified shareholder structure is more desirable is addressed in detail.

Based on 400 international banks, the analysis shows that ownership concentration reduces bank performance. Ownership concentration also has a negative impact on bank stability captured by accounting measures. Beta as market-based measure gives mixed results. For lower levels of ownership concentration, there is increased risk; for higher levels, risk decreases. The interaction of regulation and ownership concentration shows, that for performance reasons, shareholders try to evade regulation. However, this only applies to some regulatory measures and not consistently to all.

The course of investigation within this thesis is organized as follows: all chapters are numbered with Roman numerals. The first and the sixth chapter are the main introduction and the main conclusion and outline how the four studies are related to the overall topic of bank governance and how they are interrelated. The chapters II to V present the four studies. The second ordering level, indicated by Arabic numerals, provides a structure within each study.

II The Evident Banking Expertise of Supervisory Board Members of German Cooperative and Savings Banks[1]

Abstract

In 2009, new requirements on the expertise of the supervisory board members of German Banks were released. Following the existing requirement of the Stock Corporation Act (AktG), prospective members have to prove relevant expertise. This leads to a harmonization of requirements independent of the legal status of the bank. In the three-sector structure of the German banking system, cooperative banks and savings banks play an important role, especially for regional small- and medium-sized companies and for private households. However, due to their legal status, specific ownership structure, and business models, well-known control mechanisms such as the capital markets or control by family owners do not have an effect. Accordingly, the supervisory boards of both banking groups take on much of the responsibility of controlling, especially in regard to management monitoring. The present study – analyzing supervisory board members' assumed financial expertise – shows that savings banks have, on average, a significantly higher share of financial expertise than do cooperative banks. Bank size only influences the financial expertise of cooperative banks positively; board size does not materially influence the financial expertise of either group.

II.1 Introduction

In September 2010, the Financial Times Deutschland headlines stated that the German Federal Financial Supervisory Authority (BaFin) had demonstrated its power by rejecting supervisory board members of German banks (Luttmer, 2010). The article outlined the first review by BaFin of the supervisory boards of German banks in regard to expertise and competence. The legal basis of this review was the law to strengthen financial and insurance supervision, which came into force on July 29, 2009, and was codified in the Banking Act (KWG). The new amendment requires the members of the supervisory boards of German

---

1   This chapter is based on a joint working paper (Böhm, Froneberg, and Schiereck, 2012b).

banks to demonstrate financial expertise, which is considered necessary for exercising bank management supervision as well as for assessing and monitoring bank operations. BaFin's first review resulted in ten complaints: in one case about the lack of competence, in six cases about dubious reliability, and in three cases about too many supervisory board mandates being held by individuals (Luttmer, 2010).

Issues of banking supervision, control, and governance came to the fore with the 2008 banking crisis. This was because established supervisory mechanisms did not limit the magnitude of the financial crisis. The issues of understanding bank risks, management monitoring, and implementation of risk-minimizing compensation structures were frequently discussed (Ard and Berg, 2010; Erkens, Hung, and Matos, 2009; Kirkpatrick, 2009). Management monitoring and control is of particular importance for German banks because the prevailing two-tier system separates management and supervision (Köhler, 2010). This system is completely different from the Anglo-Saxon one-tier board system. The management of banks is overseen by the Board of Directors whereas the supervisory board is responsible for management supervision. The success of this structure requires that the governing committees be staffed such that their assigned tasks and duties are sufficiently met.

The German banking industry is divided into three sectors, private banks, public banks (which include savings banks), and cooperative banks. The legal characteristics and the internal structure of the associations in each sector differentiates the sectors (Köhler, 2010). Public-law savings banks are owned by the public authorities. In general, this is the municipality or the county in which the bank is based. There are also savings banks that are owned by an association of local authorities and/or counties. In addition to public-sector savings banks, there are so-called free savings banks, which usually operate as legal entities under private law, foundations, or associations (Büschgen, 1998). Savings banks in public-law sponsorship are characterized by public mandate, common public interest, regional principle, and a high degree of affiliation (Börner and Büschgen, 2003; Brämer, Gischer, Pfingsten, and Richter, 2010). The business policies of savings banks are specifically derived from the public mandate. The accomplishment of tasks such as ensuring region-wide access to banking services, in contrast to strict profit maximization, dominates the business strategy (Geiger, 1992). These aims were easily achievable up to 2005, through the guarantee system of public guarantee obligation and maintenance obligation. Savings banks were able to run their business activities without creditors fearing default of obligations (guarantee obligation) or the risk of filing for insolvency as a final consequence (maintenance obligation) (Engerer and Schrooten, 2004). The business area is geographically limited to the area of the owning municipality and/or counties. Accordingly, there is a horizontal division of work between savings banks, at the customer level, in the savings banks sector (Geiger, 1992). Affiliation is reflected in the vertical division of work between the hierarchy levels. In addition to locally operating primary savings banks, there are the Landesbanken at the federal state level and savings banks associations (Breuer and Mark, 2005).

Cooperative banks are owned by their members and operate as registered cooperatives (Becker and Peppmeier, 2006). They are characterized by the mandate to support their clients and the principles of self-aid, self-government, and affiliation (Hackethal, 2004). Cooperative banks work to promote regional and local enterprises and to support their members' social or cultural needs through financial services. Cooperative banks are committed to providing their members with services that would be priced higher at other, strictly profit-oriented banks (Kammlott and Schiereck, 2000). Similar to savings banks, in most cases, they limit their business activities to particular regions. This regional orientation is derived from its corporate purpose of member support, which is codified in § 1 of the Cooperative Act (GenG). Since this is not statutory, there are also cooperative institutions with nationwide operations, such as the Deutsche Apotheker- und Ärztebank eG. As with savings banks, there is a horizontal distribution of work in the cooperative banking sector at the primary level, resulting in limited competition between cooperative banks.

Beyond business focus and corporate strategy, the different ownership structures result in peculiarities with respect to the control mechanisms (corporate governance) at cooperative as well as savings banks. Savings banks cannot be acquired by other banks or companies outside the savings bank sector, as they are owned by the respective local or regional public authority. However, the ownership of a savings bank is not a fungible asset like tradable shares (Pfingsten, 2010). Mergers within the savings bank sector are possible only through explicit approval from the owning municipality or county. Consequently, a partial sale of shares similar to a joint-stock corporation is not possible. Therefore, although savings banks are either merged or are incorporated by another savings bank, political aspects play a dominant role in the decision-making process (Drees, Keisers, and Schiereck, 2006). Public ownership allows another special feature: savings banks are publicly owned and are consequently not directly owned by individuals or enterprises, but only indirectly by citizens. However, these citizens do not possess any control rights (Böhm-Dries, Eggers, and Hortmann, 2010).

The shareholder structure of cooperative banks – characterized by its members – leads to dispersed ownership. There is no option to acquire all the shares of the institution. Company shares generally cannot be acquired by a third party (Schiereck and Timmreck, 2001). Additionally, the value of the company shares is not based on the current value of the company, so these company shares cannot be compared to the shares of listed companies (Theurl, 2002). Hence, the consolidation process takes place only within the sector, similar to savings banks. Each member has one vote that is independent of factual ownership (one member, one vote). In terms of the supervision of business activities, this leads to critical issues. The ultimate owners have the opportunity to exercise control via their vote at the general annual assembly. However, the increasing size and complexity of business activities, on the one hand, and the free-rider problem arising from the "one member, one vote" principle, on the other hand, can impact corporate control negatively (Kammlott and Schiereck, 2000).

Because of the ownership structures of both banking groups, based on the underlying legal characteristics, there is no corporate control via the capital markets. However, capital markets are effective control instruments that immediately indicate shortcomings in profitability and efficiency (Manne, 1965). Consequently, there is no so-called "market for corporate control" in this way. Additionally, the governance structures of both banking groups are not driven towards value maximization to solve the problem between management and owners in terms of value maximization (Jensen and Ruback, 1983). Family-owned companies solve the agency problem through the identities of owner and manager. This second option is not applicable to either banking group, too. As a result, the supervisory boards of savings banks and cooperative banks play an important role in the supervision of management. Additionally, the new requirements on expertise shed light on the question of evident and assumable financial expertise and the qualifications of supervisory board members. This raises the question of whether the supervisory boards of German cooperative and savings banks are staffed such that there is evident financial expertise on the supervisory board.

Despite the importance of supervisory board members in German savings and cooperative banks, no detailed analysis has yet been performed, although research has alluded to such analysis in specific corporate governance papers (Cihák and Hesse, 2007). This study aims at systematically analyzing the evident financial expertise of supervisory board members who exercise management supervision in German savings and cooperative banks for the first time. This study is based on more than 400 institutions for the period from 2004 to 2009.

The analysis shows that savings banks have a higher share of supervisory board members with assumable financial expertise than do cooperative banks. This is partially driven by the savings banks laws, which ensure employee representation of one-third on the supervisory board in nearly all federal states.[2] Both banking groups have a relatively high proportion of supervisory board members whose bank-related economic expertise is not immediately obvious. Regarding outsiders – supervisory board members who are not employed at the respective savings bank – the results on financial expertise converge between savings and cooperative banks. However, savings banks still have a higher share. There are also differences in the compositions of the boards. The supervisory boards of cooperative banks show a significantly higher share of self-employed individuals than do the supervisory boards of savings banks. This can be traced back to the statuary employee representation of savings banks, on the one hand, and the observable high presence of local and regional politicians on the supervisory boards, on the other hand. Cooperative banks, conversely, have a high number of entrepreneurs, which is in line with the goal of member sponsorship. This result is further supported by the fact that more executive employees, (managing) partners, and owners are members of the supervisory boards of cooperative banks than of the supervisory boards of savings banks.

The study is structured as follows: Chapter II.2 briefly introduces the German banking sector, the background of the legislative regulations in each sector, and the revision of the requirements of supervisory board members. Chapter II.3 outlines the methodology for the assessment of professional background. Chapter II.4 includes the database, Chapter II.5 presents the results of the analysis, and Chapter II.6 concludes the study and provides an outlook for the future.

II.2 German Banking Sector and Legal Background

The total assets of the German banking sector were EUR 7.5 trillion at the end of 2009. These assets are allocated to 1,939 banks, of which 1,157 belong to the cooperative banks sector and 431 to the savings banks sector.[3] The cooperative and savings banks that are considered in the present study account for approximately 16% of the total assets of the German banking sector. The regional focus and characteristics of both banking groups indicate a focus on traditional credit and deposit taking activities. This is documented by the

---

2   Notice has been taken of potential conflicts of interests arising from working and exercising supervisory mandates at the same bank. This applies to executive employees in particular. However, this is not further discussed and analyzed in the present study.

3   A further 351 banks comprise commercial banks, state banks, cooperative central banks, mortgage banks, building associations, and banks with specific functions (Deutsche Bundesbank, 2011).

relatively high share of both banking groups in the overall credit volume to domestic enterprises and private households. In this category, they account for 42%. Their share of savings deposits of domestic individuals is 77% (Deutsche Bundesbank, 2011).

There is no law that consolidates all legal requirements concerning banking institutions in Germany. The KWG is a central German banking law and is effective for individual institutions as well as for banking groups of all three sectors (Koetter, Nestmann, Stolz, and Wedow, 2004). Further relevant acts can be divided into institutional and business oriented laws. The savings banks laws (SpG) of the federal states and the GenG are institutional laws. Examples of business-orientated acts are the Securities Trading Act (WpHG), the Act for the Prevention of Money Laundering (GwG), and the Act for Deposit Insurance and Investors' Compensation (EAEG).

Savings banks are governed by the savings banks laws of the federal states (Claussen, 2003). However, these laws do not apply to so-called free savings banks. There is no savings banks law in Hamburg, as the free Hamburger Sparkasse (HASPA) has the legal status of a stock corporation (Hackethal, 2004). By and large, the key aspects of savings banks laws do not differ materially. Generally, the laws govern legal status, ownership, objectives of the bank, and organizational structure. Concerning the supervisory board, the laws regulate the following key aspects: term, chair, appointment of remaining members, employee representatives, limitations to appointments, duties of the board, and competence requirements for individual members.[4] Additionally, there are further detailed regulations for the individual savings bank in its respective charter (Hartmann-Wendels, Pfingsten, and Weber, 2007). With the exception of the Bavarian Savings Banks Law, the savings bank laws require that a third of the supervisory members be elected by the employees. In only Bavaria, the chief executive officer (CEO) has a seat and voting rights on the supervisory board.[5] In Lower Saxony, the Personnel Representation Act regulates employee representation on the supervisory board.[6]

Remarkably, there are significant regional differences in the requirements of individuals' expertise, which are stated in the savings banks laws in addition to the KWG.[7] While 10 out of 15 laws prescribe expertise as a target requirement, only in five states is individual expertise compulsory. A review of members' expertise by local and/or regional governing bodies is currently

---

4   E.g. cf §§11ff. Savings Banks Law of Baden-Wuerttemberg.

5   Cf. §6, para. 1, Savings Banks Law of Bavaria.

6   Cf. §11, para. 1, no. 3, Savings Banks Law of Lower Saxony.

7   According to the version of the savings banks laws of February 2011.

compulsory only in the Savings Banks Law of the federal state North Rhine-Westphalia.[8] Four savings banks laws hold that at least one member has to have the required expertise in accounting and audit of financial statements if the respective savings bank participates in the organized market.

Cooperative banks are governed by the GenG in addition to the KWG. The Act refers to cooperatives in general, and not to credit cooperatives in particular. In comparison to the savings banks laws, the GenG has only general requirements for the determination of the supervisory board. The only requirement that is specific to individuals, states that in capital market-oriented cooperatives, in the sense of § 264d, Commercial Code (HGB), at least one member of the supervisory board needs to have expertise in accounting or auditing.

The modification of the KWG leads to a homogenization of the requirements of supervisory board members across the three sectors. According to § 24, para. 1, no. 15, KWG, newly elected supervisory board members have to provide documents for the assessment of their expertise and reliability. The required expertise depends on the size, complexity, and systematic relevance of the institution (BaFin and Deutsche Bundesbank, 2010). This implies that the supervisory boards of larger institutions should have a higher degree of financial expertise. According to § 36, para. 3, sentence 4 KWG, controlling bodies have to exercise their duties such that potential misconduct of the management board can be discovered. The mere presence of supervisory board members on the supervisory board is insufficient (Böhm-Dries, Eggers, and Hortmann, 2010).

The joint bulletin by BaFin and Deutsche Bundesbank (2010) does not specifically prescribe the requirements that have to be satisfied by members and how these members should be assessed. However, the bulletin outlines that, for individuals who are members of the supervisory board because of mandates, expertise is assumed. Among these members are mayors and district administrators who head the governing bodies of the supporting organization. The same applies for employee representatives in codetermined controlling and administration bodies. For merchants, in terms of §§ 1ff., HGB, and foresters, farmers (who are obliged to keep books of accounts), and other entrepreneurs, in terms of § 141 German fiscal code (AO), expertise can also be assumed. However, this depends on the size and business model of the company. The bulletin also states that expertise can be acquired through several activities, such as experience in other sectors, public authority, or through political mandate. If a member lacks expertise, this expertise can be acquired through additional educational training (BaFin and Deutsche Bundesbank, 2010).

---

8   Cf. § 12, para. 1, Savings Banks Law North Rhine-Westphalia.

II.3 Methodology

The present study focuses on cooperative and savings banks with the legal status of registered cooperative and public law savings banks, respectively. Hence, cooperative and savings banks with the legal status of stock corporations and private limited companies are excluded. At the moment, there is no public commercial database that provides historical data on the individual members of the supervisory boards of German banks. For this reason, the analysis is based on a unique, manually collected dataset derived from publicly available annual reports. The main criterion for the assumption of financial expertise is the stated professional background of the member. This approach follows other studies that were conducted in relation to the US-American Sarbanes-Oxley Act (SOX), which was released in 2002. SOX comprises requirements for the Audit Committees of companies whose securities are traded in the United States. Related studies analyze the impact of financial expertise in general and knowledge in accounting and auditing in particular on the risk and performance of companies (e.g., Carcello, Hollingsworth, Klein, and Neal, 2008; Dhaliwal, Naiker, and Navissi, 2006; Güner, Malmendier, and Tate, 2008; Hau and Thum, 2008; Hermalin and Weisbach, 2003). These studies mainly used individuals' professional backgrounds as indications of qualifications. Only Hau and Thum (2008) additionally considered the educational background.

First, supervisory board members are grouped into self-employed, employed, retired persons, and others (Level 1). The category "others" comprises individuals who cannot be assigned to an occupation due to the lack of available information or insufficient data granularity. Second, these categories are further detailed as follows (Level 2). The category "self-employed persons" comprises owners, partners, managing partners, entrepreneurs, merchants, and self-employed persons with freelance professions, e.g., architects. The category "employed persons" includes all employees, public officers, and politicians.

Level 1: Employment	Self-employed persons	Employed persons	Retirees	Others
Level 2: Occupation	Partner	Member of management boards	Retired self-employed person	
	Managing Partner	Bank employee	Retired employed person	
	Merchant, Owner, Entrepreneur	Other employee or public officer with explicit financial focus		
	Freelance professional	Other employee or public officer without explicit financial focus		
		Politician		
Level 3: Occupation groups	Executive management (CEO, partner, managing partner, owner, entrepreneur, merchant)			
	Chartered accountant, registered auditor, tax consultang			

In order to analyze the supervisory board composition, certain groups of job descriptions are evaluated, independent of the differentiation between self-employed and employed persons (Level 3). The first group includes executives such as chief executives, partners, managing partners, entrepreneurs, and merchants. The second group comprises chartered accountants, registered auditors, and tax consultants. Additionally, politicians are categorized into federal, federal state, regional, and local to increase granularity. Due to their legal status and public ownership, savings banks have close ties to regional and local politics.

The classification of politicians with regard to their assumable financial expertise is complex. In the present dataset, ministers, state secretaries, and members of parliament at the federal and federal state level are federal politicians or federal state politicians, respectively. The number of members of the European parliament is not material to the dataset, and these members are classified as federal politicians. At the regional and local level, the identification of politicians is much more complex. Due to the multitude of administrative bodies at the regional and local levels, a multi-level approach is applied to categorize regional and local politicians. The objective of this is to differentiate between politicians in the strict sense and holders of political electoral office.

Individuals who are potential mandatory members of the supervisory boards due to their mandates are identifiable straight away. The joint bulletin by BaFin and Deutsche Bundesbank (2010) states that, for example, mayors and district administrators are potential mandatory members. However, cross-federal state analysis requires a methodology for the classification of electoral office at the regional and local levels. There are remarkable differences between the federal states and subsequent differences in public authorities and their organizational structures. For example, this is evident in the formerly effective divergent Northern and Southern council regulations. The differences can be delineated by three essential characteristics: split of competencies, management structure, and management of public authorities. In the past, a trend towards the Southern council regulation has been observed (Gabriel and Holtmann, 2005; Naßmacher and Naßmacher, 2007). The Southern council regulation is characterized by the division of responsibilities of the public administrative authority and the governing body, identity of chairs of the administrative authority and the respective legislative body, as well as the sole management of the public authority with the right to give directives to the respective authority. After changes to the charters of local authorities, the head of the administration is the supreme representative of the municipality in most states (Gabriel and Holtmann, 2005; Naßmacher and Naßmacher, 2007).

First, a differentiation between full-time and voluntary electoral offices is made. Individuals officiating in political electoral offices voluntarily are not considered as politicians in this study. For instance, these include honorary county councils, city councils, and municipal councils. This criterion can be applied consistently nationwide. For the further differentiation of full-time professionals, the hierarchical level of the function is considered. In our analysis, we classify the concerned person as a politician if he is the head of the administration. This selection step assures that politicians in the present dataset are directly elected. In this context, the county administrators in Baden-Wuerttemberg are an exception as they are indirectly elected through the county council.

In the second step, persons who are subject to directives and who have to report to the head of the administration do not count as politicians in the present analysis. Therefore, district administrators, lord mayors, and mayors are consistently counted nationwide as politicians. Furthermore, there are few federal states in which city directors, presidents of regional committees, presidents of local committees, and presidents of regional committees are also counted as politicians if all the criteria outlined above are satisfied. Corresponding to the outlined approach, other holders of state-specific functions are not counted as politicians even though they are indirectly or directly elected and represent a political position and/or party, such as full-time city councilors in Bavaria, magistrates in Hessen, and (county) deputies in several federal states. All of these persons violate the criterion regarding heading the administration. If the function is exercised full-time, the office holders are typically responsible for particular divisions or departments, respectively. At the same time, they are subject to the directives of the head of the administration (Gabriel and Holtmann, 2005).

The quality of data on individual supervisory board members provided in the annual reports has not been consistent. For this reason, the following assumptions have been applied for the present analysis:

- For the information merchant, we assume a merchant in terms of § 1, HGB.
- For information entrepreneurs, we assume that the person is a managing partner/owner of a company.
- A farmer is treated as self-employed, if not otherwise explicitly stated.
- In cases of jobs based on apprenticeships, which could suggest both self-employed and employed occupations, an employed occupation has been assumed if no further information is available.
- If the academic title is the only available information, no classification is attributed (others).

For the determination of board size, as well as for further analysis, we do not consider the following board members:

- Advisory members,
- Honorary members,
- Members with tenures of less than half a year.

For analysis of board competence, based on the methodology outlined above, assumable financial expertise is assigned to certain job descriptions. The main idea behind this is the obvious relation to financial issues. For instance, financial expertise is expected in the case of managing directors of companies. For the assigning of financial expertise, we generally considered the information available over the time frame 2004-2009. For this study, professional backgrounds are assigned financial expertise as follows:

Table II.2: *Assignment of financial expertise*

Level 1: Employment	Self-employed persons with assumed financial expertise	Employed persons with assumed financial expertise	Retired persons with assumed financial expertise
Level 2: Occupation	Entrepreneur, Merchant, Owner	Non-bank employee with assumed financial focus (e.g. member of management board)	Retired self-employed person with assumed financial expertise
	Managing Partner	Bank employee	Retired employed person with assumed financial expertise
	Partner	Public officer with assumed financial focus (e.g. treasurer) Federal and State Minister, State Secretary	
		Local and regional politician	

With regard to the holders of electoral office, who are not counted as politicians, an individual evaluation is conducted in order to determine how close their activities are related to financial and business issues. Financial expertise is attributed based on this evaluation. Due to the legislative requirements outlined in Chapter II.2, there is a significantly higher expected share of employee representatives on the boards of savings banks than on those of cooperative banks. For this reason, the analysis is conducted twice. First, the overall financial expertise of the board is analyzed. Second, the focus shifts to so-called outside financial expertise. This refers to the financial expertise of board members who are not employees of the respective supervised bank. The composition of the boards, which is not regulated by legal requirements, will be compared. Retired persons are categorized on the basis of their last available professional occupation. For instance, a retired person is assigned financial expertise when he or she is a former managing director of company. The classification of financial expertise for professional occupation is geared to the outline of BaFin and Deutsche Bundesbank (2010). Only farmers are treated differently, as their job description significantly differs from the occupational focus of managers. For consistency reasons, publicly irreproducible information cannot be considered in this study.

II.4 Data

Our analysis is based on a unique, manually collected dataset derived from publicly available annual reports. The financial statements are either provided by the individual bank or by the Bundesanzeiger via the Unternehmensregister or LexisNexis databases. In total, our dataset comprises the characteristics of supervisory board members of 257 cooperative banks and 209 savings banks. A total of 39,365 data points at the individual level were collected. In order to secure the highest possible degree of data quality, the cooperative and savings banks included satisfy the following criteria. The analysis is based on a balanced panel. For this reason, the data on the considered banks must be available through the years 2004-2009. Furthermore, only a maximum of 10% of the board members can belong to the "other" category. Due to the relative difficulty of applying this to small boards, a maximum of one person in absolute terms can belong to this category, even if the ratio rises to above 10%. This refers in particular to boards with a size of up to nine persons, as one person in the "other" category makes up more than 10% of the board. If a financial institution has been eliminated due to lack of data or too high a representation of the category "other," the succeeding institution in the size ranking is included.

First, the largest 200 banks (Top 200) in each sector are analyzed over the period 2004-2009. For banks that are listed in the 2009 ranking under a different name due to merger(s) that have taken place in the interim, the name of the acquiring entity was applied for the former years. In order to account for potential distortions due to mergers in the cooperative and savings bank sector, the analysis is repeated for a merger-controlled panel over the same time horizon. For the merger adjustments, a blackout period of three years is introduced for the respective institution (merger year plus the two previous years). This eliminates banks that were involved in merger activities in the period between 2002 and 2009. The merger-controlled sample includes 150 institutions in each sector (Top 150). Data on the merger history of each bank was accessed via the Hoppenstedt Banken database. The largest 200 cooperative banks and 200 savings banks of 2009 account for 57% and 71% of total assets of all banks in their sectors, respectively. The 150 merger-controlled institutions account for 35% and 45% of total assets of their respective sectors. In the Top 200, the average total assets of the cooperative banks amounted to EUR 1.9 billion, and the average total assets of the savings banks amounted to EUR 3.8 billion (Top 150: EUR 1.6 billion and EUR 3.2 billion, respectively). We refer constantly to the results of the Top 200 institutions if the merger-controlled panel (Top 150) does not show any different qualitative results.

II.5 Empirical Results

Board size analysis reveals that supervisory boards of savings banks are on average 35% larger than those of cooperative banks. The average size of savings banks' supervisory boards is 17 board members, compared with 12 board members at cooperative banks. Basically, these results represent the expected variance due to bank size differences between cooperative and savings banks. The differences in board size are also driven by mandatory employee representation in savings banks. Apart from actual bank size, the savings bank laws lead to one-third of the board members being employee representatives – except in the case of the Bavarian savings banks. When considering the size of boards without employee representatives, the average numbers of board members in both sectors converge.

Table II.3: Supervisory board composition (mean values 2004-2009).

Variable	Cooperative banks		Savings banks	
	Top 200	Top 150	Top 200	Top 150
Board size	12	11	17	16
Insider	1	1	4	4
Outsider	12	10	13	12
Self-employed individuals	39.6%	39.7%	12.6%	13.5%
Employed individuals	50.2%	49.6%	73.3%	72.5%
Retirees	9.2%	9.7%	12.7%	12.6%
Others	1.0%	0.9%	1.4%	1.3%
Politicians (officiating)	2.2%	2.3%	24.4%	24.7%
Federal politicians	0.1%	0.3%	0.8%	0.7%
State politicians	0.2%	0.2%	2.6%	2.6%
Regional politicians	0.0%	0.0%	5.9%	5.5%
Local politicians	1.8%	1.9%	15.2%	15.8%
Executive employees / Owners / Partners	33.3%	34.7%	11.8%	12.2%
Accountants / Auditors / Tax consultants	7.2%	7.3%	1.2%	1.3%

The composition of the supervisory boards, based on the employment of members, reveals significant differences between both banking groups. Self-employed persons roughly account for three times as many members of the supervisory boards of cooperative banks than of savings banks. This observation matches the fundamental expectation that cooperative banks are motivated to promote their members and regional and local enterprises. Conversely, savings banks have a significantly higher share of employed persons than cooperative banks (73% vs. 50%). This is due to the fact that savings banks have a comparatively high share of employee representatives and politicians. The results remain robust when excluding insiders from the analysis. The share of retired persons is only slightly higher at savings banks. However, it is remarkable that there are some institutions in either the savings or the cooperative banking sector that have a share of more than 50% retired persons on the board.

Public ownership and the consequent legal requirements regarding the representation of public office holders lead to the high presence and importance of politicians on the supervisory boards of savings banks. This assumption is confirmed by this analysis (see Appendix II.7.4). At savings banks, politicians account for approximately a quarter of the board, on average. The representation of the owning governing body is shown by the fact that local and regional politicians are primarily on these boards. When retired politicians are included in the analysis, the share of politicians on the supervisory board increases to 28%, on average (see Appendix II.7.5). In contrast, at cooperative banks, politicians hardly play a role, with a share of 2% on average. Only the cooperative bank with the highest politician share (25%) is in line with the average share of the savings banks.

A differentiation within the cooperative banking group between employed and self-employed persons shows that financial expertise is distributed over both categories almost equally. For approximately 50% of the persons in each category, financial expertise can be assumed. The same share applies for savings banks with regard to self-employed persons. In regard to employed persons, employee representatives and the high share of politicians indicate that financial expertise can be assumed for the majority of these employed persons (see Appendix II.7.6). Apart from the attribution to employed or self-employed persons, two groups are of high relevance because for both groups, financial expertise can be assumed with high certainty: persons in executive positions and auditors, tax consultants, and accountants. Comparing the two groups it is evident that savings banks have a subordinated role in contrast to cooperative banks (see Appendix II.7.7). Directors, managing directors, and entrepreneurs/owners represent, on average, 33% of the supervisory boards of cooperative banks, but only 12% in savings banks; auditors, tax consultants, and accountants account for 7% of cooperative banks' supervisory boards and 1% in savings banks, on average.

Overall, the analysis of assumed financial expertise indicates a higher share of expertise on the supervisory boards of savings banks than on those of cooperative banks. For around two-thirds of the board, financial expertise can be assumed. Therefore, the supervisory boards of savings banks significantly outperform the average of approximately 48% at cooperative banks (see Table II.4). The results remain robust considering the merger-controlled panel. However, the results converge only when considering outsiders. The financial expertise of outsiders accounts for approximately 53% at savings banks and approximately 45% at cooperative banks. When considering the merger-controlled panel, there is no significant difference to the base analysis (54% vs. 46%).

Hau and Thum (2008) analyze the financial expertise of 29 large German banks on the basis of 14 characteristics which are used to gauge financial expertise. For this reason both studies' results are only partially comparable. The criteria financial market experience, banking experience, top-level financial management experience, and multiple board memberships are closest to our methodology. But contrary to our results, they provide competence values between 31% and 40% for private banks and only between 10% and 30% for public banks.

Table II.4:   Financial expertise (mean values 2004-2009).

Variable	Cooperative banks		Savings banks	
	Top 200	Top 150	Top 200	Top 150
Financial expertise	47.8%	47.5%	65.0%	65.5%
Outside financial expertise	45.2%	45.8%	53.2%	53.8%

Based on the characteristics of both banking sectors, the following hypotheses have been developed for comparing the two sectors:

H1: *The statuary employee representation and the assumed financial literacy of potential mandatory members, lead to significantly more financial expertise at savings banks.*

H2: *Since cooperative and savings banks have a similar business model, their outside financial expertise does not differ significantly.*

H3: *Cooperative banks are explicitly dedicated to local and regional enterprises and merchants and have therefore a significantly higher share of self-employed individuals on their supervisory boards.*

H4: *The statuary employee representation leads to a significantly higher share of employed individuals on savings banks' supervisory boards.*

H5: *Since both banking groups operate locally and foster local and regional enterprises and local public investments, there is no significant difference in the share of executive employees on both banking groups' supervisory boards.*

The following Table II.5 presents significance of the mean comparison tests between the both groups and provides evidence on the hypotheses.

Table II.5: *Comparison of mean values (mean values 2004-2009).*

Variable		Mean	Std. error	t	df	p-value
Top 200						
Financial expertise	Cooperative banks	47.7642	0.6602	-20.8182	2229.7100	0.0000
	Savings banks	64.9789	0.4980			
Outside financial expertise	Cooperative banks	45.2461	0.6705	-8.4056	2397.3900	0.0000
	Savings banks	53.1539	0.6599			
Self-employed individuals	Cooperative banks	39.5510	0.6782	36.7786	1585.8700	0.0000
	Savings banks	12.6191	0.2761			
Employed individuals	Cooperative banks	50.2240	0.6623	-30.7596	1830.7500	0.0000
	Savings banks	73.3169	0.3535			
Executive employees	Cooperative banks	33.3130	0.6059	32.8389	1586.4700	0.0000
	Savings banks	11.8263	0.2469			
Top 150						
Financial expertise	Cooperative banks	47.5350	0.7581	-18.8507	1674.5600	0.0000
	Savings banks	65.4584	0.5738			
Outside financial expertise	Cooperative banks	45.8105	0.7883	-7.3056	1796.4100	0.0000
	Savings banks	53.8369	0.7652			
Self-employed individuals	Cooperative banks	39.7042	0.8478	28.7784	1166.0000	0.0000
	Savings banks	13.5196	0.3304			
Employed individuals	Cooperative banks	49.6071	0.7964	-25.5930	1338.5800	0.0000
	Savings banks	72.4959	0.4070			
Executive employees	Cooperative banks	34.7240	0.7561	27.6554	1177.2900	0.0000
	Savings banks	12.2170	0.3012			

Confidence level: 95%

The following Table II.6 shows expertise levels of banks clustered by bank and board size. The differentiation by bank size – by creating groups of 50 financial institutions each – shows that savings banks with more total assets do not have a higher share of financial expertise than do smaller banks (for the development over time, see Appendices II.7.9, II.7.10). On the other hand, larger cooperative banks show higher average financial expertise than do smaller banks. However, this is only significant for overall board expertise but not for outside expertise (for significance levels, see Appendix II.7.14). The similar analysis of board size also shows no consistent evidence that the assumed financial expertise is determined by the number of board members (see Appendices II.7.11, II.7.12, II.7.15).

Table II.6: Financial expertise clustered by bank and board size (largest banks in bank and board size in Cluster 1, smallest banks in Cluster 4).

Variable	Cooperative banks				Savings banks			
Clustered by bank size	1	2	3	4	1	2	3	4
Top 200								
Financial expertise	54.5%	49.6%	45.8%	41.3%	64.4%	65.0%	64.9%	65.6%
Outside financial expertise	46.7%	47.9%	45.1%	41.3%	48.5%	55.9%	53.2%	55.1%
Top 150								
Financial expertise	51.5%	47.4%	43.7%	-	66.3%	65.1%	64.9%	-
Outside financial expertise	46.9%	47.1%	43.4%	-	54.5%	54.0%	53.0%	-
Clustered by board size	1	2	3	4	1	2	3	4
Top 200								
Financial expertise	49.9%	45.8%	50.9%	44.5%	64.5%	65.4%	64.2%	65.8%
Outside financial expertise	43.5%	44.5%	49.7%	43.3%	50.2%	52.4%	49.0%	61.0%
Top 150								
Financial expertise	45.4%	47.7%	49.5%	-	67.6%	61.2%	67.5%	-
Outside financial expertise	42.3%	46.5%	48.6%	-	56.5%	44.2%	60.7%	-

The following table shows the distribution of cooperative and savings bank across four expertise clusters.

Table II.7: Distribution of banks across expertise clusters (based on mean values 2004-2009).

Variable	Cooperative banks				Savings banks			
	0%-25%	26%-50%	51%-75%	76%-100%	0%-25%	26%-50%	51%-75%	76%-100%
Top 200								
Financial expertise	29	76	69	26	1	44	97	58
Outside financial expertise	36	76	69	19	23	72	67	38
Top 150								
Financial expertise	19	62	48	21	1	30	77	42
Outside financial expertise	23	62	47	18	18	48	56	28

II.6 Conclusion

The financial crisis has once more illustrated the relevance of effective supervision of financial institutions. For effective supervision, a comprehensive understanding of financial issues (financial expertise) is unconditionally necessary. For smaller institutions, in particular, some doubts arise. In fact, the analysis of the professional background of the supervisory board of savings banks and cooperative banks shows a relatively high degree of assumable financial expertise, though this is not entirely consistent. The comparison between cooperative banks and savings banks shows that a higher share of financial expertise can be assumed for savings banks. Comparing our results with the study of Hau and Thum (2008) underlines the relatively high levels of financial expertise of the more than 400 cooperative and savings banks in our sample. The values of their criteria which come closest to our methodology provide expertise ratios of 31%-40% for private banks and 10%-30% for public banks based on a sample of 29 large German banks.

Savings banks benefit from the legal requirements of employee representation and the fact that employees of banks are assigned financial expertise by the regulatory bodies. Adjusted for insiders, the quotients of cooperative and savings banks converge. However, the boards of savings banks still have a higher share of financial expertise. It is remarkable that there is no significant difference between the values with or without the adjustment for mergers. Contrary to initial expectations, neither bank size nor board size increases financial expertise consistently across both sectors. Financial expertise in only cooperative banks increases with an increase in bank size. This is of high relevance as the requirements of board members also depend on the size of the institution. In summary, around 50% or more in both banking groups have financial expertise. As the requirements on financial expertise of supervisory board members refer to the whole board, and not to a certain quota, a question remains: What are the consequences that would be applied by the regulatory authorities for the remainder of the board?

A detailed view on the composition of the boards shows significant differences in terms of the share of self-employed persons versus that of employed persons, politicians, and the volatility of the composition. Cooperative banks have on average three times as many self-employed persons than do savings banks. Conversely, savings banks have a much higher share of employed persons. This can be traced back to the employees of savings banks as employee representatives who make up, on average, 26% of the board. Considering financial expertise, the source of financial expertise in savings banks is mainly employed persons. Although cooperative banks have a relevant share of financial expertise through self-employed persons, financial expertise is mainly represented by employed persons. Apart from the differentiation between employed and self-employed people, it is noticeable that board members at cooperative banks have more executive positions than do those at savings banks.

The comparatively higher share of politicians at savings banks is in line with expectations based on the legal characteristics of savings banks. Notwithstanding this, the share exceeds the magnitude expected through the savings banks laws, which list mandatory members. In particular, the maximum values of up to two-thirds of politicians on the board are a remarkable factor. Current office holders, retired regional and local politicians, and banking employees account, on average, for around 50% of the supervisory board financial expertise. In the light of the assumed expert knowledge of both groups, by BaFin and Deutsche Bundesbank, a relatively high degree of financial expertise can be consequently assumed for boards of savings banks by definition. In regard to outside financial expertise, it can be stated that cooperative banks and savings banks converge. The reason behind is a higher number of self-employed persons and executives in the supervisory boards of cooperative banks.

With regard to the volatility of financial expertise, bank employees are stabilizing members. Financial expertise in individual cooperative banks ranges from 0% to 100%. On the other hand, savings banks have a minimum level that is required by savings banks laws. Excluding insiders, the results converge in terms of distribution and range. This leads to the conclusion that, in general, the focus on the election process of "freely eligible" members of the controlling body is comparable between both banking sectors.

The methodology of the classification is an approximation of evident banking expertise. It is therefore left to subsequent studies, which will have a broader basis, to evaluate specific individual personal data to refine the findings. The quality of supervision is another area of investigation. From our point of view, it cannot be concluded that persons who do not have financial expertise according to the underlying classifications of this study do not have financial expertise at all.

On the basis of this investigation, on the one hand, corporate governance discussions of the three sector structure of the German banking system can be extended to a broader basis. On the other hand, the heterogeneity of the shown data allows further investigation. For instance, the relationship of controlling quality and risk-adjusted performance are further avenues of research.

II.7 Appendix

Appendix II.7.1: No. of institutions and supervisory board size (absolute numbers)

	Cooperative banks						Savings banks					
Top 200	2009	2008	2007	2006	2005	2004	2009	2008	2007	2006	2005	2004
No of banks	200	200	200	200	200	200	200	200	200	200	200	200
Board size												
Mean	12	12	12	12	13	13	17	17	17	17	17	17
Median	12	12	12	12	12	12	15	15	15	15	15	15
Std. Dev.	4.9	4.4	4.1	4.3	4.4	4.6	4.8	5.0	4.9	5.1	5.3	6.5
Min	6	5	5	5	5	5	8	8	8	8	7	7
Max	37	33	30	33	32	32	38	39	39	36	38	48
Insider												
Mean	1	1	1	1	1	1	5	4	4	4	4	5
Median	0	0	0	0	0	0	5	5	5	5	5	5
Std. Dev.	2.0	2.1	1.9	2.0	2.0	1.9	2.5	2.7	2.7	2.7	2.7	3.1
Min	0	0	0	0	0	0	0	0	0	0	0	0
Max	9	10	9	10	10	10	12	12	12	11	12	16
Outside												
Mean	12	11	11	12	12	12	12	12	12	12	12	13
Median	11	11	11	11	12	12	11	12	12	12	11	12
Std. Dev.	4.4	3.9	3.6	3.8	4.1	4.5	3.5	3.6	3.5	3.6	3.7	4.4
Min	5	5	5	5	5	5	6	6	6	6	6	6
Max	37	33	30	33	32	32	27	27	27	27	27	32

	Cooperative banks						Savings banks					
Top 150	2009	2008	2007	2006	2005	2004	2009	2008	2007	2006	2005	2004
No of banks	150	150	150	150	150	150	150	150	150	150	150	150
Board size												
Mean	10	10	11	11	11	11	16	16	16	16	16	16
Median	9	9	10	10	10	11	15	15	15	15	15	15
Std. Dev.	3.4	3.4	3.6	3.8	3.8	4.0	4.0	4.0	3.9	4.2	4.3	4.5
Min	5	4	4	4	4	5	8	8	8	8	7	7
Max	26	27	30	33	32	32	31	33	32	33	32	31
Insider												
Mean	0	0	0	0	0	0	4	4	4	4	4	4
Median	0	0	0	0	0	0	5	5	5	5	5	5
Std. Dev.	1.4	1.5	1.3	1.4	1.4	1.4	2.2	2.4	2.3	2.4	2.4	2.5
Min	0	0	0	0	0	0	0	0	0	0	0	0
Max	9	10	9	10	10	10	11	12	11	11	11	11
Outside												
Mean	10	10	10	11	11	11	12	12	12	12	12	12
Median	9	9	10	10	10	10	11	11	11	11	11	11
Std. Dev.	3.1	3.2	3.4	3.7	3.6	3.8	3.1	3.2	3.2	3.3	3.3	3.3
Min	5	4	4	4	4	5	7	7	7	7	6	6
Max	26	27	30	33	32	32	27	27	27	27	27	27

Appendix II.7.2: Total supervisory board composition, self-employed, employees, retirees, other (in % of total supervisory board size)

Top 200	Cooperative banks						Savings banks					
	2009	2008	2007	2006	2005	2004	2009	2008	2007	2006	2005	2004
Self-employed individuals												
Mean	40.1%	39.6%	39.4%	39.4%	39.2%	39.5%	12.5%	12.6%	13.0%	12.7%	12.5%	12.4%
Median	44.1%	44.4%	41.7%	41.7%	40.0%	42.9%	11.1%	12.3%	12.0%	12.5%	11.1%	11.1%
Std. Dev.	23.7%	24.1%	23.6%	23.2%	23.3%	23.4%	9.5%	9.4%	9.9%	9.6%	9.7%	9.5%
Min	0.0%	0.0%	0.0%	0.0%	0.0%	0.0%	0.0%	0.0%	0.0%	0.0%	0.0%	0.0%
Max	91.7%	91.7%	88.9%	83.3%	83.3%	83.3%	41.7%	38.9%	41.7%	41.7%	47.1%	47.4%
Employed individuals												
Mean	50.9%	51.6%	50.6%	49.8%	49.7%	48.7%	73.8%	73.4%	73.1%	72.7%	74.4%	72.5%
Median	50.0%	50.0%	50.0%	44.9%	45.2%	44.7%	73.9%	73.2%	73.3%	72.7%	73.3%	73.3%
Std. Dev.	22.4%	23.4%	23.2%	22.8%	23.2%	22.7%	11.9%	12.3%	12.9%	12.2%	11.9%	12.3%
Min	0.0%	0.0%	0.0%	0.0%	0.0%	0.0%	41.7%	36.4%	36.4%	36.4%	36.4%	41.7%
Max	100.0%	100.0%	100.0%	100.0%	100.0%	100.0%	100.0%	100.0%	100.0%	100.0%	100.0%	100.0%
Retirees												
Mean	7.9%	7.7%	8.9%	9.6%	10.2%	10.7%	12.5%	12.7%	12.6%	13.3%	11.7%	13.5%
Median	6.3%	5.9%	6.1%	7.1%	7.1%	7.1%	11.1%	11.1%	11.1%	11.1%	10.0%	12.9%
Std. Dev.	10.6%	10.5%	11.9%	12.1%	12.8%	12.8%	10.0%	10.3%	10.1%	10.1%	9.4%	9.7%
Min	0.0%	0.0%	0.0%	0.0%	0.0%	0.0%	0.0%	0.0%	0.0%	0.0%	0.0%	0.0%
Max	63.6%	77.8%	77.8%	66.7%	66.7%	66.7%	55.6%	47.4%	46.7%	46.7%	40.0%	40.0%
Other												
Mean	1.0%	1.0%	1.0%	1.1%	1.0%	1.1%	1.2%	1.2%	1.3%	1.4%	1.4%	1.7%
Median	0.0%	0.0%	0.0%	0.0%	0.0%	0.0%	0.0%	0.0%	0.0%	0.0%	0.0%	0.0%
Std. Dev.	2.6%	2.7%	2.8%	2.8%	2.7%	2.9%	2.6%	2.7%	2.7%	2.8%	2.8%	2.9%
Min	0.0%	0.0%	0.0%	0.0%	0.0%	0.0%	0.0%	0.0%	0.0%	0.0%	0.0%	0.0%
Max	10.0%	14.3%	14.3%	14.3%	14.3%	14.3%	11.1%	12.5%	12.5%	12.5%	12.5%	12.5%

Top 150	2009	2008	2007	2006	2005	2004	2009	2008	2007	2006	2005	2004
Self-employed individuals												
Mean	40.5%	40.1%	40.1%	39.4%	39.0%	39.2%	13.8%	13.8%	13.9%	13.4%	13.4%	12.9%
Median	43.8%	43.7%	40.8%	39.2%	40.0%	40.0%	13.3%	13.3%	13.3%	13.3%	13.3%	11.8%
Std. Dev.	26.1%	26.0%	25.7%	25.1%	24.8%	25.3%	10.0%	9.8%	10.2%	9.8%	9.9%	9.9%
Min	0.0%	0.0%	0.0%	0.0%	0.0%	0.0%	0.0%	0.0%	0.0%	0.0%	0.0%	0.0%
Max	88.9%	90.9%	88.9%	88.9%	90.0%	87.5%	41.7%	38.9%	41.7%	41.7%	47.1%	47.4%
Employed individuals												
Mean	51.2%	51.3%	49.5%	48.7%	48.8%	48.2%	72.4%	72.1%	72.0%	71.9%	73.8%	72.8%
Median	50.0%	50.0%	46.4%	45.5%	45.8%	48.3%	73.3%	72.7%	73.3%	72.5%	73.3%	73.3%
Std. Dev.	24.0%	24.3%	24.2%	23.9%	23.8%	23.4%	12.1%	12.3%	12.6%	12.1%	11.7%	12.5%
Min	9.1%	9.1%	0.0%	0.0%	0.0%	0.0%	41.7%	36.4%	36.4%	36.4%	36.4%	41.7%
Max	100.0%	100.0%	100.0%	100.0%	100.0%	100.0%	100.0%	100.0%	100.0%	100.0%	100.0%	100.0%
Retirees												
Mean	7.4%	7.6%	9.4%	10.9%	11.3%	11.7%	12.7%	12.9%	12.8%	13.3%	11.4%	12.8%
Median	0.0%	0.0%	7.7%	8.3%	9.1%	8.7%	12.5%	12.5%	11.1%	12.5%	9.3%	11.1%
Std. Dev.	10.5%	10.6%	11.9%	12.3%	13.2%	13.0%	10.3%	10.6%	10.3%	10.5%	9.8%	10.1%
Min	0.0%	0.0%	0.0%	0.0%	0.0%	0.0%	0.0%	0.0%	0.0%	0.0%	0.0%	0.0%
Max	63.6%	77.8%	77.8%	66.7%	66.7%	66.7%	55.6%	47.4%	46.7%	46.7%	38.9%	38.9%
Other												
Mean	1.0%	1.0%	1.0%	1.0%	0.9%	0.9%	1.1%	1.2%	1.3%	1.4%	1.5%	1.6%
Median	0.0%	0.0%	0.0%	0.0%	0.0%	0.0%	0.0%	0.0%	0.0%	0.0%	0.0%	0.0%
Std. Dev.	2.9%	3.0%	2.9%	2.9%	2.8%	2.8%	2.6%	2.8%	2.8%	2.9%	2.9%	2.9%
Min	0.0%	0.0%	0.0%	0.0%	0.0%	0.0%	0.0%	0.0%	0.0%	0.0%	0.0%	0.0%
Max	16.7%	16.7%	16.7%	16.7%	16.7%	16.7%	11.1%	12.5%	12.5%	12.5%	12.5%	12.5%

Appendix II.7.3: Outside supervisory board composition, self-employed, employees, retirees, other (in % of outside supervisory board members)

Top 200	Cooperative banks						Savings banks					
	2009	2008	2007	2006	2005	2004	2009	2008	2007	2006	2005	2004
Self-employed individuals												
Mean	42.4%	42.1%	41.6%	41.7%	41.2%	41.5%	12.5%	12.6%	13.0%	12.7%	12.5%	12.4%
Median	45.7%	44.4%	44.4%	46.6%	44.1%	44.4%	11.1%	12.3%	12.0%	12.5%	11.1%	11.1%
Std. Dev.	25.3%	25.8%	25.3%	24.8%	24.7%	24.7%	9.5%	9.4%	9.9%	9.6%	9.7%	9.5%
Min	0.0%	0.0%	0.0%	0.0%	0.0%	0.0%	0.0%	0.0%	0.0%	0.0%	0.0%	0.0%
Max	91.7%	100.0%	100.0%	100.0%	100.0%	100.0%	41.7%	38.9%	41.7%	41.7%	47.1%	47.4%
Employed individuals												
Mean	48.1%	48.7%	47.9%	47.0%	47.0%	46.0%	73.8%	73.4%	73.1%	72.7%	74.4%	72.5%
Median	46.0%	46.0%	45.8%	42.9%	42.9%	41.7%	73.9%	73.2%	73.3%	72.7%	73.3%	73.3%
Std. Dev.	23.7%	24.7%	24.4%	24.0%	24.0%	23.5%	11.9%	12.3%	12.9%	12.2%	11.9%	12.3%
Min	0.0%	0.0%	0.0%	0.0%	0.0%	0.0%	41.7%	36.4%	36.4%	36.4%	36.4%	41.7%
Max	100.0%	100.0%	100.0%	100.0%	100.0%	100.0%	100.0%	100.0%	100.0%	100.0%	100.0%	100.0%
Retirees												
Mean	8.4%	8.2%	9.4%	10.2%	10.8%	11.4%	12.5%	12.7%	12.6%	13.3%	11.7%	13.5%
Median	6.5%	6.1%	6.5%	7.4%	7.4%	8.0%	11.1%	11.1%	11.1%	11.1%	10.0%	12.9%
Std. Dev.	11.7%	11.1%	12.5%	12.8%	13.7%	13.9%	10.0%	10.3%	10.1%	10.1%	9.4%	9.7%
Min	0.0%	0.0%	0.0%	0.0%	0.0%	0.0%	0.0%	0.0%	0.0%	0.0%	0.0%	0.0%
Max	70.0%	77.8%	77.8%	66.7%	66.7%	70.0%	55.6%	47.4%	46.7%	46.7%	40.0%	40.0%
Other												
Mean	1.1%	1.1%	1.1%	1.2%	1.0%	1.1%	1.2%	1.2%	1.3%	1.4%	1.4%	1.7%
Median	0.0%	0.0%	0.0%	0.0%	0.0%	0.0%	0.0%	0.0%	0.0%	0.0%	0.0%	0.0%
Std. Dev.	2.8%	2.9%	3.0%	3.0%	2.8%	3.1%	2.6%	2.7%	2.7%	2.8%	2.8%	2.9%
Min	0.0%	0.0%	0.0%	0.0%	0.0%	0.0%	0.0%	0.0%	0.0%	0.0%	0.0%	0.0%
Max	11.1%	14.3%	14.3%	14.3%	14.3%	14.3%	11.1%	12.5%	12.5%	12.5%	12.5%	12.5%

Top 150												
	2009	2008	2007	2006	2005	2004	2009	2008	2007	2006	2005	2004
Self-employed individuals												
Mean	41.6%	41.3%	41.2%	40.5%	40.0%	40.2%	18.5%	18.1%	18.1%	17.4%	17.4%	16.5%
Median	44.1%	43.7%	41.7%	40.0%	40.0%	40.8%	18.2%	18.2%	18.2%	17.9%	18.2%	16.7%
Std. Dev.	27.0%	27.0%	26.6%	26.0%	25.6%	26.1%	13.1%	12.3%	12.7%	11.9%	12.0%	11.7%
Min	0.0%	0.0%	0.0%	0.0%	0.0%	0.0%	0.0%	0.0%	0.0%	0.0%	0.0%	0.0%
Max	90.9%	100.0%	100.0%	100.0%	100.0%	100.0%	62.5%	50.0%	50.0%	50.0%	50.0%	50.0%
Employed individuals												
Mean	49.7%	49.9%	48.2%	47.3%	47.3%	46.8%	62.4%	63.1%	63.1%	62.8%	65.3%	64.0%
Median	50.0%	49.1%	46.2%	44.4%	44.9%	44.9%	63.6%	63.6%	63.1%	62.5%	66.7%	64.7%
Std. Dev.	24.7%	25.2%	24.9%	24.7%	24.4%	23.7%	16.3%	15.3%	15.5%	15.2%	14.4%	16.2%
Min	9.1%	0.0%	0.0%	0.0%	0.0%	0.0%	16.7%	30.0%	30.0%	30.0%	30.0%	20.0%
Max	100.0%	100.0%	100.0%	100.0%	100.0%	100.0%	100.0%	100.0%	100.0%	100.0%	100.0%	100.0%
Retirees												
Mean	7.8%	7.9%	9.7%	11.3%	11.8%	12.1%	17.6%	17.3%	17.0%	17.9%	15.3%	17.3%
Median	0.0%	0.0%	7.7%	9.1%	9.5%	10.0%	16.0%	15.4%	14.3%	14.3%	11.1%	13.3%
Std. Dev.	11.3%	10.8%	12.2%	12.7%	13.9%	13.7%	14.7%	14.0%	13.8%	14.6%	13.5%	14.3%
Min	0.0%	0.0%	0.0%	0.0%	0.0%	0.0%	0.0%	0.0%	0.0%	0.0%	0.0%	0.0%
Max	70.0%	77.8%	77.8%	66.7%	66.7%	66.7%	83.3%	70.0%	70.0%	70.0%	58.3%	58.3%
Other												
Mean	1.0%	1.0%	1.0%	1.0%	0.9%	0.9%	1.5%	1.6%	1.7%	1.9%	2.0%	2.2%
Median	0.0%	0.0%	0.0%	0.0%	0.0%	0.0%	0.0%	0.0%	0.0%	0.0%	0.0%	0.0%
Std. Dev.	2.9%	3.0%	2.9%	3.0%	2.8%	2.8%	3.5%	3.6%	3.7%	3.8%	3.9%	4.1%
Min	0.0%	0.0%	0.0%	0.0%	0.0%	0.0%	0.0%	0.0%	0.0%	0.0%	0.0%	0.0%
Max	16.7%	16.7%	16.7%	16.7%	16.7%	16.7%	12.5%	14.3%	14.3%	14.3%	14.3%	15.4%

Appendix II.7.4:   Differentiation between politicians (in % of total supervisory board size)

Top 200	Cooperative banks						Savings banks					
	2009	2008	2007	2006	2005	2004	2009	2008	2007	2006	2005	2004
Politicians (total)												
Mean	2.3%	2.2%	2.2%	2.2%	2.1%	2.1%	23.8%	24.8%	24.7%	24.1%	24.7%	24.1%
Median	0.0%	0.0%	0.0%	0.0%	0.0%	0.0%	25.5%	26.5%	25.0%	22.2%	25.0%	22.6%
Std. Dev.	4.6%	4.6%	4.7%	4.5%	4.5%	4.6%	13.8%	14.5%	14.0%	14.3%	14.6%	14.4%
Min	0.0%	0.0%	0.0%	0.0%	0.0%	0.0%	0.0%	0.0%	0.0%	0.0%	0.0%	0.0%
Max	25.0%	25.0%	25.0%	25.0%	25.0%	23.5%	61.5%	75.0%	60.0%	62.5%	62.5%	62.5%
Federal politicians												
Mean	0.1%	0.1%	0.1%	0.1%	0.0%	0.0%	0.8%	0.7%	0.8%	0.7%	0.8%	0.8%
Median	0.0%	0.0%	0.0%	0.0%	0.0%	0.0%	0.0%	0.0%	0.0%	0.0%	0.0%	0.0%
Std. Dev.	1.1%	1.1%	1.0%	1.0%	0.5%	0.5%	2.3%	2.3%	2.3%	2.2%	2.3%	2.4%
Min	0.0%	0.0%	0.0%	0.0%	0.0%	0.0%	0.0%	0.0%	0.0%	0.0%	0.0%	0.0%
Max	11.1%	11.1%	11.1%	11.1%	7.7%	7.7%	14.3%	14.3%	14.3%	14.3%	15.4%	15.4%
State politicians												
Mean	0.2%	0.2%	0.2%	0.2%	0.2%	0.4%	2.6%	2.7%	2.7%	2.6%	2.5%	2.3%
Median	0.0%	0.0%	0.0%	0.0%	0.0%	0.0%	0.0%	0.0%	0.0%	0.0%	0.0%	0.0%
Std. Dev.	1.3%	1.3%	1.4%	1.4%	1.5%	2.1%	4.3%	4.3%	4.3%	4.2%	4.3%	3.9%
Min	0.0%	0.0%	0.0%	0.0%	0.0%	0.0%	0.0%	0.0%	0.0%	0.0%	0.0%	0.0%
Max	11.1%	11.1%	12.5%	12.5%	12.5%	20.0%	21.4%	21.4%	21.4%	21.4%	23.1%	20.0%
Regional politicians												
Mean	0.0%	0.0%	0.0%	0.0%	0.0%	0.0%	5.8%	6.0%	6.1%	5.9%	5.9%	5.5%
Median	0.0%	0.0%	0.0%	0.0%	0.0%	0.0%	6.3%	6.5%	6.7%	6.5%	6.3%	5.9%
Std. Dev.	0.0%	0.0%	0.0%	0.0%	0.0%	0.0%	4.6%	4.8%	4.9%	4.7%	4.7%	4.5%
Min	0.0%	0.0%	0.0%	0.0%	0.0%	0.0%	0.0%	0.0%	0.0%	0.0%	0.0%	0.0%
Max	0.0%	0.0%	0.0%	0.0%	0.0%	0.0%	22.2%	22.2%	23.8%	23.8%	23.8%	28.6%
Local politicians												
Mean	1.9%	1.8%	1.9%	1.8%	1.8%	1.7%	14.6%	15.4%	15.1%	15.0%	15.5%	15.4%
Median	0.0%	0.0%	0.0%	0.0%	0.0%	0.0%	11.1%	11.1%	11.1%	11.8%	13.3%	13.3%
Std. Dev.	4.3%	4.3%	4.4%	4.2%	4.3%	4.0%	12.6%	12.7%	12.5%	12.7%	12.7%	12.4%
Min	0.0%	0.0%	0.0%	0.0%	0.0%	0.0%	0.0%	0.0%	0.0%	0.0%	0.0%	0.0%
Max	25.0%	25.0%	25.0%	25.0%	25.0%	23.5%	50.0%	54.5%	50.0%	53.3%	53.3%	53.3%

Appendix II.7.4: Differentiation between politicians (in % of total supervisory board size) - *continued*

Top 150	Cooperative banks						Savings banks					
	2009	2008	2007	2006	2005	2004	2009	2008	2007	2006	2005	2004
Politicians (total)												
Mean	2.3%	2.2%	2.2%	2.2%	2.4%	2.2%	23.9%	25.0%	24.8%	24.4%	24.9%	25.0%
Median	0.0%	0.0%	0.0%	0.0%	0.0%	0.0%	26.5%	26.7%	25.0%	21.4%	24.6%	25.0%
Std. Dev.	5.2%	4.8%	4.8%	4.7%	4.9%	4.8%	14.1%	14.7%	14.4%	14.7%	15.1%	14.7%
Min	0.0%	0.0%	0.0%	0.0%	0.0%	0.0%	0.0%	0.0%	0.0%	0.0%	0.0%	0.0%
Max	25.0%	25.0%	25.0%	25.0%	25.0%	23.5%	61.5%	75.0%	61.5%	62.5%	75.0%	69.2%
Federal politicians												
Mean	0.3%	0.3%	0.3%	0.3%	0.2%	0.2%	0.8%	0.8%	0.8%	0.7%	0.6%	0.7%
Median	0.0%	0.0%	0.0%	0.0%	0.0%	0.0%	0.0%	0.0%	0.0%	0.0%	0.0%	0.0%
Std. Dev.	1.6%	1.7%	1.7%	1.6%	1.3%	1.2%	2.5%	2.5%	2.5%	2.3%	2.3%	2.3%
Min	0.0%	0.0%	0.0%	0.0%	0.0%	0.0%	0.0%	0.0%	0.0%	0.0%	0.0%	0.0%
Max	11.1%	11.1%	11.1%	11.1%	11.1%	9.1%	14.3%	14.3%	14.3%	14.3%	15.4%	15.4%
State politicians												
Mean	0.1%	0.1%	0.1%	0.1%	0.2%	0.3%	2.5%	2.7%	2.8%	2.7%	2.7%	2.5%
Median	0.0%	0.0%	0.0%	0.0%	0.0%	0.0%	0.0%	0.0%	0.0%	0.0%	0.0%	0.0%
Std. Dev.	1.1%	1.1%	1.1%	1.0%	1.1%	1.6%	4.3%	4.5%	4.5%	4.5%	4.4%	4.0%
Min	0.0%	0.0%	0.0%	0.0%	0.0%	0.0%	0.0%	0.0%	0.0%	0.0%	0.0%	0.0%
Max	11.1%	11.1%	11.1%	11.1%	11.1%	11.1%	21.4%	21.4%	21.4%	21.4%	23.1%	15.4%
Regional politicians												
Mean	0.0%	0.0%	0.0%	0.0%	0.0%	0.0%	5.4%	5.6%	5.5%	5.4%	5.5%	5.6%
Median	0.0%	0.0%	0.0%	0.0%	0.0%	0.0%	6.3%	6.3%	6.3%	6.1%	6.3%	6.3%
Std. Dev.	0.0%	0.0%	0.0%	0.0%	0.0%	0.0%	4.1%	4.1%	4.1%	4.0%	4.2%	4.1%
Min	0.0%	0.0%	0.0%	0.0%	0.0%	0.0%	0.0%	0.0%	0.0%	0.0%	0.0%	0.0%
Max	0.0%	0.0%	0.0%	0.0%	0.0%	0.0%	20.0%	20.0%	20.0%	20.0%	20.0%	20.0%
Local politicians												
Mean	1.9%	1.8%	1.8%	1.8%	2.0%	1.8%	15.2%	15.9%	15.7%	15.6%	16.1%	16.3%
Median	0.0%	0.0%	0.0%	0.0%	0.0%	0.0%	11.8%	13.3%	13.2%	13.3%	13.3%	13.5%
Std. Dev.	4.8%	4.4%	4.4%	4.3%	4.5%	4.3%	12.7%	12.8%	12.8%	13.0%	13.3%	12.7%
Min	0.0%	0.0%	0.0%	0.0%	0.0%	0.0%	0.0%	0.0%	0.0%	0.0%	0.0%	0.0%
Max	25.0%	25.0%	25.0%	25.0%	25.0%	23.5%	50.0%	54.5%	53.8%	53.8%	66.7%	61.5%

Appendix II.7.5: Officiating and retired politicians (in % of total supervisory board size)

Top 200	Cooperative banks						Savings banks					
	2009	2008	2007	2006	2005	2004	2009	2008	2007	2006	2005	2004
Politicians (total)												
Mean	2.8%	2.7%	2.7%	2.8%	2.8%	3.0%	27.6%	28.6%	28.4%	28.1%	28.3%	27.8%
Median	0.0%	0.0%	0.0%	0.0%	0.0%	0.0%	27.8%	27.8%	27.8%	27.4%	28.6%	26.7%
Std. Dev.	5.5%	5.6%	5.5%	5.3%	5.5%	5.9%	14.9%	15.3%	14.8%	15.3%	15.3%	15.7%
Min	0.0%	0.0%	0.0%	0.0%	0.0%	0.0%	0.0%	0.0%	0.0%	0.0%	0.0%	0.0%
Max	31.3%	31.3%	31.3%	31.3%	33.3%	35.3%	61.5%	75.0%	64.3%	64.3%	62.5%	62.5%

Top 150	Cooperative banks						Savings banks					
	2009	2008	2007	2006	2005	2004	2009	2008	2007	2006	2005	2004
Politicians (total)												
Mean	3.0%	3.2%	3.1%	3.3%	3.4%	3.3%	27.8%	29.0%	28.8%	28.8%	28.8%	28.8%
Median	0.0%	0.0%	0.0%	0.0%	0.0%	0.0%	27.8%	27.8%	27.8%	27.8%	29.8%	28.8%
Std. Dev.	6.5%	6.3%	6.2%	6.1%	6.3%	6.6%	15.1%	15.7%	15.2%	15.4%	15.6%	15.5%
Min	0.0%	0.0%	0.0%	0.0%	0.0%	0.0%	0.0%	0.0%	0.0%	0.0%	0.0%	0.0%
Max	33.3%	31.3%	31.3%	31.3%	33.3%	35.3%	69.2%	75.0%	69.2%	69.2%	75.0%	69.2%

31

Appendix II.7.6: Self-employed and employees with assumed financial expertise (in % of total supervisory board size)

	Cooperative banks						Savings banks					
Top 200	2009	2008	2007	2006	2005	2004	2009	2008	2007	2006	2005	2004
Self-employed individuals with financial expertise												
Mean	19.1%	19.0%	18.4%	18.0%	18.3%	18.8%	6.6%	6.5%	6.7%	6.4%	6.3%	6.2%
Median	15.7%	15.4%	16.7%	16.0%	15.4%	16.7%	5.6%	5.6%	5.6%	5.6%	5.6%	5.6%
Std. Dev.	17.6%	17.7%	17.5%	17.0%	17.2%	17.6%	7.7%	7.3%	7.3%	6.9%	7.2%	7.1%
Min	0.0%	0.0%	0.0%	0.0%	0.0%	0.0%	0.0%	0.0%	0.0%	0.0%	0.0%	0.0%
Max	75.0%	75.0%	71.4%	69.2%	73.3%	83.3%	37.5%	37.5%	33.3%	33.3%	33.3%	33.3%
Employed individuals with financial expertise												
Mean	27.3%	27.5%	26.9%	25.7%	25.0%	24.1%	54.6%	53.1%	52.6%	52.5%	53.1%	52.3%
Median	25.0%	23.9%	23.9%	25.0%	22.2%	21.4%	52.6%	52.4%	50.0%	52.4%	53.3%	52.6%
Std. Dev.	19.6%	20.1%	19.6%	19.3%	19.2%	18.9%	15.8%	16.2%	16.0%	15.9%	15.8%	15.6%
Min	0.0%	0.0%	0.0%	0.0%	0.0%	0.0%	10.0%	9.1%	9.1%	9.1%	9.1%	14.3%
Max	91.7%	100.0%	100.0%	100.0%	100.0%	90.9%	93.8%	93.3%	93.3%	95.8%	93.3%	93.3%

Top 150	2009	2008	2007	2006	2005	2004	2009	2008	2007	2006	2005	2004
Self-employed individuals with financial expertise												
Mean	18.8%	19.1%	18.8%	18.2%	18.3%	18.0%	7.2%	7.1%	7.1%	6.7%	6.6%	6.5%
Median	16.0%	16.7%	16.7%	16.7%	16.0%	16.7%	5.9%	5.9%	5.9%	5.9%	5.6%	5.6%
Std. Dev.	17.5%	17.6%	17.5%	17.2%	17.1%	16.6%	8.3%	7.8%	7.7%	7.3%	7.4%	7.5%
Min	0.0%	0.0%	0.0%	0.0%	0.0%	0.0%	0.0%	0.0%	0.0%	0.0%	0.0%	0.0%
Max	75.0%	75.0%	71.4%	69.2%	77.8%	71.4%	37.5%	37.5%	33.3%	33.3%	33.3%	33.3%
Employed individuals with financial expertise												
Mean	28.7%	27.0%	25.9%	25.0%	24.4%	23.9%	54.3%	52.9%	52.3%	52.4%	53.2%	53.1%
Median	25.0%	22.5%	22.2%	22.2%	21.1%	19.1%	52.9%	51.2%	50.0%	50.0%	53.3%	53.3%
Std. Dev.	21.0%	21.4%	20.6%	20.7%	20.3%	20.1%	15.6%	15.7%	15.6%	15.5%	15.4%	15.6%
Min	0.0%	0.0%	0.0%	0.0%	0.0%	0.0%	10.0%	9.1%	9.1%	9.1%	9.1%	14.3%
Max	87.5%	85.7%	85.7%	85.7%	75.0%	75.0%	93.8%	93.3%	93.3%	95.8%	93.3%	93.3%

Appendix II.7.7: Cross-category groups with assumed financial expertise (in % of total supervisory board size)

Top 200	Cooperative banks						Savings banks					
	2009	2008	2007	2006	2005	2004	2009	2008	2007	2006	2005	2004
Executives / Managing Partners / Partners, Owners												
Mean	34.9%	34.7%	33.8%	32.5%	32.0%	31.9%	12.6%	11.9%	11.6%	11.6%	11.6%	11.6%
Median	33.3%	33.3%	33.3%	30.4%	33.3%	33.3%	11.1%	11.1%	11.1%	11.1%	11.1%	10.6%
Std. Dev.	20.7%	20.9%	21.1%	21.2%	21.0%	21.0%	9.6%	8.7%	8.3%	8.1%	8.3%	8.4%
Min	0.0%	0.0%	0.0%	0.0%	0.0%	0.0%	0.0%	0.0%	0.0%	0.0%	0.0%	0.0%
Max	91.7%	90.9%	92.3%	100.0%	92.3%	92.3%	37.5%	37.5%	35.7%	35.7%	38.5%	38.5%
Accountants / Auditors / Tax consultants												
Mean	7.6%	7.6%	7.3%	6.9%	6.9%	6.8%	1.3%	1.3%	1.3%	1.1%	1.1%	1.1%
Median	6.7%	7.1%	7.1%	6.5%	6.7%	6.9%	2.8%	2.7%	2.6%	2.6%	2.6%	2.4%
Std. Dev.	7.9%	8.0%	7.4%	7.5%	7.4%	7.0%	2.8%	2.7%	2.6%	2.6%	2.6%	2.4%
Min	0.0%	0.0%	0.0%	0.0%	0.0%	0.0%	0.0%	0.0%	0.0%	0.0%	0.0%	0.0%
Max	33.3%	33.3%	33.3%	37.5%	37.5%	40.0%	12.5%	11.1%	11.1%	14.3%	13.3%	11.1%

Top 150	Cooperative banks						Savings banks					
	2009	2008	2007	2006	2005	2004	2009	2008	2007	2006	2005	2004
Executives / Managing Partners / Partners, Owners												
Mean	37.5%	36.3%	35.2%	33.9%	33.0%	32.4%	13.1%	12.2%	12.0%	11.9%	11.9%	12.1%
Median	37.5%	33.3%	33.3%	33.3%	33.3%	31.0%	12.5%	12.5%	12.1%	12.5%	11.4%	11.1%
Std. Dev.	23.2%	23.4%	23.1%	23.0%	22.0%	21.3%	10.1%	9.1%	8.8%	8.5%	8.8%	8.8%
Min	0.0%	0.0%	0.0%	0.0%	0.0%	0.0%	0.0%	0.0%	0.0%	0.0%	0.0%	0.0%
Max	100.0%	88.9%	88.9%	90.0%	85.7%	90.0%	37.5%	37.5%	35.7%	35.7%	38.5%	38.5%
Accountants / Auditors / Tax consultants												
Mean	7.8%	7.5%	7.4%	6.9%	7.1%	7.0%	1.5%	1.5%	1.4%	1.3%	1.3%	1.1%
Median	7.7%	7.4%	8.0%	7.1%	7.1%	7.1%	0.0%	0.0%	0.0%	0.0%	0.0%	0.0%
Std. Dev.	8.2%	8.0%	7.6%	7.4%	7.7%	7.3%	3.0%	2.9%	2.8%	2.8%	2.8%	2.5%
Min	0.0%	0.0%	0.0%	0.0%	0.0%	0.0%	0.0%	0.0%	0.0%	0.0%	0.0%	0.0%
Max	33.3%	33.3%	33.3%	33.3%	33.3%	33.3%	12.5%	11.1%	11.1%	14.3%	13.3%	11.1%

Appendix II.7.8:   Financial expertise (in % of total supervisory board size) and outside financial expertise (in % of outside supervisory board members)

	Cooperative banks						Savings banks					
Top 200	2009	2008	2007	2006	2005	2004	2009	2008	2007	2006	2005	2004
Financial expertise												
Mean	49.1%	48.9%	48.3%	47.2%	46.8%	46.2%	66.4%	65.4%	64.8%	64.7%	64.7%	63.9%
Median	50.0%	50.0%	50.0%	46.9%	46.7%	46.4%	66.7%	64.2%	63.6%	66.7%	66.7%	66.7%
Std. Dev.	22.3%	23.1%	23.0%	23.4%	22.7%	22.9%	17.4%	17.6%	16.9%	17.4%	17.3%	17.0%
Min	0.0%	0.0%	0.0%	0.0%	0.0%	0.0%	20.0%	20.0%	20.0%	20.0%	23.1%	21.4%
Max	100.0%	100.0%	100.0%	100.0%	100.0%	100.0%	100.0%	100.0%	100.0%	100.0%	100.0%	100.0%
Outside financial expertise												
Mean	46.6%	46.4%	45.9%	44.7%	44.2%	43.6%	54.0%	53.9%	53.2%	52.9%	52.9%	51.9%
Median	48.3%	45.8%	46.2%	44.4%	44.4%	42.9%	55.1%	53.8%	53.8%	51.7%	50.0%	50.0%
Std. Dev.	22.9%	23.5%	23.5%	23.6%	23.0%	23.0%	24.0%	23.2%	22.3%	22.8%	22.8%	22.3%
Min	0.0%	0.0%	0.0%	0.0%	0.0%	0.0%	0.0%	4.8%	4.8%	4.8%	7.1%	0.0%
Max	100.0%	100.0%	100.0%	100.0%	100.0%	100.0%	100.0%	100.0%	100.0%	100.0%	100.0%	100.0%
Top 150	2009	2008	2007	2006	2005	2004	2009	2008	2007	2006	2005	2004
Financial expertise												
Mean	50.1%	48.7%	48.0%	46.9%	46.2%	45.3%	67.0%	65.9%	65.2%	65.1%	64.9%	64.6%
Median	50.0%	50.0%	48.7%	45.3%	45.8%	45.5%	66.7%	66.7%	66.7%	66.7%	66.7%	66.7%
Std. Dev.	22.3%	23.3%	22.9%	23.4%	22.1%	22.4%	17.3%	17.5%	17.0%	17.2%	17.0%	17.4%
Min	0.0%	0.0%	0.0%	0.0%	0.0%	0.0%	20.0%	20.0%	20.0%	20.0%	23.1%	21.4%
Max	100.0%	100.0%	100.0%	100.0%	100.0%	100.0%	100.0%	100.0%	100.0%	100.0%	100.0%	100.0%
Outside financial expertise												
Mean	48.2%	47.0%	46.3%	45.2%	44.5%	43.6%	54.9%	54.7%	53.8%	53.4%	53.2%	53.1%
Median	50.0%	46.2%	45.3%	43.7%	44.4%	44.4%	57.1%	56.3%	54.5%	54.8%	51.9%	53.6%
Std. Dev.	23.6%	24.3%	23.8%	24.2%	22.9%	23.1%	23.9%	23.2%	22.4%	22.9%	22.8%	22.9%
Min	0.0%	0.0%	0.0%	0.0%	0.0%	0.0%	0.0%	0.0%	0.0%	0.0%	0.0%	0.0%
Max	100.0%	100.0%	100.0%	100.0%	100.0%	100.0%	100.0%	100.0%	100.0%	100.0%	100.0%	100.0%

Appendix II.7.9: Financial expertise clustered by bank size (in % of total supervisory board size)

	Cooperative banks						Savings banks					
Top 200	2009	2008	2007	2006	2005	2004	2009	2008	2007	2006	2005	2004
Financial expertise Group 1	n=50; average total assets: EUR 4.55 bn						n=50; average total assets 2009: EUR 7.76 bn					
Mean	55.1%	54.8%	55.5%	55.1%	53.6%	52.6%	64.0%	64.5%	64.6%	64.4%	64.8%	64.1%
Median	55.8%	53.6%	58.3%	55.9%	55.1%	56.3%	65.3%	66.0%	66.7%	66.7%	66.7%	66.7%
Std. Dev.	26.0%	26.3%	25.9%	25.8%	25.1%	25.2%	15.7%	15.1%	15.1%	15.1%	14.5%	14.5%
Min	0.0%	0.0%	0.0%	0.0%	0.0%	0.0%	27.8%	38.1%	38.1%	37.5%	37.0%	38.1%
Max	100.0%	100.0%	100.0%	100.0%	100.0%	100.0%	93.3%	93.3%	93.3%	93.3%	88.2%	93.8%
Financial expertise Group 2	n=50; average total assets 2009: EUR 1.46 bn						n=50; average total assets 2009: EUR 3.38 bn					
Mean	49.7%	51.2%	50.1%	48.7%	48.9%	48.8%	67.5%	65.3%	64.8%	64.8%	64.3%	63.1%
Median	53.6%	54.2%	50.0%	46.6%	46.6%	48.7%	66.7%	66.7%	66.7%	66.7%	66.7%	65.8%
Std. Dev.	22.9%	23.4%	23.2%	23.1%	22.0%	22.6%	18.5%	19.5%	18.8%	18.9%	18.4%	17.6%
Min	0.0%	0.0%	0.0%	0.0%	0.0%	0.0%	20.0%	20.0%	20.0%	20.0%	27.3%	30.8%
Max	100.0%	100.0%	100.0%	100.0%	100.0%	100.0%	100.0%	100.0%	100.0%	100.0%	96.7%	93.3%
Financial expertise Group 3	n=50; average total assets 2009: EUR 0.99 bn						n=50; average total assets 2009: EUR 2.33 bn					
Mean	48.3%	47.9%	46.4%	43.7%	44.5%	43.6%	66.2%	65.7%	64.8%	64.5%	64.9%	63.4%
Median	50.0%	44.9%	44.4%	44.4%	44.9%	44.9%	61.5%	62.8%	61.8%	64.9%	66.7%	66.7%
Std. Dev.	19.5%	20.5%	20.1%	21.0%	20.6%	19.9%	17.7%	18.2%	16.9%	18.6%	19.1%	19.2%
Min	11.1%	11.1%	0.0%	0.0%	0.0%	0.0%	38.1%	35.7%	35.7%	35.7%	35.7%	21.4%
Max	83.3%	100.0%	88.9%	88.9%	83.3%	83.3%	100.0%	100.0%	96.2%	100.0%	100.0%	100.0%
Financial expertise Group 4	n=50; average total assets 2009: EUR 0.76 bn						n=50; average total assets 2009: EUR 1.70 bn					
Mean	43.4%	41.9%	41.3%	41.1%	40.1%	39.8%	68.0%	66.0%	65.0%	65.1%	64.8%	64.9%
Median	43.3%	40.0%	39.3%	38.0%	38.7%	40.0%	65.7%	62.5%	62.0%	62.5%	62.5%	66.7%
Std. Dev.	19.3%	20.4%	20.5%	21.7%	21.3%	21.9%	17.7%	17.9%	17.1%	17.2%	17.3%	16.8%
Min	12.5%	0.0%	0.0%	0.0%	0.0%	0.0%	23.1%	23.1%	23.1%	23.1%	23.1%	26.7%
Max	90.0%	90.9%	92.3%	92.3%	92.3%	92.3%	100.0%	100.0%	100.0%	94.4%	94.4%	94.4%

Top 150	2009	2008	2007	2006	2005	2004	2009	2008	2007	2006	2005	2004
Financial expertise Group 1	n=50; average total assets 2009: EUR 3.36 bn						n=50; average total assets 2009: EUR 5.53 bn					
Mean	52.0%	52.1%	52.6%	50.7%	50.7%	51.1%	67.4%	66.5%	65.9%	65.9%	66.4%	65.7%
Median	55.1%	55.1%	55.6%	54.5%	54.2%	55.6%	71.8%	70.2%	69.9%	67.5%	66.7%	66.7%
Std. Dev.	25.5%	26.3%	25.7%	25.4%	25.2%	26.2%	16.0%	16.6%	16.5%	15.9%	15.4%	15.6%
Min	0.0%	0.0%	0.0%	0.0%	0.0%	0.0%	28.6%	28.6%	28.6%	28.6%	28.6%	30.8%
Max	100.0%	100.0%	100.0%	100.0%	100.0%	100.0%	100.0%	100.0%	100.0%	100.0%	93.3%	93.8%
Financial expertise Group 2	n=50; average total assets 2009: EUR 0.80 bn						n=50; average total assets 2009: EUR 2.54 bn					
Mean	49.6%	48.6%	46.8%	46.8%	47.1%	45.5%	66.5%	65.6%	65.2%	64.6%	64.3%	64.6%
Median	50.0%	46.2%	43.7%	43.7%	48.3%	45.6%	64.8%	61.7%	62.1%	64.9%	62.4%	66.7%
Std. Dev.	18.6%	20.4%	20.0%	21.3%	20.0%	19.5%	18.0%	18.2%	17.3%	18.7%	18.6%	18.9%
Min	16.7%	0.0%	0.0%	0.0%	0.0%	0.0%	20.0%	20.0%	20.0%	20.0%	30.0%	21.4%
Max	85.7%	100.0%	88.9%	88.9%	85.7%	85.7%	100.0%	100.0%	96.2%	100.0%	100.0%	100.0%
Financial expertise Group 3	n=50; average total assets 2009: EUR 0.57 bn						n=50; average total assets 2009: EUR 1.62 bn					
Mean	48.7%	45.5%	44.6%	43.1%	40.8%	39.4%	67.0%	65.7%	64.5%	64.6%	64.1%	63.6%
Median	48.3%	44.4%	40.0%	40.0%	37.2%	36.0%	66.7%	65.7%	62.5%	62.5%	62.5%	65.7%
Std. Dev.	22.5%	22.9%	22.3%	23.2%	20.1%	19.8%	18.2%	18.0%	17.4%	17.3%	17.3%	17.7%
Min	0.0%	0.0%	0.0%	0.0%	0.0%	0.0%	23.1%	23.1%	23.1%	23.1%	23.1%	26.7%
Max	100.0%	88.9%	88.9%	90.0%	83.3%	88.9%	100.0%	100.0%	100.0%	94.4%	94.4%	94.4%

Appendix II.7.10: Outside financial expertise clustered by bank size (in % of outside supervisory board members)

	Cooperative banks						Savings banks					
Top 200	2009	2008	2007	2006	2005	2004	2009	2008	2007	2006	2005	2004
Out. financial expertise Group 1	n=50; average total assets: EUR 4.55 bn						n=50; average total assets 2009: EUR 7.76 bn					
Mean	47.3%	47.0%	48.2%	47.5%	45.8%	44.6%	48.1%	48.5%	48.7%	48.5%	49.0%	48.4%
Median	50.0%	50.0%	51.7%	52.3%	47.2%	44.2%	53.6%	50.9%	51.3%	50.0%	50.0%	50.0%
Std. Dev.	28.2%	27.8%	28.2%	27.5%	26.8%	25.8%	23.0%	22.3%	22.6%	22.2%	21.4%	20.5%
Min	0.0%	0.0%	0.0%	0.0%	0.0%	0.0%	0.0%	4.8%	4.8%	4.8%	7.1%	11.1%
Max	100.0%	100.0%	100.0%	100.0%	100.0%	100.0%	90.0%	90.0%	90.0%	90.0%	81.8%	90.0%
Out. financial expertise Group 2	n=50; average total assets 2009: EUR 1.46 bn						n=50; average total assets 2009: EUR 3.38 bn					
Mean	48.1%	49.5%	48.3%	47.0%	47.2%	47.1%	57.5%	56.8%	56.1%	56.0%	55.3%	53.5%
Median	50.0%	51.9%	50.0%	46.6%	46.6%	45.9%	60.0%	58.3%	58.7%	56.9%	56.7%	50.0%
Std. Dev.	22.8%	23.4%	23.0%	22.9%	21.8%	23.1%	23.0%	22.5%	21.7%	21.8%	21.7%	21.4%
Min	0.0%	0.0%	0.0%	0.0%	0.0%	0.0%	13.3%	12.5%	12.5%	12.5%	12.5%	4.2%
Max	100.0%	100.0%	100.0%	100.0%	100.0%	100.0%	100.0%	100.0%	100.0%	100.0%	95.0%	90.0%
Out. financial expertise Group 3	n=50; average total assets 2009: EUR 0.99 bn						n=50; average total assets 2009: EUR 2.33 bn					
Mean	47.7%	47.3%	45.8%	43.1%	43.8%	42.9%	53.6%	54.5%	53.5%	52.8%	53.3%	51.3%
Median	50.0%	44.9%	44.4%	44.4%	44.9%	44.9%	52.3%	56.4%	56.1%	50.0%	57.7%	50.0%
Std. Dev.	20.5%	21.7%	21.3%	22.1%	21.7%	21.0%	25.5%	24.5%	22.9%	25.1%	25.7%	25.6%
Min	0.0%	0.0%	0.0%	0.0%	0.0%	0.0%	7.1%	7.1%	7.1%	7.7%	7.1%	7.1%
Max	83.3%	100.0%	88.9%	88.9%	83.3%	83.3%	100.0%	100.0%	94.1%	100.0%	100.0%	100.0%
Out. financial expertise Group 4	n=50; average total assets 2009: EUR 0.76 bn						n=50; average total assets 2009: EUR 1.70 bn					
Mean	43.4%	41.9%	41.3%	41.1%	40.1%	39.8%	56.8%	55.7%	54.7%	54.5%	54.2%	54.5%
Median	43.3%	40.0%	39.3%	38.0%	38.7%	40.0%	51.9%	51.5%	50.0%	50.0%	50.0%	54.5%
Std. Dev.	19.3%	20.4%	20.5%	21.7%	21.3%	21.9%	24.1%	23.0%	21.7%	22.0%	22.2%	21.5%
Min	12.5%	0.0%	0.0%	0.0%	0.0%	0.0%	8.3%	8.3%	8.3%	8.3%	8.3%	0.0%
Max	90.0%	90.9%	92.3%	92.3%	92.3%	92.3%	100.0%	100.0%	100.0%	91.7%	91.7%	91.7%

Top 150	2009	2008	2007	2006	2005	2004	2009	2008	2007	2006	2005	2004
Out. financial expertise Group 1	n=50; average total assets 2009: EUR 3.36 bn						n=50; average total assets 2009: EUR 5.53 bn					
Mean	47.6%	47.5%	48.0%	46.0%	45.9%	46.4%	55.3%	54.9%	54.1%	54.1%	54.6%	54.0%
Median	53.6%	53.8%	54.7%	54.5%	51.9%	54.2%	60.0%	59.4%	59.4%	59.2%	59.2%	58.3%
Std. Dev.	27.8%	28.7%	28.1%	27.5%	27.4%	28.3%	22.0%	22.1%	22.0%	21.3%	20.2%	20.2%
Min	0.0%	0.0%	0.0%	0.0%	0.0%	0.0%	10.0%	10.0%	10.0%	10.0%	18.8%	11.1%
Max	100.0%	100.0%	100.0%	100.0%	100.0%	100.0%	100.0%	100.0%	100.0%	100.0%	90.0%	90.0%
Out. financial expertise Group 2	n=50; average total assets 2009: EUR 0.80 bn						n=50; average total assets 2009: EUR 2.54 bn					
Mean	49.3%	48.2%	46.5%	46.5%	46.8%	45.2%	55.0%	54.8%	54.2%	53.5%	52.9%	53.6%
Median	50.0%	46.2%	43.7%	43.7%	48.3%	45.6%	54.2%	53.8%	53.8%	51.9%	51.9%	50.0%
Std. Dev.	19.4%	21.1%	20.7%	21.9%	20.6%	20.1%	24.5%	24.0%	23.0%	24.7%	25.0%	24.8%
Min	0.0%	0.0%	0.0%	0.0%	0.0%	0.0%	7.1%	7.1%	7.1%	7.7%	7.1%	7.1%
Max	85.7%	100.0%	88.9%	88.9%	85.7%	85.7%	100.0%	100.0%	94.1%	100.0%	100.0%	100.0%
Out. financial expertise Group 3	n=50; average total assets 2009: EUR 0.57 bn						n=50; average total assets 2009: EUR 1.62 bn					
Mean	47.8%	45.4%	44.5%	43.0%	40.7%	39.3%	54.4%	54.3%	53.0%	52.7%	52.0%	51.7%
Median	45.3%	44.4%	40.0%	40.0%	37.2%	36.0%	50.0%	51.5%	50.0%	50.0%	50.0%	52.3%
Std. Dev.	23.3%	22.8%	22.3%	23.2%	20.0%	19.7%	25.5%	23.8%	22.8%	23.0%	23.2%	23.9%
Min	0.0%	0.0%	0.0%	0.0%	0.0%	0.0%	0.0%	0.0%	0.0%	0.0%	0.0%	0.0%
Max	100.0%	88.9%	88.9%	90.0%	83.3%	88.9%	100.0%	100.0%	100.0%	91.7%	91.7%	91.7%

Appendix II.7.11: Financial expertise clustered by supervisory board size (in % of total supervisory board size)

Top 200	Cooperative banks						Savings banks					
	2009	2008	2007	2006	2005	2004	2009	2008	2007	2006	2005	2004
Financial expertise Group 1	n=50; average board size: 18 members						n=50; average board size: 23 members					
Mean	50.9%	51.0%	50.7%	49.9%	48.8%	48.0%	63.9%	64.9%	65.4%	64.9%	64.5%	63.5%
Median	53.3%	51.7%	50.0%	50.0%	50.0%	48.7%	61.9%	64.2%	63.6%	64.3%	66.7%	65.0%
Std. Dev.	22.7%	22.9%	21.9%	22.3%	21.5%	21.4%	17.9%	17.4%	17.3%	17.1%	17.0%	16.4%
Min	5.3%	5.3%	4.5%	0.0%	0.0%	0.0%	27.8%	38.1%	38.1%	37.5%	37.0%	36.1%
Max	93.8%	94.1%	92.6%	92.6%	86.7%	86.7%	100.0%	100.0%	100.0%	100.0%	96.7%	93.3%
Financial expertise Group 2	n=50; average board size: 13 members						n=50; average board size: 17 members					
Mean	48.5%	47.1%	46.1%	44.6%	44.4%	43.8%	67.0%	66.0%	66.3%	65.3%	65.0%	62.9%
Median	45.5%	45.5%	41.7%	40.1%	35.7%	40.0%	63.9%	61.8%	62.5%	62.5%	61.8%	63.4%
Std. Dev.	22.6%	23.7%	23.8%	24.0%	23.8%	24.3%	14.9%	15.3%	15.1%	15.8%	16.1%	16.6%
Min	16.7%	0.0%	0.0%	0.0%	0.0%	0.0%	46.7%	31.3%	33.3%	38.1%	37.5%	35.0%
Max	100.0%	100.0%	100.0%	100.0%	100.0%	100.0%	100.0%	100.0%	100.0%	94.4%	94.4%	94.4%
Financial expertise Group 3	n=50; average board size: 11 members						n=50; average board size: 15 members					
Mean	50.3%	51.6%	51.8%	50.8%	49.8%	51.2%	65.6%	64.6%	63.6%	63.7%	63.8%	63.8%
Median	50.0%	52.3%	55.6%	50.0%	50.0%	50.0%	64.3%	63.3%	66.7%	66.7%	66.7%	66.7%
Std. Dev.	18.5%	20.4%	20.0%	21.0%	18.6%	18.9%	16.8%	17.9%	17.2%	17.8%	17.7%	17.9%
Min	11.1%	10.0%	11.1%	11.1%	11.1%	20.0%	40.0%	35.7%	28.6%	28.6%	28.6%	21.4%
Max	100.0%	100.0%	100.0%	100.0%	100.0%	91.7%	100.0%	100.0%	93.3%	100.0%	93.3%	93.8%
Financial expertise Group 4	n=50; average board size: 8 members						n=50; average board size: 12 members					
Mean	46.7%	46.1%	44.8%	43.3%	44.1%	41.9%	69.1%	65.9%	64.0%	64.9%	65.5%	65.3%
Median	50.0%	47.2%	44.4%	43.7%	44.4%	44.4%	71.4%	66.7%	66.7%	66.7%	66.7%	66.7%
Std. Dev.	25.4%	25.3%	25.7%	25.9%	26.2%	25.7%	19.8%	20.1%	18.3%	19.1%	18.8%	17.5%
Min	0.0%	0.0%	0.0%	0.0%	0.0%	0.0%	20.0%	20.0%	20.0%	20.0%	23.1%	30.8%
Max	100.0%	100.0%	100.0%	100.0%	100.0%	100.0%	100.0%	100.0%	92.9%	93.3%	100.0%	100.0%

Top 150	Cooperative banks						Savings banks					
	2009	2008	2007	2006	2005	2004	2009	2008	2007	2006	2005	2004
Financial expertise Group 1	n=50; average board size: 15 members						n=50; average board size: 20 members					
Mean	48.5%	46.3%	45.6%	44.4%	44.1%	43.6%	68.2%	68.2%	68.7%	67.8%	67.1%	65.6%
Median	46.2%	46.2%	46.2%	44.5%	44.5%	45.6%	66.0%	65.0%	69.9%	68.7%	68.4%	67.4%
Std. Dev.	22.1%	23.5%	22.9%	23.2%	22.6%	22.7%	16.0%	16.3%	16.2%	16.3%	16.3%	16.6%
Min	11.8%	0.0%	0.0%	0.0%	0.0%	0.0%	38.1%	38.1%	38.1%	38.1%	38.1%	38.1%
Max	100.0%	100.0%	100.0%	100.0%	100.0%	100.0%	100.0%	100.0%	100.0%	100.0%	94.4%	94.4%
Financial expertise Group 2	n=50; average board size: 10 members						n=50; average board size: 15 members					
Mean	48.4%	49.0%	48.1%	48.1%	46.7%	45.9%	62.6%	61.6%	60.7%	60.6%	61.0%	60.9%
Median	50.0%	49.7%	47.2%	44.4%	44.9%	45.5%	60.0%	60.0%	60.0%	60.0%	60.0%	60.0%
Std. Dev.	18.4%	20.1%	18.9%	19.1%	18.5%	20.3%	15.7%	16.4%	16.1%	15.8%	15.7%	17.4%
Min	0.0%	0.0%	0.0%	0.0%	0.0%	0.0%	33.3%	33.3%	28.6%	28.6%	28.6%	21.4%
Max	88.9%	100.0%	88.9%	90.0%	83.3%	91.7%	100.0%	100.0%	93.3%	93.3%	93.8%	93.8%
Financial expertise Group 3	n=50; average board size: 8 members						n=50; average board size: 12 members					
Mean	53.4%	50.8%	50.3%	48.1%	47.8%	46.5%	70.2%	67.9%	66.2%	66.7%	66.7%	67.5%
Median	52.8%	50.0%	50.0%	50.0%	50.0%	47.7%	74.2%	73.0%	67.9%	69.2%	67.9%	69.6%
Std. Dev.	25.8%	26.2%	26.5%	27.4%	25.1%	24.4%	19.4%	19.2%	18.0%	18.9%	18.6%	17.7%
Min	0.0%	0.0%	0.0%	0.0%	0.0%	0.0%	20.0%	20.0%	20.0%	20.0%	23.1%	30.8%
Max	100.0%	100.0%	100.0%	100.0%	100.0%	100.0%	100.0%	100.0%	92.9%	100.0%	100.0%	100.0%

Appendix II.7.12: Outside financial expertise clustered by supervisory board size (in % of outside supervisory board members)

Top 200	Cooperative banks						Savings banks					
	2009	2008	2007	2006	2005	2004	2009	2008	2007	2006	2005	2004
Out. financial expertise Group 1	n=50; average board size: 18 members						n=50; average board size: 23 members					
Mean	44.3%	44.4%	44.6%	43.7%	42.4%	41.6%	49.7%	50.7%	51.3%	50.5%	50.2%	48.8%
Median	46.4%	46.1%	48.3%	48.3%	43.7%	39.6%	52.8%	50.0%	51.3%	52.5%	50.0%	46.9%
Std. Dev.	23.4%	23.0%	22.3%	22.1%	21.9%	21.3%	25.9%	25.7%	25.6%	25.1%	24.7%	23.4%
Min	0.0%	0.0%	0.0%	0.0%	0.0%	0.0%	0.0%	4.8%	4.8%	4.8%	7.1%	4.2%
Max	87.5%	88.9%	88.9%	88.9%	80.0%	85.7%	100.0%	100.0%	100.0%	100.0%	95.0%	90.0%
Out. financial expertise Group 2	n=50; average board size: 13 members						n=50; average board size: 17 members					
Mean	47.3%	46.0%	44.9%	43.4%	43.2%	42.2%	53.4%	53.5%	53.8%	52.2%	51.9%	49.4%
Median	45.5%	45.5%	41.7%	40.1%	35.7%	40.0%	50.0%	50.0%	50.0%	50.0%	50.0%	50.0%
Std. Dev.	22.0%	23.0%	23.3%	23.1%	22.8%	23.6%	20.9%	20.1%	20.3%	21.3%	21.4%	21.5%
Min	9.1%	0.0%	0.0%	0.0%	0.0%	0.0%	20.0%	20.0%	20.0%	18.8%	18.2%	11.1%
Max	100.0%	100.0%	100.0%	100.0%	100.0%	100.0%	100.0%	100.0%	100.0%	91.7%	91.7%	91.7%
Out. financial expertise Group 3	n=50; average board size: 11 members						n=50; average board size: 15 members					
Mean	49.3%	50.4%	50.5%	49.5%	48.4%	50.1%	49.5%	49.8%	48.4%	48.6%	48.7%	49.1%
Median	50.0%	50.0%	55.6%	50.0%	50.0%	50.0%	50.0%	50.0%	50.0%	50.0%	50.0%	50.0%
Std. Dev.	19.4%	21.1%	20.8%	21.8%	19.2%	18.8%	25.0%	24.6%	23.5%	24.3%	24.3%	24.1%
Min	0.0%	0.0%	0.0%	0.0%	11.1%	20.0%	10.0%	10.0%	10.0%	10.0%	10.0%	0.0%
Max	100.0%	100.0%	100.0%	100.0%	100.0%	90.0%	100.0%	100.0%	90.0%	100.0%	90.0%	90.0%
Out. financial expertise Group 4	n=50; average board size: 8 members						n=50; average board size: 12 members					
Mean	45.6%	44.9%	43.6%	42.1%	42.9%	40.7%	63.3%	61.5%	59.3%	60.5%	61.0%	60.5%
Median	50.0%	47.2%	44.4%	42.9%	44.4%	44.4%	64.6%	62.5%	61.3%	62.5%	62.5%	61.3%
Std. Dev.	26.5%	26.8%	27.0%	27.2%	27.6%	27.1%	22.0%	20.5%	18.0%	18.8%	18.9%	18.0%
Min	0.0%	0.0%	0.0%	0.0%	0.0%	0.0%	20.0%	20.0%	20.0%	20.0%	23.1%	30.8%
Max	100.0%	100.0%	100.0%	100.0%	100.0%	100.0%	100.0%	100.0%	90.0%	90.0%	100.0%	100.0%

Top 150	2009	2008	2007	2006	2005	2004	2009	2008	2007	2006	2005	2004
Out. financial expertise Group 1	n=50; average board size: 15 members						n=50; average board size: 20 members					
Mean	45.0%	43.2%	42.7%	41.5%	41.0%	40.3%	57.1%	57.7%	58.3%	56.7%	55.7%	53.7%
Median	45.3%	43.7%	40.8%	37.1%	36.3%	37.9%	58.3%	58.6%	59.0%	59.2%	58.3%	56.9%
Std. Dev.	24.0%	24.4%	23.5%	23.5%	23.0%	23.1%	21.7%	21.9%	22.0%	22.3%	22.0%	22.4%
Min	0.0%	0.0%	0.0%	0.0%	0.0%	0.0%	7.1%	7.1%	7.1%	7.7%	7.1%	7.1%
Max	100.0%	100.0%	100.0%	100.0%	100.0%	100.0%	100.0%	100.0%	100.0%	100.0%	91.7%	91.7%
Out. financial expertise Group 2	n=50; average board size: 10 members						n=50; average board size: 15 members					
Mean	47.3%	47.8%	46.8%	46.9%	45.4%	45.0%	45.0%	44.8%	43.6%	43.5%	43.7%	44.6%
Median	50.0%	45.5%	44.4%	43.1%	44.4%	44.9%	41.4%	40.0%	40.0%	40.0%	40.0%	40.0%
Std. Dev.	19.1%	20.6%	19.6%	19.9%	19.1%	20.5%	23.7%	23.4%	22.6%	22.4%	22.5%	23.4%
Min	0.0%	0.0%	0.0%	0.0%	0.0%	0.0%	0.0%	0.0%	0.0%	0.0%	0.0%	0.0%
Max	88.9%	100.0%	88.9%	90.0%	83.3%	90.0%	100.0%	100.0%	90.0%	90.0%	90.9%	90.9%
Out. financial expertise Group 3	n=50; average board size: 8 members						n=50; average board size: 12 members					
Mean	52.4%	50.0%	49.5%	47.2%	47.0%	45.6%	62.6%	61.4%	59.3%	60.1%	60.0%	60.9%
Median	52.8%	50.0%	50.0%	50.0%	50.0%	47.7%	66.7%	62.5%	62.5%	62.5%	61.3%	62.5%
Std. Dev.	26.8%	27.4%	27.7%	28.5%	26.2%	25.5%	23.3%	21.2%	19.4%	20.8%	21.0%	20.2%
Min	0.0%	0.0%	0.0%	0.0%	0.0%	0.0%	12.5%	18.2%	18.2%	18.2%	10.0%	10.0%
Max	100.0%	100.0%	100.0%	100.0%	100.0%	100.0%	100.0%	100.0%	90.0%	100.0%	100.0%	100.0%

Appendix II.7.13: T-Test, comparison of mean values financial expertise and outside financial expertise between cooperative and savings banks over time

	Top 200						Top 150					
Financial expertise	2009	2008	2007	2006	2005	2004	2009	2008	2007	2006	2005	2004
Levene Test												
F	10.779	11.403	16.480	15.184	11.478	13.314	6.098	10.275	12.447	12.129	8.568	7.211
Significance	0.001	0.001	0.000	0.000	0.001	0.000	0.014	0.001	0.000	0.001	0.004	0.008
T Test												
T	-8.647	-7.994	-8.172	-8.511	-8.878	-8.756	-7.333	-7.213	-7.379	-7.671	-8.218	-8.350
df (equal variances)	398.000	398.000	398.000	398.000	398.000	398.000	298.000	298.000	298.000	298.000	298.000	298.000
Significance (two-sided)	0.000	0.000	0.000	0.000	0.000	0.000	0.000	0.000	0.000	0.000	0.000	0.000
df (different variances)	375.457	372.071	365.902	367.051	372.019	367.706	280.996	276.454	274.737	273.989	279.669	280.460
Significance (two-sided)	0.000	0.000	0.000	0.000	0.000	0.000	0.000	0.000	0.000	0.000	0.000	0.000
Outside financial expertise	2009	2008	2007	2006	2005	2004	2009	2008	2007	2006	2005	2004
Levene Test												
F	2.411	0.431	0.031	0.012	0.296	0.003	0.674	0.011	0.153	0.068	0.147	0.121
Significance	0.121	0.512	0.860	0.912	0.587	0.954	0.412	0.916	0.696	0.794	0.701	0.728
T Test												
T	-3.141	-3.201	-3.208	-3.559	-3.797	-3.670	-2.434	-2.784	-2.786	-3.035	-3.301	-3.555
df (equal variances)	398.000	398.000	398.000	398.000	398.000	398.000	298.000	298.000	298.000	298.000	298.000	298.000
Significance (two-sided)	0.002	0.001	0.001	0.000	0.000	0.000	0.016	0.006	0.006	0.003	0.001	0.000
df (different variances)	397.051	397.925	396.910	397.500	397.960	397.603	297.948	297.315	296.938	297.062	297.981	297.977
Significance (two-sided)	0.002	0.001	0.001	0.000	0.000	0.000	0.016	0.006	0.006	0.003	0.001	0.000

Confidence level: 95%

Appendix II.7.14: T-Test, comparison of mean values of financial expertise and outside financial expertise of banks clustered by bank size

		Cluster 1 vs. 2	Cluster 1 vs. 3	Cluster 1 vs. 4	Cluster 2 vs. 3	Cluster 2 vs. 4	Cluster 3 vs. 4
		t (p-value)	t (p-value)	t (p-value)	t (p-value)	t (p-value)	t (p-value)
Top 200							
Financial expertise	Cooperative banks	2.9376*** 0.0036	4.4992*** 0.0000	7.2798*** 0.0000	2.0716** 0.0392	4.3519*** 0.0000	2.8218*** 0.0051
	Savings banks	-0.3936 0.6942	-0.3804 0.7039	-0.8960 0.3710	0.0368 0.9707	-0.4398 0.6604	-0.5178 0.6050
Outside financial expertise	Cooperative banks	-0.6284 0.5302	0.8173 0.4144	2.8828*** 0.0042	1.4697 0.1427	3.4688*** 0.0006	2.2880** 0.0228
	Savings banks	-3.9633*** 0.0001	-2.5484** 0.0113	-3.6695*** 0.0003	1.2928 0.1971	0.4462 0.6558	-1.0215 0.3078
Top 150							
Financial expertise	Cooperative banks	-0.4722 0.6371	0.6365 0.5249	n/a	1.1141 0.2662	n/a	n/a
	Savings banks	4.8476*** 0.0000	0.0543 0.9568	n/a	-4.4112*** 0.0000	n/a	n/a
Outside financial expertise	Cooperative banks	-1.4641 0.1442	-0.3112 0.7558	n/a	0.8978 0.3700	n/a	n/a
	Savings banks	6.6849*** 0.0000	-2.4480** 0.0149	n/a	-8.8421*** 0.0000	n/a	n/a

Confidence level: 95%
* indicates significance at the 10% level, ** at the 5% level, and *** at the 1% level, respectively.

Appendix II.7.15: T-Test, comparison of mean values of financial expertise and outside financial expertise of of banks clustered by board size

		Cluster 1 vs. 2	Cluster 1 vs. 3	Cluster 1 vs. 4	Cluster 2 vs. 3	Cluster 2 vs. 4	Cluster 3 vs. 4
		t (p-value)	t (p-value)	t (p-value)	t (p-value)	t (p-value)	t (p-value)
Top 200							
Financial expertise	Cooperative banks	1.2460	0.6197	2.7528***	-0.6146	1.6805*	2.6308***
		0.2137	0.5359	0.0063	0.5393	0.0939	0.0090
	Savings banks	-0.7156	0.2279	-0.8805	0.9676	-0.2703	-1.1494
		0.4748	0.8199	0.3793	0.3340	0.7871	0.2513
Outside financial expertise	Cooperative banks	-1.8542*	-2.4440**	0.1402	-0.4633	1.6973*	2.3797**
		0.0647	0.0151	0.8886	0.6435	0.0907	0.0180
	Savings banks	-1.2232	0.6015	-6.1808***	2.0529**	-4.9134***	-7.0605***
		0.2222	0.5479	0.0000	0.0410	0.0000	0.0000
Top 150							
Financial expertise	Cooperative banks	-0.4722	0.6365	n/a	1.1141	n/a	n/a
		0.6371	0.5249		0.2662		
	Savings banks	4.8476***	0.0543	n/a	-4.4112***	n/a	n/a
		0.0000	0.9568		0.0000		
Outside financial expertise	Cooperative banks	-1.4641	-0.3112	n/a	0.8978	n/a	n/a
		0.1442	0.7558		0.3700		
	Savings banks	6.6849***	-2.4480**	n/a	-8.8421***	n/a	n/a
		0.0000	0.0149		0.0000		

Confidence level: 95%

* indicates significance at the 10% level, ** at the 5% level, and *** at the 1% level, respectively.

Appendix II.7.16: Distribution average (outside) financial expertise per sector, Top 200 banks

Financial expertise	Cooperative banks (Top 200)

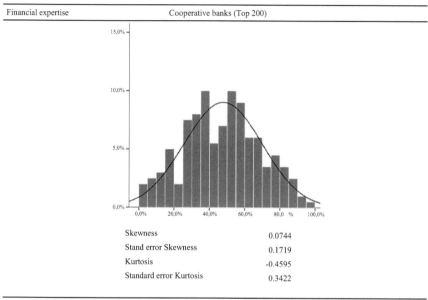

Skewness	0.0744
Stand error Skewness	0.1719
Kurtosis	-0.4595
Standard error Kurtosis	0.3422

Savings banks (Top 200)

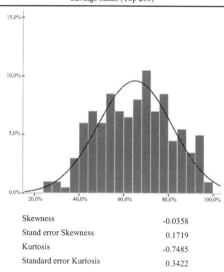

Skewness	-0.0358
Stand error Skewness	0.1719
Kurtosis	-0.7485
Standard error Kurtosis	0.3422

Cooperative banks (Top 200)

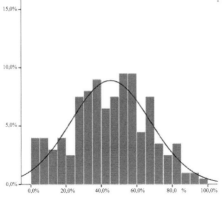

Skewness	0.0009
Stand error Skewness	0.1719
Kurtosis	-0.4034
Standard error Kurtosis	0.3422

Savings banks (Top 200)

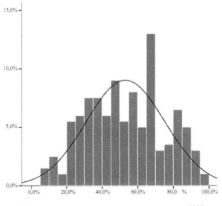

Skewness	-.0232
Stand error Skewness	.1719
Kurtosis	-.8678
Standard error Kurtosis	.3422

43

Appendix II.7.17: Distribution average (outside) financial expertise per sector, Top 150 banks

Financial expertise	Cooperative banks (Top 150)

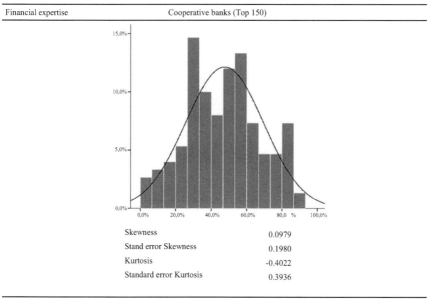

Skewness	0.0979
Stand error Skewness	0.1980
Kurtosis	-0.4022
Standard error Kurtosis	0.3936

Savings banks (Top 150)

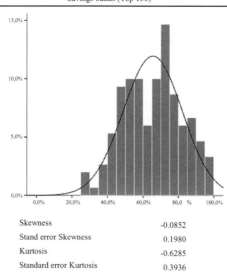

Skewness	-0.0852
Stand error Skewness	0.1980
Kurtosis	-0.6285
Standard error Kurtosis	0.3936

Cooperative banks (Top 150)

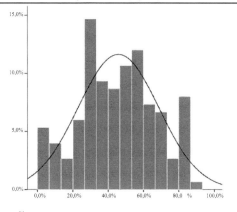

Skewness	0.0259
Stand error Skewness	0.1980
Kurtosis	-0.4375
Standard error Kurtosis	0.3936

Savings banks (Top 150)

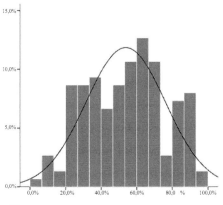

Skewness	-0.0770
Stand error Skewness	0.1980
Kurtosis	-0.8150
Standard error Kurtosis	0.3936

III Financial Expertise in Supervisory Boards, Bank Performance and Risk-Taking: Evidence from German Savings Banks

Abstract

The present study investigates whether and how financial expertise of supervisory board members influences the risk-return profile of German savings banks. The results provide empirical evidence for the discussions on the relevance of competence in internal bank governance structures. Financial expertise is assumed on the basis of the professional background of the supervisory board members. We find that performance is positively impacted by financial expertise. However, the positive influence on performance comes at the price of an increase in risk.

III.1 Introduction

In recent years, banks have expanded, changed, and discarded various business models. The reasons for these exceptional industry dynamics can be found in shifts between regulation and deregulation, macroeconomic and political trends, industry competition, and changing customer demands (e.g., Dermine, 2003; DeYoung, Hunter, and Udell, 2004; Goddard, Molyneux, Wilson, and Tavakoli, 2007). Consequently, bank managers have constantly adjusted their banks' risk-return profile through bank activities, asset mix, funding strategies, the matching of assets and liabilities, etc. So far, theoretical evidence has not given a clear answer about which business model is ultimately optimal, and the 2008 banking crisis has proved that not all business models and their risk-return profiles are equally feasible (Demirgüç-Kunt and Huizinga, 2010; Diamond, 1991; Rajan, 1992; Stein, 2002).

Healthy risk-return profiles are not only important for the stability and profitability of individual banks, but also for the whole financial system. In contrast to other industries, failures of single firms in the banking industry have a systemic dimension. Large banks, which are considered "too big to fail," require rescue measures by governments as their failures are likely to result in the collapse of the whole financial system (Hoggarth, Reidhill, and Sinclair, 2004; Kaufman, 2002). However, turbulences of smaller banks are not less important. Because of the expected chain reaction when a couple of weak, and not necessarily large, banks fail together, regulators might face a "too many to fail" problem, which could end in a systemic collapse as well, unless countermeasures are taken (Acharya and Yorulmazer, 2007; Brown and Dinç, 2011).

Banks can hardly be fully crisis resilient. Their business model is associated with uncertainty about liquidity needs and a maturity mismatch between assets and liabilities, which results in inherently fragile financial institutions (Bhattacharya, Boot, and Thakor, 1998; Diamond and Rajan, 2001). Furthermore, despite the threats to the financial system, it is desirable that banks take some risks to finance economic growth (Levine, 2006; Rajan and Zingales, 1998). Banks collect and channel savings to wealth-increasing projects of companies and private households, and facilitate the trading, hedging, and pooling of risks (Kroszner, Laeven, and Klingebiel, 2007; Levine, 1997; Pang and Wu, 2009).

To ensure balanced risk-return profiles and to keep each bank and the whole banking system stable, regulators and governments take their chance in strengthening bank governance structures and enforcing bank regulations. Plenty of regulation sets limits to bank managers' discretion in calibrating banks' risk-return profiles. For example, there are limitations to bank activities as well as capital and funding requirements (Barth, Caprio, and Levine, 2008). During and after the banking crisis, insufficient industry expertise has been acknowledged as an important shortcoming in internal bank governance (Ard and Berg, 2010; Choundhry, 2011; Kirkpatrick, 2009). The banking business models themselves are complex, and have become even more complex in recent years (Mehran, Morrison, and Shapiro, 2011). Thus, superior financial expertise of board members is considered a potential measure to manage increased risk and to create more stable banks with balanced risk-return profiles from inside. Recommendations include paying "closer attention to the overall balance of the board in relation to the risk strategy of the business, taking into account the experience, behavioural and other qualities of individual directors" (Walker, 2009). In particular, independent directors in a one-tier system and supervisory board members in a two-tier system are mandated to supervise bank management and the risk-return profile of the bank (Hopt and Leyens, 2004; John and Senbet, 1998; Jungmann, 2006). This mandate holds especially for supervisory boards in two-tier systems as they are separated from the management board and explicitly assigned management monitoring. However, no final empirical evidence has been found so far to the question whether, and how, greater financial expertise in internal governance influences banks' risk-return profiles.

This study explores how financial expertise in internal control mechanisms influences a bank's risk-return profile. As banks' profiles are affected by many other factors as well, it is difficult to provide empirical evidence on the actual influence of financial experts. Regulation, business models, and competition in the banking market directly influence performance and risk of banks. Moreover, banks in different countries have divergent governance structures with either a one- or two-tier system across borders. Both aspects will distort the analysis of who or what mainly affected the risk-return profile of the banks.

The German savings bank sector provides a rather homogeneous environment for the examination of financial expertise in supervisory boards on a bank's risk-return profile. All banks within the sector operate in the same regulatory environment, and have similar business models, strategies, and organizational structures. Savings banks provide universal banking services to customers, and have a clear focus with traditional lending and deposit taking. Their business purpose requires them to operate within a clearly defined and limited geographical area and foster regional economic development (Hackethal, 2004; Hakenes, Schmidt, and Xie, 2009; Schmidt, 2009).

The 431[9] German savings banks have the common German two-tier board system that separates management and supervision (Hackethal, 2004; Hopt and Leyens, 2004). German savings banks represent the only banking group in Europe that is still publicly owned (Kleff and Weber, 2005). Typically, the owner is the county or city in which the bank is located, which entails close ties to local and regional authorities (Fischer and Pfeil, 2004).[10] From a governance perspective, they only differentiate themselves considerably from exchange-listed commercial banks by the fact that they do not have a so-called "market for corporate control" (Manne, 1965). Thus, they lack one important governance mechanism, but at the same time, the potentially distorting influences of capital markets are absent.

German savings banks' supervisory boards are equipped with more power than the supervisory boards in the other German banking sectors. They have far-reaching competencies that allow them to influence the bank's profile directly (Böhm-Dries, Eggers, and Hortmann, 2010). In this respect, though they have a two-tier board structure, they also have features of a one-tier system. They are responsible for the overall bank strategy guidelines, and assign operating instructions to the management (Wingendorf, 2005). Such instructions and approvals can include the closure of branches, the acquisition of equity stakes in

---

9   As of the end of 2009 (Deutsche Bundesbank, 2011).
10   In cases where several cities or counties have a savings bank together there is an association which owns the bank.

49

other companies, the employment of executives, and the distribution of profits.[11] Furthermore, a credit committee allows the board to directly intervene in the lending policies and guidelines (Hackethal, 2004). Following the calls for more expertise, and in response to the financial crisis, German legislation has been modified to enhance the quality of internal control and stability of the banking system. Since 2009, prospective supervisory board members need to demonstrate relevant expertise, depending on the size, complexity, and systemic importance of the respective bank (BaFin and Deutsche Bundesbank, 2010).

Based on a unique, manually collected sample with more than 200 institutions, this study examines if German savings banks' risk-return profile is influenced by supervisory board members' financial expertise. The remainder of this study is structured as follows: Chapter III.2 provides an overview of the related literature. Special attention is paid to the effect of the financial expertise of board members, board composition, performance, and the political influence on savings banks' operations. Chapter III.3 introduces the data and research methodology and describes the empirical model. In Chapter III.4, summary statistics and regression results are reported. The section also shows the results based on different measures and outlier treatments for robustness checks. Chapter III.5 concludes the study.

III.2   Related Literature

Empirical studies related to the impact of financial expertise on performance and risk, can be divided into three categories: board competence and expertise, board composition and size, and the stability and performance of savings banks.

Cross-industry studies analyzing the impact of board members' expertise on performance and risk still provide mixed results. For example, Davidson, Xie, and Xu (2004), DeFond, Hann, and Hu (2005), Dhaliwal, Naiker, and Navissi (2006), Fernandes and Fich (2009), and Lee, Rosenstein, and Wyatt (1999) report positive relationships between financial expertise and performance measures. Dhaliwal, Naiker, and Navissi (2006) define three types of expertise: accounting, finance, and supervisory. They test the relationship between expertise and accruals quality and show a significant positive relation between accounting expertise and accruals quality. Davidson, Xie, and Xu (2004), DeFond, Hann, and Hu (2005), Fernandes and Fich (2009), and Lee, Rosenstein, and Wyatt (1999) follow a different approach for performance measurement, using capital markets measures such as stock price movement and abnormal

---

11   See, for example, the savings bank law of the state of Baden-Wuerttemberg.

returns. Their studies suggest that capital markets reward competence on the boards as capital markets react positively to the announcement of new directors who are considered financial experts. Fernandes and Fich (2009) additionally point out that, particularly during crises, financial expertise pays off.

Carcello, Hollingsworth, Klein, and Neal (2008), Güner, Malmendier, and Tate (2008), Rosenstein and Wyatt (1990), and Minton, Taillard, and Williamson (2010) do not report consistent effects. According to Carcello, Hollingsworth, Klein, and Neal (2008), expertise is unrelated to real earnings management. They conclude that other governance mechanisms are as good as financial expertise in regard to the quality of financial reporting. Güner, Malmendier, and Tate (2008) focus on bankers on boards and find no significant influence on decisions as long as there are no conflicts of interest between the bankers' interests and those of the concerned company. In such cases, bankers can be detrimental to shareholder wealth. According to Rosenstein and Wyatt (1990), all occupations are equally valuable to shareholders, with regard to share price reactions. Minton, Taillard, and Williamson (2010) analyze the impact of financial expertise on bank risk and a report that greater board expertise is even associated with higher risk levels. All studies outlined above have in common that professional experience is the main source for assuming financial expertise.

With regard to the German two-tier system, only two studies provide evidence of a link between expertise and effectiveness of supervisory boards. Kaplan (1994) shows that supervisory board monitoring works efficiently, as indicated by management turnover, resulting from poor firm performance. The importance of German bank supervisory board financial expertise is addressed by Hau and Thum (2009) with a sample of the 29 largest German banks. In this analysis, 14 biographical criteria are defined to gauge the competence of the supervisory board members. The results suggest that bank losses due to the financial crisis are correlated to the monitoring ability of the supervisory board members. Higher expertise levels are associated with fewer crisis-related losses.

The second related area of literature deals with board size and board composition. Theoretically, larger boards are supposed to be less effective as they might increase agency problems such as free-rider incentives (Jensen, 1993). Empirical studies support this view (Eisenberg, Sundgren, and Wells, 1998; Yermack, 1996). Both studies measure the relationship between board size and Tobin's Q as the proxy for firm value. They document that board size negatively affects firm value. However, studies that focus on the banking industry do not back the idea of larger boards being less effective (Adams and Mehran, 2008; Andres and Vallelado, 2008). On the contrary, larger boards in banking firms may increase effectiveness in monitoring and in advising management.

Board composition was mainly analyzed in regard to the proportion of outside directors. Most studies do not report a significant impact of board composition on firm performance (Hermalin and Weisbach, 2003). Regardless of whether accounting-based performance numbers or capital market-based measures have been used, board composition does not have a significant influence on firm performance, for example, on Tobin's Q (Bhagat and Black, 2000; Hermalin and Weisbach, 1991; Klein, 1998; Mehran, 1995). Bermig and Frick (2010) confirm the missing consistent link between board composition and valuation and performance based on a sample of listed German firms in the period between 1998 and 2007.

The third related area of literature deals with the risk, stability, and performance of savings banks. It has been analyzed at the national as well as the international level (Beck, Hesse, Kick, and Westernhagen, 2009; Cihák and Hesse, 2007; Westman, 2010). Overall, German savings banks are relatively stable. Beck, Hesse, Kick, and Westernhagen (2009) show that with regard to z-score, German savings banks are more stable than German commercial banks, but less stable than cooperative banks. With respect to distress probability, savings banks in Germany are even the least risky banks. International comparisons confirm that savings banks are more stable than commercial banks, but that profitability is higher for commercial banks than for savings banks (Cihák and Hesse, 2007; Westman, 2010). As regards efficiency, Altunbas, Evans, and Molyneux (2001) find no major difference between the three sectors based on a sample of 1,511 German banks.

Apart from the studies on board competence and expertise, board size and composition, and the stability and performance of savings banks, the close link between savings banks and politics has also been the focus of research. The results suggest that politicians are inclined to use local state-owned savings banks as tools to implement political objectives (Illueca, Norden, and Udell, 2009; Kleff and Weber, 2005; Sapienza, 2004; Vins, 2008). In the context of local elections, German savings banks are less inclined to lay off employees and close branches, especially in economically weak areas (Vins, 2008). There is also evidence that the payout policy of savings banks is influenced by local authorities. Indebtedness per inhabitant and personnel expenses per inhabitant have a significant positive impact on the payout decision (Kleff and Weber, 2005). Italian state-owned banks have been shown to systematically charge lower interest rates than privately owned competitors (Sapienza, 2004). This effect is even more evident when considering electoral results. The stronger the political party in the borrowing firm's area, the lower the interest rates to be paid. In the case of Spain, research shows that banks in which the regional government has a stake in the board of directors are more likely to expand in provinces that are close to the political party (Illueca, Norden, and Udell, 2009).

Summing up, existing evidence shows that financial expertise of board members can influence the risk-return profile of firms. However, previous studies mainly deal with the issues of board size and board composition in countries with one-tier board systems. Most studies that focus on the relationship between financial expertise and firm performance do not consider banks in particular. Additionally, the financial expertise of bank supervisory boards in two-tier board systems was largely neglected. The study of Hau and Thum (2009) is most similar to the present analysis, but focuses on a relatively small sample of 29 large-scale German banks and bank losses only during the banking crisis years.

III.3 Data and Methodology

III.3.1 Sample and Data

The sample consists of the 200 largest German savings banks in terms of total assets as of the end of 2009 (Top 200). Savings banks that are not held by public authorities are excluded from the dataset. The banks in the dataset fulfil the following requirement to allow a clear and unbiased analysis of financial expertise in supervisory boards. Since individual board members are counted in the category "other" if a classification of financial expertise cannot be derived, a threshold is defined that limits the number of "others" per bank. Only a maximum of 10% of the overall supervisory board, or one individual for supervisory boards of up to nine individuals, is allowed to be classified as "other". If a savings bank has not been included in the analysis due to a too high a representation of the category "other," the succeeding institution in the size ranking is included.

The sample covers 71% of the total assets of the German savings bank sector as of the end of 2009. The largest savings bank in the sample has total assets of EUR 29.3 billion and the smallest savings bank EUR 1.5 billion. The mean of total assets in the sample is EUR 3.8 billion. In order to account for potential distortions due to merger activities, a lockout period is introduced for a merger-controlled panel. Banks that were involved in mergers over the panel horizon, and the two years preceding this horizon, are excluded. The merger-controlled balanced panel comprises the largest 150 savings banks that fulfill these criteria (Top 150). The revised sample covers 45% of the total assets of the sector as of 2009 with a mean total asset value of EUR 3.2 billion. The largest savings bank of the merger-controlled sample has total assets of EUR 15.6 billion, and the smallest savings bank EUR 1.4 billion.

As no database provides historical data on individuals on the supervisory boards of German savings banks, the information was manually collected from each bank's annual report[12]. The dataset comprises a total of 20,989 data points at the individual level. The Hoppenstedt Banken database was used to research the merger history of each savings bank. Balance sheet and Profit & Loss statement data were taken from the BAKIS database. BAKIS is the joint information system of the German Federal Financial Supervisory Authority (BaFin) and Deutsche Bundesbank, and contains unique bank-specific data. Macroeconomic and structural control variables are taken from the Regionaldatenbank Deutschland of the German Federal Statistical Office.

III.3.2 Hypotheses and Model

Based on the discussions on financial expertise in internal bank governance, we examine whether the financial expertise has an impact on performance and risk. The following two hypotheses are tested:

Hypothesis 1: The (outside) financial expertise of the supervisory board members is unrelated to (risk-adjusted) performance.

Hypothesis 2: The (outside) financial expertise of the supervisory board members is unrelated to stability and risk.

The empirical examination is based on a panel analysis to capture changes over time. In order to include effects between banks, regressions are run with random effects. The estimated model is of the following form:

$$DV_{it} = \alpha + \beta FE_{it} + \gamma B_{it} + \delta M_{it} + \varepsilon_{it} \qquad (\text{III.1})$$

where *DV* is the dependent variable of savings bank *i* at time *t*. Dependent performance variables are return on risk-weighted assets (RORWA) and return on equity (ROE). The dependent variables for stability and risk are z-score and non-performing loans ratio (NPL ratio). FE is the proxy for financial expertise, B is a vector of bank-specific variables, M is a vector of macroeconomic and structural control variables, and ε is the error term. Vector B comprises (a) bank size, (b) bank size growth, (c) bank efficiency, (d) bank loan volume growth, (e) bank claims on monetary financial institutions (MFI), (f) bank claims on non-

---

12   Hardcopies were provided by individual banks or published by the Bundesanzeiger and accessed via the Unternehmensregister or LexisNexis databases.

monetary financial institutions (non-MFI), and (g) supervisory board size. Vector M comprises the macroeconomic and structural control variables (h) East/West dummy, (i) local Gross Domestic Product (GDP) per capita, and (j) population.

III.3.3 Financial Expertise

The financial expertise of the supervisory board members is gauged based on their professional backgrounds. This methodology is in line with previous studies (e.g., Davidson, Xie, and Xu, 2004; Dhaliwal, Naiker, and Navissi, 2006; Minton, Taillard, and Williamson, 2010). With the help of publicly available data in the annual reports the groups presented in Table III.1 have been constituted according to occupations, which allow assumptions to be made regarding the financial expertise of the supervisory board members.

Table III.1: Professional backgrounds with assumed financial expertise.

Level 1: Employment	Self-employed persons with assumed financial expertise	Employed persons with assumed financial expertise	Retired persons with assumed financial expertise
Level 2: Occupation	Entrepreneur, Merchant, Owner	Non-bank employee with assumed financial focus (e.g. member of management board)	Retired self-employed person with assumed financial expertise
	Managing Partner	Bank employee	Retired employed person with assumed financial expertise
	Partner	Public officer with assumed financial focus (e.g. treasurer) Federal and State Minister, State Secretary	
		Local and regional politician	

The main idea behind the applied methodology is the obvious relation to financial issues. For instance, financial expertise is expected to be given in the case of the managing directors of companies. The definition of financial expertise mainly follows that of the German regulatory bodies (BaFin and Deutsche Bundesbank, 2010).[13] The regulatory bodies do not explicitly specify the required competence levels, but indicate occupations and experiences that allow assumptions to be made regarding financial expertise. Professional experience in other areas may also be sufficient. Additionally, they outline that supervisory board members can gain relevant expertise through similar supervisory mandates and professional activities in the banking sector.

---

13   In contrast to the occupations outlined by BaFin and Deutsche Bundesbank (2010), farmers are not assigned general financial expertise in the present study. This is due to the high degree of variation in the size and administrative complexity of the farming business.

Furthermore, regulatory bodies consider potential mandatory members, such as mayors and district administrators, whose board presence is legally required, to be financially literate (BaFin and Deutsche Bundesbank, 2010).

To account for differences in the declarations in the annual reports, several assumptions concerning tenure, employment classification, and politicians have been applied. If no professional background was assignable, the individual was counted in the category "other". For the identification of local and regional politicians, a more detailed methodology has been applied, taking into consideration full-time employment vs. voluntary service and the authorization to give instructions. Both criteria must be fulfilled for local and regional politicians to be counted as financial experts (for further details see Appendix III.6.1).

Most federal state-based laws on savings banks guarantee a high degree of employee representation. Together with local and regional politicians, this guarantees a relatively stable base of financial expertise at savings banks. Accordingly, two sets of regressions are run. The first analysis focuses on the financial expertise of the total supervisory board, and the second analysis concentrates on outside financial expertise. For the analysis of outside financial expertise, individuals who are employed at the respective savings bank are excluded. This eliminates the effects on board expertise of savings banks laws and enhances comparability between savings banks located in different federal states.

III.3.4   Measurement of Performance and Risk

Performance is captured by two numbers. RORWA measures risk-adjusted performance and is defined as operating result divided by risk-weighted assets. ROE is used as the second performance measure and is defined as operating result divided by equity. In both cases, the operating result is used to avoid distortions due to undisclosed hidden reserves already accounted for in the annual net profit. These reserves are typically used when banks are in trouble (Beck, Hesse, Kick, and Westernhagen, 2009).

The primary risk measure is the z-score, which has become a widely used risk indicator in empirical studies on the banking industry (e.g., Boyd and Runkle, 1993; Laeven and Levine, 2009). The z-score measures the distance to default (Roy, 1952). Insolvency is defined as the state in which a bank's capital is not sufficient to absorb losses. A higher z-value indicates a more stable bank. Prob(-ROA<CAR) expresses the probability of insolvency, where ROA is the return on assets and CAR is the capital assets ratio. Assuming profits to be

normally distributed, the inverse probability of insolvency becomes (ROA+CAR)/σ(ROA), where σ(ROA) is the standard deviation of ROA (Boyd and Runkle, 1993). For each year, the standard deviation of ROA is calculated for the period from 1994 to the year under consideration. ROA is calculated as operating result divided by total assets. CAR is defined as Tier-1 equity divided by total assets. The second risk measure is the NPL ratio, which is defined as classified non-performing loans divided by total assets. A higher ratio indicates a higher risk based on the loan portfolio of each savings bank. Due to the strong focus on lending business, this risk measure is highly relevant to savings banks.

III.3.5   Control Variables

The empirical model controls for bank-specific issues as well as for macroeconomic and structural aspects. To account for different bank sizes and growth rates, the logarithm of total assets and the annual change in total assets is used, and for different efficiency levels, the cost-income ratio (CIR). CIR is defined as the ratio of general administrative expenses to operating result. Different levels of lending engagements are accounted for by the growth rate of the total loan volume. Additionally, the ratios of claims on MFI to total assets and claims on non-MFI to total assets are taken into account. As larger boards tend to incentivize free-riding, there might be negative effects of the supervisory board size on performance and risk (Jensen, 1993). For this reason, we control for the size of the supervisory board.

As savings banks have legally specified business areas, it is important in which region the bank is located. These structural issues are captured by an index differentiating between urban and rural areas and using a binary variable identifying federal states that used to be in the former German Democratic Republic. The latter variable is important to long-term business relationships. Savings banks in Eastern German federal states worked in a different structure until 1990. Following regional development planning, which differentiates between regional, district, and county centers, an index with five clusters is applied to separate sparsely populated areas from densely populated and metropolitan areas. For the differentiation between district and regional centers, areas with up to 1,000,000 inhabitants are divided into four clusters of 250,000 inhabitants each. The fifth cluster is assigned to areas with more than 1,000,000 inhabitants. For differences in economic development, the local GDP per capita is taken into account. GDP per capita within the business area was adjusted for mergers during the panel horizon in order to include the effects of macroeconomic changes. Table III.2 summarizes the control variables in use.

Table III.2: Definition of control variables and sources.

Bank level control variables	Description	Source
a. Bank size	Ln of total assets	BAKIS (Deutsche Bundesbank)
b. Bank size growth	Year-to-year change in total assets	BAKIS (Deutsche Bundesbank)
c. Bank efficiency	General administrative expenses to operating result (CIR)	BAKIS (Deutsche Bundesbank)
d. Bank loan volume growth	Year-to-year change in total loans	BAKIS (Deutsche Bundesbank)
e. Bank claims on MFI	Claims on MFI divided by total assets	BAKIS (Deutsche Bundesbank)
f. Bank claims on non-MFI	Claims on non-MFI divided by total assets	BAKIS (Deutsche Bundesbank)
g. Bank supervisory board size	Number of supervisory board members	Annual reports

Macroeconomic and structural control variables		
h. East/West	Binary variable separating Eastern and Western federal state	Annual reports
i. GDP per capita	GDP of business area divided by population within business area	Regionaldatenbank Deutschland
j. Population	Index based on population within business area	Regionaldatenbank Deutschland

III.4   Results

III.4.1   Summary Statistics

The examination of the board composition in Table III.3 reveals that insiders have a considerable stake in the board, as they account for a quarter of the supervisory board. Supported by this large fraction, supervisory boards are dominated by employed people, who make up almost three quarters of the board. On the other hand, self-employed people play a minor role. Together with retired individuals, they account for almost the same proportion of the board, around 13% each. Expectations about the close ties to local and regional politics are met, since on average 21% of the supervisory board are politicians who officiate at the local and regional level. Counting officiating and retired politicians of all levels drives the number up to 28%. For the merger-controlled savings banks, see Appendix III.6.2.

Table III.3: Supervisory board composition, Top 200 savings banks.

Variables	Mean	Std. Dev.	Coeff. of variation	Min	Max
Insider (%)	24.71	12.33	49.90	0.00	41.67
Outsider (%)	75.29	12.33	16.38	58.33	100.00
Employment					
Employed individuals (%)	73.32	12.24	16.70	36.36	100.00
Self-employed individuals (%)	12.62	9.57	75.80	0.00	47.37
Retired individuals (%)	12.71	9.95	78.25	0.00	55.56
Others (%)	1.35	2.77	204.11	0.00	12.50
Politicians (officiating)					
Federal politicians (%)	0.76	2.29	299.94	0.00	15.38
Federal state politicians (%)	2.57	4.22	164.08	0.00	23.08
Regional politicans (%)	5.88	4.69	79.74	0.00	28.57
Local politicians (%)	15.15	12.57	82.97	0.00	54.55
Officiating and retired politicians (%)	28.13	15.19	54.00	0.00	75.00

Despite similar business models, savings banks show a relatively wide distribution of performance, with coefficients of variation of 74.08% for RORWA and 62.11% for ROE. RORWA ranges from -2.92% to 8.65% and ROE from -61.76% to 67.79%. The average performance is 1.33% in terms of RORWA and 13.60% in terms of ROE. Risk and stability metrics show a similar variation, with coefficients of 54.41% for z-score and 71.38% for the NPL ratio. Z-score ranges from 2.87 to 77.02 with an average of 19.40. The minimum NPL ratio in the sample is close to zero, at 0.04%, and reaches a maximum of 11.56%. The average NPL ratio is 2.11%.

Financial expertise has a floor of 20.00% due to the legally required employee representation and reaches an average of 64.98%. With bank employees excluded from the data, 53.15% of outside members, on average, have some financial expertise. A comparison of the financial expertise of the entire supervisory board with that of outsiders indicates that there is much more variation in the expertise of the "freely eligible" (outside) members, as was expected.

Concerning the other bank-level variables, bank size growth and loan volume growth show the largest variation within the sample. Results indicate that, over the years, savings banks shift their assets toward more profitable lending business without growing in total bank size. Whereas average bank growth is 0.25%, the loan volume grows at an average rate of 2.86%. Bank efficiency is relatively homogeneous among all banks as indicated by the low coefficient of variation of 11.20%. Despite a wide range between minimum and maximum values, savings banks do not vary much in their non-MFI engagement, but in their inter-bank activities as the coefficient of variation for claims on MFI indicates. The results remain qualitatively the same in the merger-controlled panel with the Top 150 (see Appendix III.6.3).

Table III.4: Summary statistics, Top 200 savings banks.

Dependent variables	Mean	Std. Dev.	Coeff. of variation	Min	Max
RORWA (%)	1.33	0.99	74.08	-2.92	8.65
ROE (%)	13.60	8.45	62.11	-61.76	67.79
z-score	19.40	10.56	54.41	2.87	77.02
NPL ratio (%)	2.11	1.51	71.38	0.04	11.56
Bank level variables					
Financial expertise (%)	64.98	17.25	26.55	20.00	100.00
Outside financial expertise (%)	53.15	22.86	43.01	0.00	100.00
Bank size (ln '000s of EUR)	21.78	0.60	2.77	20.56	24.16
Bank efficiency (%)	65.29	7.32	11.20	36.00	95.51
Bank size growth (%)	0.25	3.34	1,323.23	-16.29	18.26
Board size	16.81	5.29	31.46	7.00	48.00
Loan growth (%)	2.86	9.80	342.62	-14.70	104.87
Claims on MFI (%)	9.85	6.55	66.58	0.00	44.37
Claims on non-MFI (%)	58.91	12.00	20.37	24.21	85.36
Macroeconomic and structural variables					
East/West	0.13	0.34	258.80	0.00	1.00
GDP per capita ('000s of EUR)	27.49	7.62	27.73	14.12	72.20
Population	1.73	0.90	51.96	1.00	5.00

To explore differences in performance, risk, and stability between banks with different expertise levels, all savings banks are clustered by financial expertise (see Table III.5). Each cluster contains 50 banks. The banks with the highest levels of financial expertise are in Cluster 1, and those with the lowest levels are in Cluster 4. The analysis indicates that financial expertise of the supervisory board pays off. Savings banks in Cluster 1 have a significantly better average performance than the banks in Clusters 3 and 4. In contrast to the advantageous effects on performance, expertise tends to reduce stability, as banks in Clusters 1 and 2 have a significantly lower z-score than banks in Clusters 3 and 4. The NPL ratio does not show a clear trend between the clusters. The NPL ratio rises from Cluster 4 to Cluster 3 with an increasing expertise level, but then decreases from Cluster 3 to Cluster 1. The trends of the other bank-level variables are not fully monotonic across clusters, except for bank efficiency, which constantly rises with an increase in financial expertise. For the cluster analysis of the merger-controlled panel, see Appendix III.6.4.

Table III.5: Bank level variables, clustered by financial expertise, Top 200 savings banks.

Dependent variables	Cluster 1	Cluster 2	Cluster 3	Cluster 4	Delta Cluster 1-4
RORWA (%)	1.42	1.50	1.26	1.13	0.29
ROE (%)	15.20	14.31	13.07	11.82	3.37
z-score	18.65	17.38	20.67	20.89	-2.25
NPL ratio (%)	2.01	2.11	2.30	2.03	-0.01
Bank level variables					
Financial expertise (%)	86.38	71.28	58.69	43.56	42.81
Outside financial expertise (%)	81.12	61.24	43.70	26.56	54.56
Bank size (ln '000s of EUR)	21.74	21.87	21.68	21.84	-0.10
Bank efficiency (%)	64.05	64.69	65.64	66.78	-2.74
Bank size growth (%)	0.67	0.17	0.25	-0.07	0.73
Board size	17.37	16.39	16.67	16.80	0.57
Loan growth (%)	2.46	2.28	2.69	4.02	-1.56
Claims on MFI (%)	11.58	9.72	10.06	8.03	3.55
Claims on non-MFI (%)	53.55	58.24	59.75	64.11	-10.56

Table III.6 provides evidence of the significance between the clusters (see Appendix III.6.5 for the merger-controlled panel).

Table III.6: Pairwise test of the significance between expertise clusters, Top 200 savings banks.

Dependent variables	Cluster 1 vs. 2 t (p-value)	Cluster 1 vs. 3 t (p-value)	Cluster 1 vs. 4 t (p-value)	Cluster 2 vs. 3 t (p-value)	Cluster 2 vs. 4 t (p-value)	Cluster 3 vs. 4 t (p-value)
RORWA	-1.1722	2.0085 **	4.5434 ***	2.9031 ***	4.8021 ***	1.7949 *
	0.2420	0.0455	0.0000	0.0040	0.0000	0.0737
ROE	1.5491	2.9093 ***	6.0121 ***	1.7952 *	4.3481 ***	1.8871 *
	0.1224	0.0040	0.0000	0.0736	0.0000	0.0601
z-score	1.7932 *	-2.0026 **	-2.6364 ***	-3.5476 ***	-4.6260 ***	-0.2238
	0.0740	0.0461	0.0088	0.0005	0.0000	0.8230
NPL ratio	-0.8212	-2.3812 **	0.0338	-1.8113 *	0.9519	2.8269 ***
	0.4122	0.0179	0.9730	0.0711	0.3419	0.0050
Bank level variables						
Financial expertise	38.6471 ***	72.3544 ***	97.5500 ***	31.8934 ***	61.9574 ***	32.0524 ***
	0.0000	0.0000	0.0000	0.0000	0.0000	0.0000
Outside financial expertise	29.4410 ***	54.4313 ***	68.7638 ***	22.6287 ***	42.3762 ***	20.1752 ***
	0.0000	0.0000	0.0000	0.0000	0.0000	0.0000
Bank size	-3.0146 ***	1.3804	-1.9940 **	4.2496 ***	0.7161	-2.9528 ***
	0.0028	0.1685	0.0471	0.0000	0.4745	0.0034
Bank efficiency	-1.0181	-2.6110 ***	-4.4523 ***	-1.8035 *	-3.6803 ***	-2.1189 **
	0.3094	0.0095	0.0000	0.0723	0.0003	0.0349
Bank size growth	1.7965 *	1.4950	2.6986 ***	-0.0661	0.9662	1.1114
	0.0735	0.1361	0.0074	0.9473	0.3348	0.2674
Board size	2.0786 **	1.5048	1.3134	-0.8163	-1.2133	-0.3118
	0.0385	0.1334	0.1900	0.4150	0.2260	0.7554
Loan growth	0.3587	-0.6442	-2.2038 **	-1.0905	-2.1322 **	-1.4634
	0.7201	0.5200	0.0284	0.2764	0.0338	0.1445
Claims on MFI	3.4456 ***	2.7623 ***	7.0218 ***	-0.6907	3.5515 ***	4.4932 ***
	0.0007	0.0061	0.0000	0.4903	0.0004	0.0000
Claims on non-MFI	-5.0788 ***	-6.2691 ***	-11.3830 ***	-1.6453	-7.3531 ***	-4.7265 ***
	0.0000	0.0000	0.0000	0.1010	0.0000	0.0000

Confidence level: 95%
* indicates significance at the 10% level, ** at the 5% level, and *** at the 1% level, respectively.

III.4.2   Regression Results

Regression analyses confirm that financial expertise pays off for savings banks' performance. This result is consistent with previous studies that also document a positive relationship between financial expertise and performance (e.g., Davidson, Xie, and Xu, 2004; Fernandes and Fich, 2009; Lee, Rosenstein, and Wyatt, 1999). The positive relationship holds for both expertise (total supervisory board and outside financial expertise) and performance (RORWA and ROE) measures. With regard to bank risk, financial expertise tends to reduce stability and increase loan portfolio risk. This lends support to the empirical findings of Minton, Taillard, and Williamson (2010), who document higher bank risk levels associated with higher financial expertise. The detrimental impact on risk and stability suggests that financial experts explicitly advocate more risk-taking, which Acharya, Richardson, van Nieuwerburgh, and White (2011) describe as a "race to the bottom". Overall, financial experts tend to impact the risk-return profile. Since the positive impact on performance comes at the price of a negative impact on stability and on loan portfolio risk, they cannot suspend the risk-return trade-off.

Despite the large fraction of insiders, the coefficients of total board financial expertise and outside financial expertise do not differ materially in absolute terms. This observation suggests that bank employees do not exert an influence different from the majority of outsiders. The reason for this might be herding, as it was found for audit committees in audit processes (Schöndube-Pirchegger and Schöndube, 2011). Based on their findings, insiders might herd and follow the majority vote of the outside members.

As indicated by the Wald-Chi square value, all regressions are significant at the 1% level. The performance regressions show that the coefficients of total board financial expertise and outside financial expertise are significant for the impact on ROE, but not on RORWA (see Table III.7). Contrary to all other bank-level variables, loan volume growth affects performance positively. This implies that it is essentially the expansion of savings banks' core business that still drives their profitability. The negative impact of board size indicates that larger boards are detrimental to performance. This is in line with the considerations outlined by Jensen (1993) and empirically supported, for example, by Yermack (1996) and Eisenberg, Sundgren, and Wells (1998). Larger boards might lead to members' perceived lower personal responsibility for performance and, therefore, ease free-riding. Remarkably, neither population density nor the economic strength of the business area affects performance significantly.

Table III.7: *Random-effect regressions with dependent variables RORWA and ROE, Top 200 savings banks.*

Variable		RORWA (RE) Financial expertise		RORWA (RE) Out. financial expertise		ROE (RE) Financial expertise		ROE (RE) Out. financial expertise	
		Coeff.	SE (robust)	Coeff.	SE (robust)	Coeff.	SE (robust)	Coeff.	SE (robust)
Financial expertise	Financial expertise	0.0012	0.0016			0.0301	0.0165 *		
	Outside financial expertise			0.0017	0.0013			0.0283	0.0124 **
Bank level	Bank size	-0.0382	0.0887	-0.0348	0.0891	-0.6261	0.8745	-0.5957	0.8764
	Bank efficiency	-0.0481	0.0056 ***	-0.0479	0.0056 ***	-0.4764	0.0568 ***	-0.4754	0.0569 ***
	Bank size growth	-0.0112	0.0106	-0.0114	0.0106	-0.0252	0.0836	-0.0288	0.0833
	Board size	-0.0192	0.0057 ***	-0.0190	0.0056 ***	-0.1178	0.0536 **	-0.1097	0.0527 **
	Loan growth	0.0185	0.0028 ***	0.0187	0.0028 ***	0.0892	0.0206 ***	0.0922	0.0210 ***
	Claims on MFI	-0.0149	0.0049 ***	-0.0150	0.0050 ***	-0.1147	0.0440 ***	-0.1161	0.0442 ***
	Claims on non-MFI	-0.0241	0.0042 ***	-0.0236	0.0042 ***	-0.1118	0.0364 ***	-0.1079	0.0362 ***
Macroeconomic and structural environment	East/West	0.2631	0.1717	0.2744	0.1714	1.6826	1.4071	1.8522	1.4217
	GDP per capita	0.0006	0.0033	0.0001	0.0034	-0.0308	0.0438	-0.0359	0.0445
	Population	0.0136	0.0585	0.0161	0.0587	0.0719	0.4755	0.1094	0.4707
	constant	6.9872	1.8922 ***	6.8676	1.9010 ***	66.3223	19.8971 ***	65.7388	19.8536 ***
	Wald Chi²	192.59	***	194.58	***	283.96	***	282.58	***
	R-sq	0.3481		0.3489		0.2721		0.2737	
	No of observations	1,162		1,162		1,162		1,162	

* indicates significance at the 10% level, ** at the 5% level, and *** at the 1% level, respectively.
Standard errors control for clustering at the bank level.

Contrary to the performance regressions, the financial expertise coefficients are hardly significant in the risk regressions (see Table III.8). Only the influence of total board financial expertise on the NPL ratio is significant at the 10% level. The negative impact of financial expertise on risk is consistent for both measures.

Contrary to z-score, almost all bank-level control variables are significant in the regression with the NPL ratio as dependent variable. Bank size growth, board size, and loan volume growth have different impacts on stability and loan portfolio risk. Growing bank size reduces the stability, but does not similarly affect the loan portfolio risk. The negative impact of board size on the NPL ratio underlines the free-riding hypothesis from the performance regressions. The perceived lower personal responsibility in large boards might result in a less strict lending policy, which explains the negative impact on performance and the increasing effect on the NPL ratio. Loan volume growth affects stability and loan portfolio risk differently than bank size growth. It enhances banking stability, but increases the risk of the loan portfolio.

Bank employees do not exert a favourable impact on loan portfolio risk, which implies that insiders do not act as additional effective risk filters. Agency conflicts and overconfidence of the banking experts might be the reason for this.

63

Despite their sound understanding of banking business, their self-perceived expertise might lead to an overreaction to their private information and, subsequently, to an underestimation of bank risks. As a result, expertise does not neccessarily result in better risk monitoring (e.g., Chuang and Lee, 2006; Fellner, Güth, and Maciejovsky, 2004). Furthermore, Odean (1998) provides evidence that the greater expertise individuals have, the more overconfident they tend to be.

Table III.8: *Random-effect regressions with dependent variables z-score and NPL ratio, Top 200 savings banks.*

Variable		z-score (RE) Financial expertise		z-score (RE) Out. financial expertise		NPL Ratio (RE) Financial expertise		NPL Ratio (RE) Out. financial expertise	
		Coeff.	SE (robust)	Coeff.	SE (robust)	Coeff.	SE (robust)	Coeff.	SE (robust)
Financial expertise	Financial expertise	-0.0113	0.0319			0.0075	0.0039*		
	Outside financial expertise			-0.0134	0.0266			0.0031	0.0031
Bank level	Bank size	2.9669	3.0396	2.9668	3.0489	-0.3582	0.2063*	-0.3653	0.2082*
	Bank efficiency	0.0320	0.0342	0.0317	0.0344	-0.0247	0.0086***	-0.0253	0.0087***
	Bank size growth	-0.1309	0.0238***	-0.1308	0.0238***	-0.0981	0.0124***	-0.0981	0.0125***
	Board size	0.0110	0.0792	0.0063	0.0806	0.0378	0.0099***	0.0400	0.0098***
	Loan growth	0.0381	0.0074***	0.0378	0.0073***	0.0499	0.0062***	0.0500	0.0062***
	Claims on MFI	0.0249	0.0418	0.0252	0.0417	-0.0110	0.0086	-0.0109	0.0086
	Claims on non-MFI	-0.0245	0.0548	-0.0265	0.0552	0.0359	0.0105***	0.0344	0.0105***
Macroeconomic and structural environment	East/West	-7.8680	2.4781***	-7.9407	2.4781***	0.8212	0.3013***	0.8324	0.3028***
	GDP per capita	-0.0550	0.0694	-0.0548	0.0690	-0.0121	0.0074*	-0.0114	0.0073
	Population	-0.6670	1.9582	-0.6752	1.9652	0.0065	0.1085	0.0080	0.1088
	constant	42.0789	65.3565	41.8661	65.6779	8.4945	4.4823*	9.0372	4.5276**
	Wald Chi²	120.51	***	122.59	***	237.59	***	236.46	***
	R-sq	0.0423		0.0401		0.2282		0.2076	
	No of observations	1,162		1,162		1,156		1,156	

* indicates significance at the 10% level, ** at the 5% level, and *** at the 1% level, respectively.
Standard errors control for clustering at the bank level.

Supervisory boards of banks without bank merger activities between 2002 and 2009 do not influence performance and risk differently (see Appendices III.6.8 and III.6.9).

III.4.3   Robustness Checks

For robustness checks, all analyses are repeated with two outlier corrected data samples. All variables are truncated, except for the binary variable (East/West) and the index variable on population. First, all observations smaller than the 1st percentile of the distribution are set to the value of the 1st percentile.

Observations larger than the 99th percentile are set to the value of the 99th percentile. Second, all observations smaller than the 5th percentile of the distribution are set to the value of the 5th percentile, and observations larger than the 95th percentile are set to the value of the 95th percentile.

Overall, the regressions with the outlier-corrected data confirm the results of the regressions with unchanged outliers. This result underlines the robustness of the results. The models with outlier-corrected datasets have higher explanatory power than the models without outlier correction.

With regard to performance, all coefficients retain their signs from the original regressions (see Appendices III.6.10, III.6.12, III.6.14, and III.6.16). Notably, the coefficients of total board financial expertise and outside financial expertise on ROE become more significant. The effect becomes even clearer with the 5% compared to the 1% outlier treatment. Concerning risk-adjusted performance (RORWA), coefficients become significant in the case of the 5% outlier-corrected regressions. In absolute terms, the expertise coefficients only marginally increase.

Concerning stability and risk, the outlier-corrected data samples also confirm the results of the base regressions (see Appendices III.6.11, III.6.13, III.6.15, and III.6.17). Similar to the performance regressions, the expertise coefficients retain their signs from the original regressions. Moreover, they remain insignificant and the total board financial expertise coefficient in the NPL ratio regression even becomes insignificant. In absolute terms, the expertise coefficients diminish only slightly.

Summing up, the robustness tests confirm the general findings. Compared to the original regressions, there is neither a change in the signs of the expertise coefficients nor a material difference between the Top 200 panel and the merger-controlled Top 150 panel due to the outlier treatment. However, especially with regard to performance, the results become more significant.

III.5   Conclusion

The present study examines the impact of financial expertise of supervisory board members on the risk-return profile based on the example of German savings banks during the period 2004-2009.

Financial experts on supervisory boards impact the risk-return profile. However, they cannot suspend the risk-return trade-off in which an increase in performance is associated with an increase in risk. Since financial expertise positively influences bank performance significantly, it pays to have financial experts on the supervisory board. Financial experts' positive influence on performance comes at a price: an increase in loan portfolio risk and a reduction in stability. Robustness checks with outlier-corrected datasets confirm the results.

The finding that financial experts boost savings banks' performance implies that local and regional politicians and savings bank employees exert a favourable impact on performance. On average, almost 50% of savings banks' supervisory boards are made up of bank employees and local and regional politicians. The savings banks' close ties to local and regional politics are possibly beneficial, particularly for their business development. These might lead to profitable business with public authorities at a manageable risk as larger projects at the local and regional levels are often contracted out by local and regional authorities.

However, the increase in bank risk through financial expertise also suggests that local and regional politicians and bank employees do not necessarily advocate risk-minimizing strategies. They rather advocate profitable business even if that entails higher risk levels. The reason why financial experts fail in reducing loan portfolio risk and enhancing bank stability might be due to overconfidence. Individuals tend to misjudge their personal competence, and rate their own expertise higher than that of others (Fellner, Güth, and Maciejovsky, 2004; Fischhoff, Slovic, and Lichtenstein, 1977). Chuang and Lee (2006) show, in the context of investment decisions, that overconfidence can lead to an underestimation of risk, which, in turn, results in higher risk investments.

With an average value of 25% of the total supervisory board, employee representatives play a major role in savings banks' supervision and represent a notable reservoir of financial expertise. For this reason, it is notable that results hardly change between total supervisory board financial expertise and outside financial expertise. This indicates that the relatively large fraction of insiders does not make a material difference. Herding among supervisory boad members might be the reason for this observation. This follows the idea of Schöndube-Pirchegger and Schöndube (2011), who find such behaviour in audit committees. Based on their finding, we conclude that insiders on the supervisory boards follow the mainstream, and do not hold diverging opinions.

The findings of this study are deemed to be useful for the composition of boards in general, and of supervisory boards in particular. Furthermore, it provides evidence for the usefulness of some regulations to improve the stability of the banking system. Overall, savings banks seem to benefit from financial expertise because of its significant impact on performance, though not on risk. Based on these findings, banks and their owners should strive to include as many financial experts on their supervisory boards as possible. However, this should not be accompanied with an increase in board size. Free-riding incentives should rather be limited through an increase in personal responsibility. This can be done through a reduction of the supervisory board size. Smaller supervisory boards would be beneficial to bank performance, on the one hand, and to loan portfolio risk, on the other.

From a regulator's perspective the results suggest that demanding universal financial expertise in bank's internal governance mechanisms is not necessarily beneficial. For example, the results document that the new German legislation does not contribute to an enhancement of banking system stability as it was supposed to. Although expertise impacts performance positively, there is a stability-reducing and risk-increasing effect, as well.

III.6 Appendix

Appendix III.6.1:   Underlying assumptions and definition of local and regional politicians

The following assumptions have been applied for the present analysis:

- For the information merchant, we assume a merchant in terms of § 1, German Commercial Code HGB.
- For information entrepreneurs, we assume that the person is a managing partner/owner of a company.
- A farmer is treated as self-employed if not otherwise explicitly stated.
- In cases of jobs based on apprenticeships, which could suggest both self-employed and employed, employed is assumed if no further information is available.
- If the academic title is the only available information, no classification is attributed (others).

For the determination of board size, as well as for further analysis, we do not consider the following board members:

- Advisory members
- Honorary members
- Members with tenures of less than half a year.

Ministers, state secretaries, and members of parliament at the federal and federal-state level are federal politicians or federal-state politicians, respectively. The number of members of the European parliament is not material for the dataset, and these members are classified as federal politicians. For the identification of politicians at the regional and local levels, a two-step approach has been applied to differentiate between politicians in the strict sense and holders of political electoral office. This is necessary due to the multitude of administrative bodies at the regional and local levels and the heterogeneity of different federal states.

First, given the difference between full-time and voluntary electoral offices, individuals officiating voluntarily in political electoral offices are not considered politicians. These offices include honorary county councils, city councils, and municipal councils. Second, the hierarchical level of the function is considered. In our analysis, we classify the concerned person as a politician if he or she is the head of the administration. This selection step assures that politicians in our dataset are directly elected, with the exception of county administrators in Baden-Wuerttemberg.

Persons who are subject to directives and who have to report to the head of the administration do not count as politicians in the present analysis. Subsequently, district administrators, lord mayors, and mayors are consistently counted nationwide as politicians. There are a few federal states in which city directors, presidents of regional committees, presidents of local committees, and presidents of regional committees are counted as politicians if all the criteria outlined above are satisfied. Other holders of state-specific functions are not counted as politicians even though they are directly or indirectly elected and represent a political position and/or party, such as full-time city councilors in Bavaria, magistrates in Hessen, and (county) deputies in several federal states. All these persons violate the criterion regarding heading the administration. If the function is exercised full-time, the office holders are typically responsible for particular divisions or departments.

Appendix III.6.2: Supervisory board composition, Top 150 savings banks (merger-controlled panel)

Variables	Mean	Std. Dev.	Coeff. of Variation	Min	Max
Insider (%)	24.58	12.16	49.46	0.00	41.67
Outsider (%)	75.42	12.16	16.12	58.33	100.00
Employment					
Employed individuals (%)	72.50	12.21	16.84	36.36	100.00
Self-employed individuals (%)	13.52	9.91	73.32	0.00	47.37
Retired individuals (%)	12.64	10.27	81.21	0.00	55.56
Others (%)	1.34	2.82	209.61	0.00	12.50
Politicians (officiating)					
Federal politicians (%)	0.74	2.37	320.61	0.00	15.38
Federal state politicians (%)	2.64	4.36	164.99	0.00	23.08
Regional politicans (%)	5.52	4.09	74.14	0.00	20.00
Local politicians (%)	15.78	12.86	81.50	0.00	66.67
Officiating and retired politicians (%)	28.64	15.39	53.73	0.00	75.00

Appendix III.6.3: Summary statistics, Top 150 savings banks (merger-controlled panel)

Dependent variables	Mean	Std. Dev.	Coeff. of Variation	Min	Max
RORWA (%)	1.39	0.94	67.68	-2.92	8.34
ROE (%)	14.15	7.61	53.74	-28.36	67.79
z-score	19.16	9.76	50.94	3.02	77.02
NPL ratio (%)	2.08	1.46	70.08	0.04	11.56
Bank level variables					
Financial expertise (%)	65.46	17.22	26.30	20.00	100.00
Outside financial expertise (%)	53.84	22.96	42.64	0.00	100.00
Bank size (ln '000s of EUR)	21.69	0.54	2.47	20.89	23.47
Bank efficiency (%)	64.55	7.29	11.29	36.00	90.25
Bank size growth (%)	0.30	3.25	1,074.99	-16.29	14.74
Board size	15.89	4.12	25.96	7.00	33.00
Loan growth (%)	2.76	9.58	347.08	-14.70	104.87
Claims on MFI (%)	9.86	6.56	66.55	0.00	44.37
Claims on non-MFI (%)	59.79	11.03	18.44	24.21	85.36
Macroeconomic and structural variables					
East/West	0.09	0.29	311.85	0.00	1.00
GDP per capita ('000s of EUR)	27.83	7.70	27.66	14.16	72.20
Population	1.56	0.74	47.39	1.00	5.00

Appendix III.6.4: Financial expertise clusters, Top 150 savings banks (merger-controlled panel)

Dependent variables	Cluster 1	Cluster 2	Cluster 3	Delta Cluster 1-3
RORWA (%)	1.58	1.36	1.22	0.36
ROE (%)	15.85	13.95	12.65	3.21
z-score	19.76	18.23	19.49	0.27
NPL ratio (%)	1.97	2.07	2.21	-0.24
Bank level variables				
Financial expertise (%)	83.78	65.96	46.64	37.14
Outside financial expertise (%)	77.32	54.81	29.38	47.95
Bank size (ln '000s of EUR)	21.69	21.75	21.64	0.06
Bank efficiency (%)	62.34	65.54	65.78	-3.44
Bank size growth (%)	0.58	0.18	0.14	0.43
Board size	16.01	16.25	15.41	0.60
Loan growth (%)	2.35	2.03	3.89	-1.54
Claims on MFI (%)	10.63	10.65	8.30	2.33
Claims on non-MFI (%)	56.82	59.14	63.39	-6.57

Appendix III.6.5: Pairwise test of significance between expertise clusters, Top 150 savings banks (merger-controlled panel).

Dependent variables	Cluster 1 vs. 2	Cluster 1 vs. 3	Cluster 2 vs. 3
	t	t	t
	(p-value)	(p-value)	(p-value)
RORWA	2.9212 ***	5.1308 ***	2.0891 **
	0.0038	0.0000	0.0375
ROE	3.2540 ***	6.2159 ***	2.3510 **
	0.0013	0.0000	0.0194
z-score	2.1519 **	0.2783	-1.5821
	0.0322	0.7810	0.1147
NPL ratio	-1.0372	-2.1583 **	-1.2316
	0.3005	0.0317	0.2191
Bank level variables			
Financial expertise	50.1895 ***	96.1220 ***	44.0866 ***
	0.0000	0.0000	0.0000
Outside financial expertise	35.2981 ***	67.3601 ***	29.7499 ***
	0.0000	0.0000	0.0000
Bank size	-1.2410	1.4256	2.4038 **
	0.2156	0.1550	0.0168
Bank efficiency	-5.1310 ***	-5.8860 ***	-0.4735
	0.0000	0.0000	0.6362
Bank size growth	1.5352	1.7050 *	0.1416
	0.1258	0.0892	0.8875
Board size	-0.6500	1.6842 *	2.6486 ***
	0.5162	0.0932	0.0085
Loan growth	0.5969	-2.3829 **	-2.2693 **
	0.5510	0.0178	0.0240
Claims on MFI	-0.0377	4.4976 ***	5.0412 ***
	0.9700	0.0000	0.0000
Claims on non-MFI	-2.7057 ***	-7.0374 ***	-5.0723 ***
	0.0072	0.0000	0.0000

Confidence level: 95%
* indicates significance at the 10% level, ** at the 5% level, and *** at the 1% level, respectively.

Appendix III.6.6: Correlation matrix, Top 200 savings banks

	RORWA	ROE	z-score	NPL ratio	Financial expertise	Outside financial expertise	Bank size	Bank efficiency
RORWA	1.0000							
ROE	0.8696*	1.0000						
z-score	0.0705*	-0.0125	1.0000					
NPL ratio	-0.0329	-0.0619*	-0.0848*	1.0000				
Financial expertise	0.1405*	0.1566*	-0.0916*	-0.0016	1.0000			
Outside financial expertise	0.1351*	0.1540*	-0.0158	-0.0667*	0.9363*	1.0000		
Bank size	-0.0712*	-0.0650*	0.0539	-0.0854*	-0.0354	-0.0971*	1.0000	
Bank efficiency	-0.4360*	-0.4502*	-0.0618*	-0.0671*	-0.1371*	-0.1211*	-0.0946*	1.0000
Bank size growth	0.0711*	0.0764*	-0.0121	-0.2163*	0.0728*	0.0999*	-0.0057	-0.0843*
Loan growth	0.1922*	0.1245*	-0.0199	0.2647*	-0.0463	-0.0916*	0.0400	-0.0617*
Claims on MFI	0.0335	0.0110	-0.1162*	-0.1288*	0.1906*	0.1928*	0.0788*	0.0166
Claims on non-MFI	-0.3786*	-0.2684*	0.3008*	0.1465*	-0.3103*	-0.2711*	0.0672*	0.1442*
Board size	-0.1860*	-0.1542*	-0.0151	0.1042*	0.0455	-0.0590*	0.4593*	0.0799*
GDP per capita	-0.0775*	-0.0824*	0.0609*	-0.0924*	0.0852*	0.1336*	0.3309*	0.0388
Population	-0.0345	-0.0508	0.0067	-0.0202	-0.0214	-0.1109*	0.6982*	0.0007
East/West	0.3249*	0.2405*	-0.2379*	0.0299	0.1416*	0.0696*	-0.1356*	-0.1037*

* significant at the 5% level

	Bank size growth	Loan growth	Claims on MFI	Claims on non-MFI	Board size	GDP per capita	Population	East/West
RORWA								
ROE								
z-score								
NPL ratio								
Financial expertise								
Outside financial expertise								
Bank size								
Bank efficiency								
Bank size growth	1.0000							
Loan growth	0.2356*	1.0000						
Claims on MFI	0.1241*	-0.0571	1.0000					
Claims on non-MFI	-0.1132*	-0.0092	-0.4472*	1.0000				
Board size	-0.0664*	0.0013	0.0108	0.0701*	1.0000			
GDP per capita	0.0776*	-0.0032	0.0701*	0.1048*	0.0019	1.0000		
Population	-0.0468	0.0269	0.0313	-0.0465	0.4273*	0.1737*	1.0000	
East/West	-0.0634*	-0.0399	0.1549*	-0.6867*	-0.1297*	-0.3150*	0.0484	1.0000

* significant at the 5% level

Appendix III.6.7: Correlation matrix, Top 150 savings banks (merger-controlled panel)

	RORWA	ROE	z-score	NPL ratio	Financial expertise	Outside financial expertise	Bank size	Bank efficiency
RORWA	1.0000							
ROE	0.8612*	1.0000						
z-score	0.0441	-0.0434	1.0000					
NPL ratio	-0.0432	-0.0492	-0.0691*	1.0000				
Financial expertise	0.1431*	0.1525*	-0.0198	-0.0181	1.0000			
Outside financial expertise	0.1215*	0.1435*	0.0294	-0.0801*	0.9412*	1.0000		
Bank size	-0.0143	0.0059	0.0831*	-0.1025*	0.0125	-0.0157	1.0000	
Bank efficiency	-0.4550*	-0.4617*	-0.0748*	-0.0974*	-0.1638*	-0.1218*	-0.1688*	1.0000
Bank size growth	0.0634	0.0616	-0.0198	-0.2083*	0.0502	0.0728*	0.0218	-0.0721*
Loan growth	0.1814*	0.1186*	-0.0141	0.2708*	-0.0472	-0.0911*	0.0173	-0.0628
Claims on MFI	0.0227	0.0197	-0.1172*	-0.1758*	0.1702*	0.1711*	0.1810*	0.0370
Claims on non-MFI	-0.4072*	-0.2707*	0.3122*	0.1781*	-0.2834*	-0.2394*	0.0128	0.1461*
Board size	-0.1331*	-0.0909*	0.0079	0.0967*	0.0895*	0.0101	0.3283*	0.0242
GDP per capita	-0.0762*	-0.0901*	0.0552	-0.0896*	0.0826*	0.1500*	0.4820*	0.0251
Population	0.0244	-0.0023	0.0527	-0.0437	0.0401	0.0055	0.6326*	-0.0818*
East/West	0.3422*	0.2281*	-0.2318*	0.0014	0.0751*	0.0124	-0.1798*	-0.1282*

* significant at the 5% level

	Bank size growth	Loan growth	Claims on MFI	Claims on non- MFI	Board size	GDP per capita	Population	East/West
RORWA								
ROE								
z-score								
NPL ratio								
Financial expertise								
Outside financial expertise								
Bank size								
Bank efficiency								
Bank size growth	1.0000							
Loan growth	0.2419*	1.0000						
Claims on MFI	0.1360*	-0.0579	1.0000					
Claims on non-MFI	-0.0941*	-0.0201	-0.4252*	1.0000				
Board size	-0.0442	0.0049	0.0618	0.0224	1.0000			
GDP per capita	0.0891*	-0.0023	0.1227*	0.0398	0.0185	1.0000		
Population	-0.0091	0.0131	0.0850*	-0.0711*	0.3390*	0.2547*	1.0000	
East/West	-0.1178*	-0.0578	0.0651	-0.6100*	-0.1377*	-0.2795*	-0.0326	1.0000

* significant at the 5% level

Appendix III.6.8: Random-effect regressions with dependent variables RORWA and ROE, Top 150 savings banks (merger-controlled panel)

Variable		RORWA (RE) Financial expertise		RORWA (RE) Out. fin. expertise		ROE (RE) Financial expertise		ROE (RE) Out. fin. expertise	
		Coeff.	SE (robust)	Coeff.	SE (robust)	Coeff.	SE (robust)	Coeff.	SE (robust)
Financial expertise	Financial expertise	0.0012	0.0019			0.0247	0.0162		
	Outside financial expertise			0.0014	0.0015			0.0269	0.0126**
Bank level	Bank size	-0.0195	0.0920	-0.0142	0.0930	0.3198	0.8935	0.4207	0.8936
	Bank efficiency	-0.0472	0.0059***	-0.0471	0.0060***	-0.4485	0.0559***	-0.4466	0.0561***
	Bank size growth	-0.0119	0.0079	-0.0120	0.0080	-0.0712	0.0657	-0.0727	0.0654
	Board size	-0.0204	0.0076***	-0.0201	0.0075***	-0.1041	0.0743	-0.0974	0.0744
	Loan growth	0.0168	0.0029***	0.0169	0.0029***	0.0777	0.0208***	0.0802	0.0210***
	Claims on MFI	-0.0142	0.0047***	-0.0143	0.0047***	-0.0905	0.0441**	-0.0917	0.0443**
	Claims on non-MFI	-0.0290	0.0048***	-0.0287	0.0048***	-0.1380	0.0398***	-0.1330	0.0394***
Macroeconomic and structural environment	East/West	0.2508	0.2471	0.2609	0.2483	0.5913	1.7904	0.7860	1.8038
	GDP per capita	-0.0022	0.0036	-0.0026	0.0037	-0.0942	0.0474**	-0.1024	0.0482**
	Population	0.0118	0.0836	0.0113	0.0838	-0.2717	0.6278	-0.2799	0.6225
	constant	6.9513	1.9569***	6.8246	1.9756***	48.1475	19.9047**	45.8273	19.9033**
	Wald Chi^2	181.54	***	180.72	***	260.13	***	260.72	***
	R-sq	0.3770		0.3770		0.2748		0.2778	
	No of observations	900		900		900		900	

* indicates significance at the 10% level, ** at the 5% level, and *** at the 1% level, respectively.
Standard errors control for clustering at the bank level.

Appendix III.6.9: Random-effect regressions with dependent variables z-score and NPL ratio, Top 150 savings banks (merger-controlled panel)

Variable		z-score (RE) Financial expertise		z-score (RE) Out. fin. expertise		NPL Ratio (RE) Financial expertise		NPL Ratio (RE) Out. fin. expertise	
		Coeff.	SE (robust)	Coeff.	SE (robust)	Coeff.	SE (robust)	Coeff.	SE (robust)
Financial expertise	Financial expertise	0.0164	0.0108			0.0044	0.0040		
	Outside financial expertise			0.0092	0.0099			0.0008	0.0032
Bank level	Bank size	-2.9337	1.5313*	-2.8600	1.5274*	-0.1331	0.2156	-0.1414	0.2197
	Bank efficiency	-0.0296	0.0178*	-0.0297	0.0178*	-0.0268	0.0084***	-0.0274	0.0085***
	Bank size growth	-0.1113	0.0152***	-0.1113	0.0153***	-0.0917	0.0126***	-0.0918	0.0126***
	Board size	0.0368	0.0063	-0.0336	0.0554	0.0382	0.0156**	0.0400	0.0155***
	Loan growth	-0.0027	0.0231***	0.0371	0.0064***	0.0478	0.0075***	0.0478	0.0075***
	Claims on MFI	0.0123	0.0322	-0.0030	0.0230	-0.0165	0.0086*	-0.0164	0.0086*
	Claims on non-MFI	-0.0445	0.0529	0.0123	0.0320	0.0267	0.0106**	0.0251	0.0105**
Macroeconomic and structural environment	East/West	-6.9327	1.8367***	-6.8153	1.8265***	0.4316	0.3410	0.4172	0.3426
	GDP per capita	0.2464	0.0471***	0.2477	0.0469***	-0.0150	0.0094	-0.0144	0.0093
	Population	0.4236	1.1016	0.3960	1.0897	-0.0555	0.1418	-0.0553	0.1435
	constant	76.7019	31.8427**	75.5080	31.7979**	4.7281	4.4803	5.2407	4.5675
	Wald Chi^2	169.17	***	165.98	***	165.8	***	163.96	***
	R-sq	0.0316		0.0326		0.2179		0.2165	
	No of observations	900		900		896		896	

* indicates significance at the 10% level, ** at the 5% level, and *** at the 1% level, respectively.
Standard errors control for clustering at the bank level.

Appendix III.6.10: Random-effect regressions with dependent variables RORWA and ROE, Top 200 savings banks, with 1% outlier-correction

Variable		RORWA (RE) Financial expertise		RORWA (RE) Out. fin. expertise		ROE (RE) Financial expertise		ROE (RE) Out. fin. expertise	
		Coeff.	SE (robust)	Coeff.	SE (robust)	Coeff.	SE (robust)	Coeff.	SE (robust)
Financial expertise	Financial expertise	0.0018	0.0015			0.0365	0.0148 **		
	Outside financial expertise			0.0021	0.0012 *			0.0328	0.0110 ***
Bank level	Bank size	-0.0620	0.0820	-0.0585	0.0824	-0.4953	0.7696	-0.4675	0.7714
	Bank efficiency	-0.0467	0.0046 ***	-0.0465	0.0046 ***	-0.4716	0.0453 ***	-0.4709	0.0455 ***
	Bank size growth	-0.0107	0.0074	-0.0110	0.0074	-0.0281	0.0632	-0.0319	0.0628
	Board size	-0.0184	0.0057 ***	-0.0179	0.0057 ***	-0.1208	0.0549 **	-0.1096	0.0546 **
	Loan growth	0.0218	0.0026 ***	0.0220	0.0026 ***	0.1030	0.0205 ***	0.1065	0.0208 ***
	Claims on MFI	-0.0134	0.0047 ***	-0.0135	0.0047 ***	-0.1218	0.0455 ***	-0.1234	0.0458 ***
	Claims on non-MFI	-0.0220	0.0035 ***	-0.0215	0.0035 ***	-0.1029	0.0333 ***	-0.0990	0.0332 ***
Macroeconomic and structural environment	East/West	0.1960	0.1555	0.2095	0.1549	1.2487	1.3608	1.4393	1.3714
	GDP per capita	-0.0006	0.0035	-0.0012	0.0035	-0.0629	0.0443	-0.0686	0.0450
	Population	0.0215	0.0493	0.0246	0.0494	0.0554	0.4186	0.0977	0.4140
	constant	7.2342	1.7781 ***	7.1237	1.7860 ***	63.2824	16.8611 ***	62.9106	16.8887 ***
	Wald Chi^2	333.25	***	333.97	***	344.46	***	340.84	***
	R-sq	0.3824		0.3837		0.2941		0.2959	
	No of observations	1,162		1,162		1,162		1,162	

* indicates significance at the 10% level, ** at the 5% level, and *** at the 1% level, respectively.
Standard errors control for clustering at the bank level.

Appendix III.6.11: Random-effect regressions with dependent variables z-score and NPL ratio, Top 200 savings banks, with 1% outlier-correction

Variable		z-score (RE) Financial expertise		z-score (RE) Out. fin. expertise		NPL Ratio (RE) Financial expertise		NPL Ratio (RE) Out. fin. expertise	
		Coeff.	SE (robust)	Coeff.	SE (robust)	Coeff.	SE (robust)	Coeff.	SE (robust)
Financial expertise	Financial expertise	-0.0122	0.0323			0.0068	0.0036 *		
	Outside financial expertise			-0.0138	0.0269			0.0026	0.0028
Bank level	Bank size	2.3528	3.1307	2.3570	3.1421	-0.3638	0.1989 *	-0.3713	0.2006 *
	Bank efficiency	0.0352	0.0365	0.0350	0.0366	-0.0252	0.0075 ***	-0.0257	0.0076 ***
	Bank size growth	-0.1372	0.0262 ***	-0.1371	0.0262 ***	-0.1081	0.0119 ***	-0.1080	0.0120 ***
	Board size	0.0170	0.1107	0.0100	0.1130	0.0406	0.0114 ***	0.0429	0.0112 ***
	Loan growth	0.0474	0.0083 ***	0.0470	0.0081 ***	0.0582	0.0053 ***	0.0583	0.0053 ***
	Claims on MFI	0.0330	0.0448	0.0332	0.0447	-0.0157	0.0083 *	-0.0157	0.0084 *
	Claims on non-MFI	-0.0231	0.0550	-0.0250	0.0553	0.0300	0.0095 ***	0.0286	0.0096 ***
Macroeconomic and structural environment	East/West	-8.0425	2.4929 ***	-8.1242	2.4948 ***	0.6625	0.2876 **	0.6733	0.2881 **
	GDP per capita	-0.0545	0.0920	-0.0544	0.0915	-0.0160	0.0083 *	-0.0152	0.0083 *
	Population	-0.4019	1.9926	-0.4076	2.0005	-0.0051	0.1018	-0.0044	0.1021
	constant	-29.5826	66.4948	-29.4682	66.8039	9.1556	4.2727 **	9.6719	4.3164 **
	Wald Chi²	128.87	***	130.53	***	359.8	***	355.9	***
	R-sq	0.0421		0.0398		0.2435		0.2414	
	No of observations	1,162		1,162		1,156		1,156	

* indicates significance at the 10% level, ** at the 5% level, and *** at the 1% level, respectively.
Standard errors control for clustering at the bank level.

Appendix III.6.12: Random-effect regressions with dependent variables RORWA and ROE, Top 200 savings banks, with 5% outlier-correction

Variable		RORWA (RE) Financial expertise		RORWA (RE) Out. fin. expertise		ROE (RE) Financial expertise		ROE (RE) Out. fin. expertise	
		Coeff.	SE (robust)	Coeff.	SE (robust)	Coeff.	SE (robust)	Coeff.	SE (robust)
Financial expertise	Financial expertise	0.0021	0.0013 *			0.0377	0.0139 ***		
	Outside financial expertise			0.0022	0.0010 ***			0.0100	0.0328 ***
Bank level	Bank size	-0.0734	0.0691	-0.0704	0.0695	-0.2713	0.6716	-0.2413	0.6729
	Bank efficiency	-0.0457	0.0037 ***	-0.0456	0.0037 ***	-0.4861	0.0399 ***	-0.4865	0.0398 ***
	Bank size growth	-0.0213	0.0052 ***	-0.0215	0.0052 ***	-0.0719	0.0565	-0.0750	0.0563
	Board size	-0.0162	0.0054 ***	-0.0156	0.0053 ***	-0.0938	0.0548 *	-0.0829	0.0547
	Loan growth	0.0300	0.0030 ***	0.0303	0.0030 ***	0.1436	0.0280 ***	0.1473	0.0282 ***
	Claims on MFI	-0.0118	0.0043 ***	-0.0119	0.0043 ***	-0.1363	0.0427 ***	-0.1369	0.0429 ***
	Claims on non-MFI	-0.0209	0.0031 ***	-0.0204	0.0030 ***	-0.1183	0.0312 ***	-0.1147	0.0311 ***
Macroeconomic and structural environment	East/West	-0.0483	0.1243	-0.0345	0.1246	0.4029	1.1990	0.6072	1.2096
	GDP per capita	-0.0049	0.0043	-0.0052	0.0043	-0.1316	0.0501 ***	-0.1344	0.0505 ***
	Population	0.0257	0.0375	0.0279	0.0376	0.0025	0.3533	0.0295	0.3506
	constant	7.4018	1.5163 ***	7.3226	1.5243 ***	62.0277	14.8510 ***	61.7143	14.8526 ***
	Wald Chi^2	690.11	***	685.87	***	502.26	***	495.87	***
	R-sq	0.3999		0.4018		0.3222		0.324	
	No of observations	1,162		1,162		1,162		1,162	

* indicates significance at the 10% level, ** at the 5% level, and *** at the 1% level, respectively.
Standard errors control for clustering at the bank level.

Appendix III.6.13: Random-effect regressions with dependent variables z-score and NPL ratio, Top 200 savings banks, with 5% outlier-correction

Variable		z-score (RE) Financial expertise		z-score (RE) Out. fin. expertise		NPL Ratio (RE) Financial expertise		NPL Ratio (RE) Out. fin. expertise	
		Coeff.	SE (robust)	Coeff.	SE (robust)	Coeff.	SE (robust)	Coeff.	SE (robust)
Financial expertise	Financial expertise	-0.0056	0.0318			0.0041	0.0033		
	Outside financial expertise			-0.0140	0.0276			0.0007	0.0025
Bank level	Bank size	1.5318	3.4903	1.5375	3.5028	-0.3850	0.1639 **	-0.3903	0.1653 **
	Bank efficiency	0.0318	0.0377	0.0314	0.0375	-0.0305	0.0063 **	-0.0309	0.0063 ***
	Bank size growth	-0.1744	0.0335 ***	-0.1738	0.0332 ***	-0.1343	0.0110 ***	-0.1342	0.0110 ***
	Board size	0.0337	0.1273	0.0259	0.1292	0.0406	0.0115 ***	0.0416	0.0114 ***
	Loan growth	0.0831	0.0151 ***	0.0826	0.0146 ***	0.0959	0.0059 ***	0.0960	0.0059 ***
	Claims on MFI	0.0376	0.0507	0.0374	0.0505	-0.0202	0.0081 **	-0.0201	0.0081 **
	Claims on non-MFI	-0.0339	0.0564	-0.0371	0.0571	0.0221	0.0079 ***	0.0208	0.0080 ***
Macroeconomic and structural environment	East/West	-8.5238	2.4488 ***	-8.5784	2.4501 ***	0.3582	0.2411	0.3626	0.2418
	GDP per capita	-0.0440	0.1279	-0.0432	0.1273	-0.0243	0.0111 **	-0.0232	0.0111 **
	Population	-0.0221	1.9757	-0.0238	1.9791	-0.0052	0.0850	-0.0076	0.0859
	constant	-12.5296	73.4407	-11.9266	73.6803	10.8109	3.4984 ***	11.2174	3.5309 ***
	Wald Chi²	151.28	***	151.88	***	659.84	***	663.41	***
	R-sq	0.0398		0.0384		0.2649		0.2636	
	No of observations	1,162		1,162		1,156		1,156	

* indicates significance at the 10% level, ** at the 5% level, and *** at the 1% level, respectively.
Standard errors control for clustering at the bank level.

Appendix III.6.14: Random-effect regressions with dependent variables RORWA and ROE, Top 150 savings banks (merger-controlled panel), with 1% outlier-correction

Variable		RORWA (RE) Financial expertise		RORWA (RE) Out. fin. expertise		ROE (RE) Financial expertise		ROE (RE) Out. fin. expertise	
		Coeff.	SE (robust)	Coeff.	SE (robust)	Coeff.	SE (robust)	Coeff.	SE (robust)
Financial expertise	Financial expertise	0.0016	0.0018			0.0276	0.0159 *		
	Outside financial expertise			0.0017	0.0014			0.0286	0.0121 **
Bank level	Bank size	-0.0482	0.0785	-0.0419	0.0796	0.1485	0.7812	0.2571	0.7838
	Bank efficiency	-0.0458	0.0051 ***	-0.0458	0.0051 ***	-0.4445	0.0497 ***	-0.4428	0.0498 ***
	Bank size growth	-0.0137	0.0075 *	-0.0138	0.0076 *	-0.0787	0.0637	-0.0809	0.0635
	Board size	-0.0203	0.0074 ***	-0.0197	0.0072 ***	-0.1117	0.0735	-0.1035	0.0736
	Loan growth	0.0213	0.0025 ***	0.0214	0.0025 ***	0.0901	0.0213 ***	0.0931	0.0215 ***
	Claims on MFI	-0.0127	0.0049 ***	-0.0128	0.0049 ***	-0.0923	0.0459 **	-0.0933	0.0462 **
	Claims on non-MFI	-0.0273	0.0041 ***	-0.0270	0.0041 ***	-0.1349	0.0367 ***	-0.1307	0.0360 ***
Macroeconomic and structural environment	East/West	0.1714	0.2308	0.1822	0.2313	-0.2946	1.7576	-0.1069	1.7645
	GDP per capita	-0.0028	0.0038	-0.0034	0.0039	-0.1175	0.0462 **	-0.1261	0.0468 ***
	Population	0.0360	0.0711	0.0352	0.0713	-0.0424	0.5380	-0.0557	0.5342
	constant	7.3129	1.7289 ***	7.1782	1.7472 ***	51.6968	17.8464 ***	49.3656	17.8738 ***
	Wald Chi^2	258.12	***	258.14	***	304.09	***	305.52	***
	R-sq	0.4016		0.4027		0.2867		0.2901	
	No of observations	900		900		900		900	

* indicates significance at the 10% level, ** at the 5% level, and *** at the 1% level, respectively.
Standard errors control for clustering at the bank level.

Appendix III.6.15: Random-effect regressions with dependent variables z-score and NPL ratio, Top 150 savings banks (merger-controlled panel), with 1% outlier-correction

Variable		z-score (RE) Financial expertise		z-score (RE) Out. fin. expertise		NPL Ratio (RE) Financial expertise		NPL Ratio (RE) Out. fin. expertise	
		Coeff.	SE (robust)	Coeff.	SE (robust)	Coeff.	SE (robust)	Coeff.	SE (robust)
Financial expertise	Financial expertise	0.0148	0.0108			0.0049	0.0039		
	Outside financial expertise			0.0084	0.0100			0.0016	0.0030
Bank level	Bank size	-2.7740	1.2591 **	-2.7197	1.2530 **	-0.1084	0.2014	-0.1126	0.2052
	Bank efficiency	-0.0281	0.0178	-0.0282	0.0178	-0.0241	0.0075 ***	-0.0246	0.0076 ***
	Bank size growth	-0.1170	0.0165 ***	-0.1170	0.0165 ***	-0.1047	0.0129 ***	-0.1048	0.0130 ***
	Board size	-0.0480	0.0530	-0.0380	0.0550	0.0367	0.0159 **	0.0387	0.0157 **
	Loan growth	0.0483	0.0060 ***	0.0486	0.0060 ***	0.0594	0.0063 ***	0.0595	0.0063 ***
	Claims on MFI	0.0055	0.0239	0.0053	0.0238	-0.0178	0.0090 **	-0.0178	0.0090 **
	Claims on non-MFI	0.0234	0.0349	0.0234	0.0346	0.0240	0.0098 **	0.0227	0.0097 **
Macroeconomic and structural environment	East/West	-6.6380	1.9260 ***	-6.5338	1.9106 ***	0.3420	0.3328	0.3352	0.3337
	GDP per capita	0.2483	0.0447 ***	0.2499	0.0445 ***	-0.0200	0.0097 **	-0.0197	0.0096 **
	Population	0.4016	1.0962	0.3781	1.0855	-0.0528	0.1293	-0.0534	0.1307
	constant	72.5048	26.7925 ***	71.6700	26.6580 ***	4.2936	4.1890	4.6911	4.2705
	Wald Chi²	207.54	***	203.65	***	252.89	***	249.44	***
	R-sq	0.0352		0.0362		0.2285		0.2268	
	No of observations	900		900		896		896	

* indicates significance at the 10% level, ** at the 5% level, and *** at the 1% level, respectively.
Standard errors control for clustering at the bank level.

Appendix III.6.16: Random-effect regressions with dependent variables RORWA and ROE, Top 150 savings banks (merger-controlled panel), with 5% outlier-correction

Variable		RORWA (RE) Financial expertise		RORWA (RE) Out. fin. expertise		ROE (RE) Financial expertise		ROE (RE) Out. fin. expertise	
		Coeff.	SE (robust)	Coeff.	SE (robust)	Coeff.	SE (robust)	Coeff.	SE (robust)
Financial expertise	Financial expertise	0.0022	0.0015			0.0309	0.0151 **		
	Outside financial expertise			0.0021	0.0011 *			0.0293	0.0111 ***
Bank level	Bank size	-0.0554	0.0630	-0.0502	0.0634	0.3618	0.7455	0.4359	0.7446
	Bank efficiency	-0.0454	0.0039 ***	-0.0454	0.0039 ***	-0.4675	0.0445 ***	-0.4671	0.0442 ***
	Bank size growth	-0.0232	0.0054 ***	-0.0234	0.0054 ***	-0.1051	0.0599 *	-0.1073	0.0598 *
	Board size	-0.0197	0.0072 ***	-0.0187	0.0071 ***	-0.1110	0.0809	-0.0971	0.0810
	Loan growth	0.0270	0.0029 ***	0.0272	0.0029 ***	0.1163	0.0280 ***	0.1195	0.0282 ***
	Claims on MFI	-0.0088	0.0045 **	-0.0088	0.0044 **	-0.0832	0.0448 *	-0.0833	0.0450 *
	Claims on non-MFI	-0.0232	0.0034 ***	-0.0230	0.0033 ***	-0.1308	0.0335 ***	-0.1276	0.0329 ***
Macroeconomic and structural environment	East/West	-0.1735	0.1471	-0.1602	0.1475	-1.0514	1.4853	-0.8572	1.4882
	GDP per capita	-0.0062	0.0046	-0.0065	0.0046	-0.1742	0.0542 ***	-0.1785	0.0547 ***
	Population	0.0374	0.0446	0.0362	0.0448	-0.1323	0.4457	-0.1503	0.4413
	constant	7.1974	1.4294 ***	7.0965	1.4306 ***	49.7215	16.8658 ***	48.2487	16.7493 ***
	Wald Chi^2	571.59	***	569.09	***	423.07	***	419.64	***
	R-sq	0.4026		0.4046		0.303		0.3064	
	No of observations	900		900		900		900	

* indicates significance at the 10% level, ** at the 5% level, and *** at the 1% level, respectively.
Standard errors control for clustering at the bank level.

Appendix III.6.17: Random-effect regressions with dependent variables z-score and NPL ratio, Top 150 savings banks (merger-controlled panel), with 5% outlier-correction

Variable		z-score (RE) Financial expertise		z-score (RE) Out. fin. expertise		NPL Ratio (RE) Financial expertise		NPL Ratio (RE) Out. fin. expertise	
		Coeff.	SE (robust)	Coeff.	SE (robust)	Coeff.	SE (robust)	Coeff.	SE (robust)
Financial expertise	Financial expertise	0.0180	0.0118			0.0038	0.0039		
	Outside financial expertise			0.0091	0.0102			0.0003	0.0030
Bank level	Bank size	-2.9837	1.3629 **	-2.9041	1.3470 **	-0.1284	0.1864	-0.1365	0.1888
	Bank efficiency	-0.0341	0.0167 **	-0.0341	0.0167 **	-0.0267	0.0072 ***	-0.0272	0.0072 ***
	Bank size growth	-0.1428	0.0198 ***	-0.1432	0.0198 ***	-0.1281	0.0125 ***	-0.1281	0.0125 ***
	Board size	-0.0950	0.0576 *	-0.0841	0.0592	0.0297	0.0188	0.0306	0.0187
	Loan growth	0.0754	0.0089 ***	0.0761	0.0089 ***	0.0901	0.0069 ***	0.0902	0.0069 ***
	Claims on MFI	0.0157	0.0254	0.0161	0.0253	-0.0170	0.0088 *	-0.0169	0.0088 *
	Claims on non-MFI	0.0276	0.0365	0.0274	0.0361	0.0227	0.0090 **	0.0213	0.0089 **
Macroeconomic and structural environment	East/West	-6.3616	1.7677 ***	-6.2481	1.7497 ***	0.2103	0.2969	0.1999	0.2980
	GDP per capita	0.2227	0.0454 ***	0.2240	0.0455 ***	-0.0268	0.0129 **	-0.0257	0.0129 **
	Population	1.1947	0.7108 *	1.1664	0.6982 *	-0.0194	0.1145	-0.0193	0.1165
	constant	77.1628	29.7426 ***	75.9599	29.3936 ***	5.2093	3.8758	5.6968	3.9269
	Wald Chi²	216.74	***	212.54	***	473.41	***	477.24	***
	R-sq	0.0295		0.0309		0.228		0.2271	
	No of observations	900		900		896		896	

* indicates significance at the 10% level, ** at the 5% level, and *** at the 1% level, respectively.
Standard errors control for clustering at the bank level.

IV Financial Expertise of Supervisory Board Members, Overconfidence, and Bank Risk-Taking[14]

Abstract

In this study, we analyze whether financial expertise in internal bank governance benefits the financial institution by reducing risk and increasing stability. Whereas behavioural finance theory questions the benefit of financial expertise, empirical studies provide evidence that financial experts do add value. Based on a study of more than 400 German banks, we find that the financial expertise of supervisory board members reduces stability and increases loan portfolio risk. This finding is robust across ownership types. With regard to performance, the results show that supervisory board competence impacts banking groups in different ways. In general, our results question the effectiveness of universal expertise in internal governance; therefore, we propose that financial institutions should have experts for specific areas on their supervisory boards.

IV.1 Introduction

In 1999 and 2006, the Basel Committee on Banking Supervision had already emphasized the high relevance of board competence for an effective governance system (Basel Committee on Banking Supervision, 1999, 2006). As one of its principles for an effective governance system, the committee demands that "board members should be qualified for their positions, have a clear understanding of their role in corporate governance and be able to exercise sound judgment about the affairs of the bank" (Basel Committee on Banking Supervision, 2006). The recent 2008 banking crisis sheds additional light on the importance of governance in general and board expertise in particular: incomplete risk information, inappropriate risk management, and insufficient industry expertise were identified as major shortcomings in bank risk governance (Ard and Berg, 2010; Choundhry, 2011; Kirkpatrick, 2009). As a consequence, increasing industry expertise on boards is considered an important and necessary measure to come to terms with banks' increasingly complex

---

14   This chapter is based on a joint working paper (Böhm, Froneberg, and Schiereck, 2012a).

business (Mehran, Morrison, and Shapiro, 2011). Although it seems perfectly logical that increasing expertise helps to overcome these shortcomings, the question remains whether this is the case in reality. Theoretical evidence and empirical studies give contradictory answers to this question.

Individuals tend to be overconfident, which can become apparent in various ways (e.g., Fischhoff, Slovic, and Lichtenstein, 1977). Such overconfidence can take various forms: overestimating one's own abilities, rating oneself better than others, or overstating the accuracy of one's own beliefs (Moore and Healy, 2007). As a consequence, decision-makers may wrongly estimate and trade-off risks and opportunities (e.g., Chuang and Lee, 2006; Cooper, Woo, and Dunkelberg, 1988; Fellner, Güth, and Maciejovsky, 2004). Moreover, Odean (1998) shows that increasing expertise levels does not resolve the problem but can even aggravate it, as overconfidence increases with expertise. In summary, with regard to improving risk governance, behavioural finance theory suggests that financial expertise is not necessarily beneficial.

Fama and Jensen (1983) consider outside directors as a source of knowledge. Consequently, increasing expertise could be beneficial. Empirical studies analyzing the impact of financial expertise on firm performance support this idea and report positive relationships. Firms with more financial experts on their boards document better stock performances and higher abnormal returns than firms with less experts (e.g., Davidson, Xie, and Xu, 2004; Lee, Rosenstein, and Wyatt, 1999). Furthermore, some studies with accounting-based measures also support these findings (e.g., Dhaliwal, Naiker, and Navissi, 2006).

In this study, we investigate whether a higher degree of financial expertise improves internal bank governance and has a positive impact on bank stability and risk. Analyzing if and how financial experts influence risk and stability of banks makes great demands on the database in terms of homogeneity to ensure comparability across a large number of banks. Different regulatory requirements, business models, and organizational structures affect bank risk and stability as well and may hide the actual influence of board members' financial expertise. However, for the robustness of the analysis, it is important to have comparable banks across different ownership types.

The German three-sector banking system represents a unique object of investigation. All banks operate under the same regulatory regime, have the common German two-tier board structure, and provide a large reservoir of comparable banks. From a governance perspective, two of the sectors, cooperative and savings banks, are characterized by a prominent similarity that is important to the present analysis. Neither type of bank has a so-called "market for corporate control" as they are not tied to capital markets for equity funding (Manne, 1965). On the one hand, this can lead to a lack of control by investors, as in large exchange-listed commercial banks. On the other hand, they do not have the distorting effects of capital markets.

Both banking groups are not exchange-listed and have a completely different ownership structure, which is probably the most striking difference between the two groups, at least from a governance perspective. Cooperative banks are strictly privately owned, whereas savings banks are publicly owned (Hackethal, 2004; Schmidt, 2009). In the case of savings banks, this results in a single shareholder who owns the bank.[15] Due to their public ownership, savings banks are closely tied to local and regional authorities (Fischer and Pfeil, 2004). Cooperative banks, on the other hand, are owned by their members, resulting in a highly fragmented ownership structure. Consequently, the governance mechanisms of cooperative banks are mainly based on social control among members due to their highly fragmented structure and the "one member, one vote" principle (Hackethal and Schmidt, 2005).

Furthermore, the supervisory boards in both sectors are authorized with different decision-making powers and responsibilities, which allows to test the actual impact of financial expertise for robustness and to be separated from structural aspects. Federal state laws on savings banks provide the supervisory boards of these banks with far-reaching responsibilities, leading to more power for savings banks than banks with other legal statuses, e.g., through the credit committee (Hackethal, 2004). Thus, the supervisory board influences the overall banking strategy at savings banks significantly. Additionally, the laws allow the supervisory board to influence the bank management directly, such as by assigning instructions to the management. Examples of these instructions and approvals include the closure of branches, the acquisition of equity stakes in other companies, the employment of executive employees, and the distribution of profits (Kleff and Weber, 2005; Vins, 2008).[16] In contrast to savings banks laws, the Cooperatives Act (GenG) does not provide such opportunities for the supervisory board to influence the operating decisions of bank management directly.

Cooperative and savings banks have a similar business model that guarantees a high degree of comparability. Both banking groups are main competitors at the local and regional levels (Engerer and Schrooten, 2004; Fischer and Pfeil, 2004). Their similarity is anchored in the charters of cooperative banks and the savings bank laws of the federal states. The overall objective of cooperative banks is to serve their members with self-aid and self-

---

15   In cases where several cities or counties have a savings bank together, there is an association that owns the bank.

16   See, for example, the savings banks law of the state of Baden-Wuerttemberg.

responsibility as guiding principles (Hackethal, 2004). They operate on a regional level and provide universal banking service with focus on typical deposit taking and lending business. The business focus of savings banks is dominated by a public mandate which requires them to operate regionally and foster regional economic development (Hackethal, 2004; Hakenes, Schmidt, and Xie, 2009; Schmidt, 2009). Like cooperative banks, the core business of savings banks is deposit taking and lending. At the end of 2009, the 1,939 German banks included 1,157 cooperative banks and 431 savings banks (Deutsche Bundesbank, 2011).

Overall, German cooperative and savings banks provide a suitable basis for the analysis. The sample of the present study comprises more than 400 German cooperative and savings banks, with more than 39,365 observations at the individual level. This study addresses the following two questions: "Does more financial expertise of supervisory board members improve bank performance, risk and stability?" and "Are these impacts significantly different across ownership types?"

The remainder of this study is structured as follows: Chapter IV.2 presents related literature on board composition and the financial expertise of board members as well as on the risk-taking and performance of cooperative and savings banks. Chapter IV.3 introduces the data, sources, and the empirical model. Chapter IV.4 provides descriptive results and presents the results of the regression analysis. Chapter IV.5 concludes the study with an evaluation of the findings.

IV.2   Related Literature

The empirical related literature can be classified into three categories. The first category deals with the impact of boards' financial expertise on performance and risk. The second category comprises studies that analyze the impact of board composition and size on firm performance. The third category focuses on the efficiency, performance, and stability of cooperative and savings banks.

The most related strand of literature is the first, which deals with the impact of financial expertise on performance and risk. In summary, studies show that higher levels of competence can pay off. However, these results are not consistent. The following studies hold that financial expertise is mainly defined by the professional experience of the individuals.

Most related studies that analyze the impact of competence on performance and risk have a similar conceptual ground but differ to a certain extent, such as in their focus on one-tier boards and non-banks. The results of several studies that use accounting-based performance indicators are mixed. Carcello, Hollingsworth, Klein, and Neal (2008) do not find expertise to be exclusively beneficial, as there are substitutes for expertise that can have the same positive effect on financial reporting. Dhaliwal, Naiker, and Navissi (2006) find a positive link between accounting expertise and accruals quality, indicating that expertise in general positively influences firm performance. Güner, Malmendier, and Tate (2008) analyze the impact of bankers on the boards and on investments. They find that bankers do exert influence but not always in the interest of shareholders, especially if there are conflicts of interest between the bankers and the shareholders. Studies with market-based measures indicate that capital markets also reward financial expertise. The appointment of financial experts to boards leads to positive stock price reactions and abnormal returns (Davidson, Xie, and Xu, 2004; DeFond, Hann, and Hu, 2005; Fernandes and Fich, 2009; Lee, Rosenstein, and Wyatt, 1999). Focusing on the recent banking crisis, Minton, Taillard, and Williamson (2010) find bank risk is positively associated with financial expertise.

Besides the analysis of the explicit impact of board competence, studies analyze, in general, the effect of board size and composition on firm performance. The results suggest that larger boards tend to reduce firm value (Eisenberg, Sundgren, and Wells, 1998; Yermack, 1996). This supports the theory that larger boards lead to free riding, which can have adverse effects on performance (Jensen, 1993). However, a more recent study shows that board size can enhance value, depending on the complexity of the firm (Coles, Daniel, and Naveen, 2008). Studies that focus especially on banks conclude that banks with larger boards do not perform worse than banks with smaller boards, and that larger boards can have a positive effect on bank performance (Adams and Mehran, 2008; Andres and Vallelado, 2008). Concerning board composition, most studies conclude that this is unrelated to firm performance (Hermalin and Weisbach, 2003). The fraction of outsiders on the boards was mostly used to proxy board composition. Insignificant relationships were reported regardless of the use of Tobin's q or accounting measures (Bhagat and Black, 2000; Hermalin and Weisbach, 1991; Klein, 1998; Mehran, 1995).

The third category of literature deals with the comparison of performance and risk across the banking sectors. These studies conclude that cooperative and savings banks are less risky and more stable than are commercial banks. However, the results are unclear about whether cooperative banks are more stable and less risky than savings banks, or vice versa. Similar to the present study, Beck, Hesse, Kick, and Westernhagen (2009) focus on German banks to analyze stability across the three sectors. This allows meaningful comparisons between banking groups, as no diverging cross-country effects between banking sectors need to be taken into account. The study concludes that commercial banks are less stable than are banks in the other two sectors. The comparison between cooperative and savings banks shows that cooperative banks face less insolvency risk than savings banks do. However, regarding distress probability, the result is the opposite. Evidence on lending risk is not consistent. Profitability is lower for both groups than for commercial banks, but savings banks are more profitable than cooperative banks. Based on an international sample of 665 banks, Goddard, Molyneux, and Wilson (2004) confirm weaker performance for German cooperative and savings banks.

As regards international banks, Westman (2010) shows, without controlling for operational and ownership characteristics, that savings and cooperative banks are less profitable and less risky than commercial banks. For international cooperative banks, Cihák and Hesse (2007) conclude that these banks are more stable than commercial banks in terms of z-score. To a lesser extent, this holds for savings banks as well. The aforementioned study covers nearly 17,000 banks from 29 countries. By going beyond mere comparison, the study shows that cooperative banks can increase the stability of the overall banking system. However, the study also concludes that non-profit banks such as cooperative banks can threaten weak commercial banks in the retail market because they eat into their market segment, forcing the commercial banks into more volatile segments such as corporate and investment banking. The results of Cihák and Hesse (2007) are backed by those of another study, which show that earnings stability is higher for both cooperative and savings banks than it is for commercial banks and that savings banks are more stable than cooperative banks (Ayadi, Llewellyn, Schmidt, Arbak, and Groen, 2010). With regard to efficiency, there is hardly any evidence of significant differences between German regional banks in the three sectors during the 1989–1996 period (Altunbas, Evans, and Molyneux, 2001).

IV.3   Data and Methodology

IV.3.1   Sample and Data

The present study is based on the 400[17] largest cooperative and savings banks as at the end of 2009. Cooperative banks that are not of the legal form of a cooperative firm and savings banks that are not publicly owned are excluded from the dataset. Since individuals are counted in the category "other," if financial expertise cannot be derived, all banks included in the panel must be

---

17 The 200 largest banks of each sector are included if the study criteria are satisfied.

below the following "other" threshold to increase the explanatory power of the analysis. A maximum of 10% of the overall supervisory board, or one individual for supervisory boards of up to nine individuals, is allowed to be classified as "other." If a cooperative or savings bank has not been included in the analysis due to lack of data or too high a representation of individuals who could not clearly be labeled either financially literate or not literate, the institution that ranks next in size is included, instead.

In the present study, two samples are analyzed. First, the 200 largest banks in each sector are included in the sample "Top 200". Second, the "Top 150" sample comprises the 150 largest banks in each sector that were not involved in mergers over the panel horizon and the two years preceding this horizon. Overall, 257 cooperative and 209 savings banks have been considered in this study. The Top 200 sample covers 21% of all German banks and accounts for 15% of the German banks' total assets.[18] In the cooperative banking sector, the largest 200 banks included in the analysis account for 57% of the total assets. The average cooperative bank in the sample has total assets of EUR 1.9 billion. The largest cooperative bank has total assets of EUR 41.4 billion, while the smallest bank has EUR 0.7 billion. With regard to the largest 200 savings banks, the sample accounts for 71% of the sector's total assets. The largest savings bank in the sample has total assets of EUR 29.3 billion, and the smallest savings bank has EUR 1.5 billion. The mean of total assets is EUR 3.8 billion. The merger-controlled banks (Top 150) account for 35% of the cooperative bank sector's total assets and 45% of the savings bank sector's total assets. The average of total assets in the merger-controlled sample is EUR 1.6 billion for cooperative banks and EUR 3.2 billion for savings banks. The total assets of cooperative banks range from EUR 0.5 billion to EUR 41.4 billion and that of savings banks from EUR 1.4 billion to EUR 15.6 billion.

Data on supervisory board members were manually collected from each bank's annual report (published by the Bundesanzeiger and accessed via the Unternehmensregister or LexisNexis databases). The merger history of each bank was accessed through the Hoppenstedt Banken database. Balance sheet and Profit & Loss statement data were taken from the BAKIS database. BAKIS is the joint information system of the German Federal Financial Supervisory Authority (BaFin) and Deutsche Bundesbank, and it contains bank-specific data. The Regionaldatenbank Deutschland of the German Federal Statistical Office provided data for macroeconomic and structural control variables.

---

18 As of the end of 2009.

IV.3.2 Hypotheses and Model

With our empirical model, we test two hypotheses on the impact of supervisory board financial expertise on the risk and performance of banks. First, we analyze whether the (outside) financial expertise of the supervisory board has an impact on the risk and performance of cooperative and savings banks. Second, we test whether the impact of (outside) financial expertise is the same across ownership types.

Hypothesis 1: *The (outside) financial expertise of the supervisory board members is unrelated to bank risk and performance.*

Hypothesis 2: *The impact of the (outside) financial expertise of the supervisory board on bank risk and performance is equal in cooperative and savings banks.*

The impact of the financial expertise of supervisory boards on bank performance and risk is analyzed based on a panel analysis via a random-effect regression model of the following general form:

$$DV_{it} = \alpha + \beta FE_{it} + \gamma B_{it} + \delta M_{it} + \theta SD_i + \varepsilon_{it} \qquad (IV.1)$$

where *DV* is the dependent variable of bank *i* at time *t*. Dependent variables for stability and risk are z-score and non-performing loans (NPL) ratio. The dependent variables for performance are return on risk-weighted assets (RORWA) and return on equity (ROE). *FE* is the financial expertise of the supervisory board, *B* comprises bank-level control variables, *M* comprises macroeconomic and structural control variables, *SD* is a dummy variable for savings banks, and ε is the error term. For a comparison of the coefficients across the two sectors, interaction effects are included in the regression model. For this reason, *FE*, *B*, and *M* are made to interact with dummy variables for cooperative and savings banks. *B* comprises (a) bank size, (b) bank size growth, (c) bank efficiency, (d) bank loan volume growth, (e) claims on monetary financial institutions (MFI), (f) claims on non-monetary financial institutions (non-MFI), and (g) supervisory board size. *M* comprises (h) East/West dummy, (i) local Gross Domestic Product (GDP) per capita, and (j) population.

The equality of the coefficients across the banking sectors is tested with the following null hypothesis (H_0):

$$H_0 : \beta_{cv} - \beta_{sv} = 0 \qquad (IV.2)$$

where β is the regression coefficient of variable *v*. *c* indicates the regression coefficient of the cooperative banking sector, and *s* indicates the coefficient of the savings banks sector. These coefficients are tested with a Wald parameter test.

IV.3.3 Financial Expertise

The financial expertise of supervisory board members is gauged based on their professional backgrounds. This follows previous studies (e.g., Davidson, Xie, and Xu, 2004; Dhaliwal, Naiker, and Navissi, 2006; Minton, Taillard, and Williamson, 2010). The financial expertise of supervisory board members is defined as outlined in Table IV.1:

Table IV.1: Professional backgrounds with assumed financial expertise.

Level 1: Employment	Self-employed persons with assumed financial expertise	Employed persons with assumed financial expertise	Retired persons with assumed financial expertise
Level 2: Occupation	Entrepreneur, Merchant, Owner	Non-bank employee with assumed financial focus (e.g. member of management board)	Retired self-employed person with assumed financial expertise
	Managing Partner	Bank employee	Retired employed person with assumed financial expertise
	Partner	Public officer with assumed financial focus (e.g. treasurer) Federal and State Minister, State Secretary	
		Local and regional politician	

The main idea behind the applied methodology is the obvious relation to financial issues. For instance, financial expertise is expected in the case of the managing directors of companies. Additionally, the definition of financial expertise mainly follows that of the German regulatory bodies (BaFin and Deutsche Bundesbank, 2010). For example, following the regulators' joint bulletin, financial expertise is assigned to potential mandatory members, such as mayors and district administrators.

As details in the annual reports differ between banks, several assumptions concerning tenure, employment classification, and politicians have been applied. For the identification of local and regional politicians, a more detailed methodology has been applied, taking into consideration full-time employment vs. voluntary service and the authorization to give instructions (for further details see Appendix IV.6.1).

Whereas the federal savings bank laws ensure a constant level of employee representation on the supervisory boards of savings banks, cooperative banks have different legal requirements that do not demand a comparable level of employee representation on the supervisory board. Thus, regression analysis is conducted twice for each sample. First, the financial expertise of the total supervisory board and its impact on risk and performance is tested. Second, employee representatives who are employed at the respective bank are excluded in order that the impact on performance and risk of the outside expertise of the "freely eligible" supervisory board members is analyzed. This enhances comparability in two ways: first, between savings banks located in different federal states and, second, between cooperative and savings banks.

IV.3.4 Measurement of Risk and Performance

Risk is measured in two ways. Z-score is applied as a stability measure and indicates the risk of insolvency. This indicator has become a widely used method to measure risk (e.g., Boyd and Runkle, 1993; Laeven and Levine, 2009). Insolvency is defined as the state in which a bank's capital is insufficient to absorb losses (Roy, 1952). The probability of insolvency is defined as prob(-ROA<CAR), where ROA is the return on assets and CAR is the capital assets ratio. Assuming that profits are normally distributed, the probability of insolvency becomes (ROA+CAR)/σ(ROA), where σ(ROA) is the standard deviation of ROA (Boyd and Runkle, 1993). A higher z-value indicates a more stable bank. ROA is calculated as operating result divided by total assets. The standard deviation of ROA is calculated over the years, from 1994 to the year under consideration. CAR is defined as Tier 1 equity divided by total assets. We use the ratio of non-performing loans to total assets to measure loan portfolio risk. Due to large engagements in the lending business, this risk measure is highly important to cooperative and savings banks.

RORWA is used as a primary performance measure and is defined as operating result divided by risk-weighted assets. RORWA performance is risk-adjusted, because a bank's risk-weighted assets are based on its specific risk profile. ROE is used for robustness checks and is defined as operating result divided by equity. We use operating result for both performance measures to avoid distortions due to undisclosed reserves. These reserves are already accounted for in the annual net profit (Beck, Hesse, Kick, and Westernhagen, 2009).

IV.3.5 Control Variables

The present study controls for bank-specific issues as well as macroeconomic and structural aspects. To account for differences in bank size and bank growth, the log of total assets and the year-to-year change in total assets are used. To control for different efficiency levels, we use the cost-income ratio (CIR), which is defined as general administrative expenses divided by operating results. To account for different levels of lending engagement, we use the annual change in total loans. In addition, the difference in activities between cooperative and savings banks is reflected by the ratios of claims on MFI to total assets and claims on non-MFI to total assets. Different board sizes may affect performance and risk due to free-riding incentives in different ways (Jensen, 1993). Accordingly, the size of the supervisory board is accounted for in the empirical analysis.

As both banking groups have clearly defined business areas, the region in which the bank is located is very important. Structural issues are captured by an index variable that separates urban and rural areas, and with a binary variable that separates federal states that used to be in the former German Democratic Republic from other federal states. Banks in the federal states of the former German Democratic Republic are assigned a value of one. The difference between urban and rural areas is based on population. In order to differentiate between regional, district, and county centers, an index is applied to separate sparsely populated areas from densely populated and metropolitan areas. Five clusters have been defined. Areas with up to 1,000,000 inhabitants are divided into four clusters of 250,000 inhabitants each. The fifth cluster is composed of areas with more than 1,000,000 inhabitants. Regional economic development is gauged by the GDP per capita of the business area. The population and the GDP per capita are adjusted for mergers during the panel horizon in order to capture the effect of macroeconomic changes. The following Table IV.2 gives an overview of the definitions and sources of all control variables.

Table IV.2: Definition of control variables and sources.

Bank level control variables	Description	Source
a. Bank size	Ln of total assets	BAKIS (Deutsche Bundesbank)
b. Bank size growth	Year-to-year change in total assets	BAKIS (Deutsche Bundesbank)
c. Bank efficiency	General administrative expenses to operating result (CIR)	BAKIS (Deutsche Bundesbank)
d. Bank loan volume growth	Year-to-year change in total loans	BAKIS (Deutsche Bundesbank)
e. Bank claims on MFI	Claims on MFI divided by total assets	BAKIS (Deutsche Bundesbank)
f. Bank claims on non-MFI	Claims on non-MFI divided by total assets	BAKIS (Deutsche Bundesbank)
g. Bank supervisory board size	Number of supervisory board members	Annual reports
Macroeconomic and structural control variables		
h. East/West	Binary variable separating Eastern and Western federal state	Annual reports
i. GDP per capita	GDP of business area divided by population within business area	Regionaldatenbank Deutschland
j. Population	Index based on population within business area	Regionaldatenbank Deutschland

IV.4   Results

IV.4.1   Summary Statistics

Employed people dominate savings banks' supervisory boards, which is mainly driven by the large fraction of insiders who account on average for 25% of the board. On the contrary, only 5% of the members of cooperative banks' supervisory boards are employed at the respective bank. Cooperative banks' supervisory boards are rather characterized by a large fraction of self-employed people who account for almost 40% of the supervisory boards and exceed the number of self-employed people at savings banks by far. Similar to insiders, politicians only play a role in savings banks. They represent a notable fraction of the supervisory boards which meets the expectation because of the public ownership of savings banks.

In summary, despite the similar business model, the supervisory board composition of the banks is quite different. Hence, the assignment of financial expertise in the two groups is driven by different employment groups, which adds robustness to the analysis of the impact of financial experts on risk and stability.

Table IV.3:   Supervisory board composition, Top 200.

Variables		Mean	Std. Dev.	Coeff. of Variation	Min	Max
Insider (%)	Cooperative banks	5.20	11.88	228.34	0.00	52.94
	Savings banks	24.71	12.33	49.90	0.00	41.67
Outsider (%)	Cooperative banks	94.80	11.88	12.53	47.06	100.00
	Savings banks	75.29	12.33	16.38	58.33	100.00
Employment						
Employed individuals (%)	Cooperative banks	50.22	22.94	45.68	0.00	100.00
	Savings banks	73.32	12.24	16.70	36.36	100.00
Self-employed individuals (%)	Cooperative banks	39.55	23.49	59.40	0.00	91.67
	Savings banks	12.62	9.57	75.80	0.00	47.37
Retired individuals (%)	Cooperative banks	9.20	11.86	128.99	0.00	77.78
	Savings banks	12.71	9.95	78.25	0.00	55.56
Other (%)	Cooperative banks	1.03	2.76	268.43	0.00	14.29
	Savings banks	1.35	2.77	204.11	0.00	12.50
Politicians (officiating)						
Federal politicians (%)	Cooperative banks	0.09	0.90	1,020.84	0.00	11.11
	Savings banks	0.76	2.29	299.94	0.00	15.38
Federal state politicians (%)	Cooperative banks	0.24	1.53	629.23	0.00	20.00
	Savings banks	2.57	4.22	164.08	0.00	23.08
Regional politicians (%)	Cooperative banks	0.00	0.00	0.00	0.00	0.00
	Savings banks	5.88	4.69	79.74	0.00	28.57
Local politicians (%)	Cooperative banks	1.83	4.24	231.21	0.00	25.00
	Savings banks	15.15	12.57	82.97	0.00	54.55
Officiating and retired politicians (%)	Cooperative banks	2.80	5.53	197.83	0.00	35.29
	Savings banks	28.13	15.19	54.00	0.00	75.00

Comparing risk and stability measures of both banking groups does not provide consistent results (see Table IV.4). Cooperative banks are more stable than savings banks in terms of z-score. But at the same time, they have a higher loan portfolio risk than savings banks in terms of the NPL ratio. Due to their larger bank size, savings banks perhaps better realize diversification benefits in their loan portfolio than cooperative banks. Contrary to risk and stability, performance measures reveal a clear picture. Savings banks' performance exceeds that of cooperative banks in both performance measures.

Savings banks' financial expertise significantly outreaches that of cooperative banks, proving that they benefit from the legally required employee representation. Furthermore, savings banks have an expertise floor at 20%. Controlling for insiders aligns the expertise values but leaves the savings banks' supervisory board more financially literate. Outside financial expertise for both groups is around 50% and ranges from 0% to 100%. This suggests that neither banking sector has fundamentally different preferences with regard to the "freely eligible" members.

As expected, savings banks are significantly larger than their cooperative competitors. Accordingly, the larger average bank size and the legally required employee representation lead to larger supervisory boards in savings banks. Contrary to bank size, as regards both growth rates, cooperative banks are ahead of savings banks. Cooperative banks are more engaged in business development and grow a lot faster than savings banks, in both total assets and loan volume. The stronger focus on growth might be caused by the more entrepreneur-staffed supervisory boards in cooperative banks. Self-employed business people might have a stronger focus on growth and business expansion, which explains the higher growth rates. Despite the stronger business expansion, profitability is lower and risk is higher for cooperative banks. The reason might be the monopolistic structures of local markets. Since those markets are limited in size and monopolistically structured, growth comes at the expense of lower profitability and more risk (Claessens and Laeven, 2003; Hempell, 2002). In general, the asset shift toward more profitable lending business as indicated by the higher loan volume growth compared to the total assets growth is consistent in both sectors.

All differences in the risk, stability, performance, and other bank-level variables between the two groups are significant, except of claims on non-MFI (see Appendices IV.6.3 and IV.6.5). Additionally, the merger-controlled panel confirms these results (see Appendix IV.6.4).

Table IV.4: Summary statistics, Top 200.

Dependent variables	Group	Mean	Std. Dev.	Coeff. of Variation	Min	Max
z-score	Cooperative banks	22.71	14.81	65.24	3.61	103.23
	Savings banks	19.40	10.56	54.41	2.87	77.02
NPL ratio (%)	Cooperative banks	2.66	1.97	74.15	0.00	13.47
	Savings banks	2.11	1.51	71.38	0.04	11.56
ROE (%)	Cooperative banks	12.19	7.56	62.04	-17.62	55.21
	Savings banks	13.60	8.45	62.11	-61.76	67.79
RORWA (%)	Cooperative banks	1.21	0.80	65.70	-1.82	6.27
	Savings banks	1.33	0.99	74.08	-2.92	8.65

Bank level variables						
Financial expertise (%)	Cooperative banks	47.76	22.87	47.88	0.00	100.00
	Savings banks	64.98	17.25	26.55	20.00	100.00
Outside financial expertise (%)	Cooperative banks	45.25	23.23	51.34	0.00	100.00
	Savings banks	53.15	22.86	43.01	0.00	100.00
Board size	Cooperative banks	12.42	4.44	35.76	5.00	37.00
	Savings banks	16.81	5.29	31.46	7.00	48.00
Bank size (ln '000s of EUR)	Cooperative banks	20.90	0.69	3.28	19.60	24.45
	Savings banks	21.78	0.60	2.77	20.56	24.16
Bank size growth (%)	Cooperative banks	2.61	4.61	176.76	-14.80	31.47
	Savings banks	0.25	3.34	1,323.23	-16.29	18.26
Bank efficiency (%)	Cooperative banks	66.48	9.55	14.37	15.98	112.92
	Savings banks	65.29	7.32	11.20	36.00	95.51
Loan growth (%)	Cooperative banks	4.98	7.44	149.52	-13.19	51.54
	Savings banks	2.86	9.80	342.62	-14.70	104.87
Claims on MFI (%)	Cooperative banks	11.89	6.59	55.47	0.06	45.65
	Savings banks	9.85	6.55	66.58	0.00	44.37
Claims on non-MFI (%)	Cooperative banks	58.67	11.39	19.41	11.17	83.57
	Savings banks	58.91	12.00	20.37	24.21	85.36

Macroeconomic and structural variables						
East/West	Cooperative banks	0.02	0.14	700.29	0.00	1.00
	Savings banks	0.13	0.34	258.80	0.00	1.00
GDP per capita ('000s of EUR)	Cooperative banks	28.04	7.32	26.12	9.39	62.04
	Savings banks	27.49	7.62	27.73	14.12	72.20
Population	Cooperative banks	2.67	1.39	52.07	1.00	5.00
	Savings banks	1.73	0.90	51.96	1.00	5.00

In order to assess how different financial expertise levels within each group are associated with risk, stability, performance, and further bank level characteristics, all banks are clustered by financial expertise (see Table IV.5). Each cluster in both groups contains 50 banks. Banks with the highest expertise levels are included in Cluster 1, and those with the lowest levels in Cluster 4.

Financial expertise tends to reduce stability. For cooperative banks, this holds consistently across all clusters. With savings banks, stability consistently diminishes from Clusters 4 to 2, but then slightly rises again in Cluster 1. Similar to z-score, the NPL ratio trend in cooperative banks is consistent across all clusters. The larger the number of financial experts on cooperative banks' supervisory boards, the higher the NPL ratio. Savings banks' NPL ratio does not show a similar pro-risk attitude of financial experts. From Cluster 4 to Cluster 3, the ratio rises with higher expertise level, but decreases from Cluster 3 to Cluster

1. Apparently, savings banks' higher performance in the high-expertise clusters is associated with higher loan portfolio risk since Clusters 2 and 3 are above Cluster 4. But since Cluster 1 has the same level as Cluster 4, there is obviously a threshold above which financial expertise has a risk-decreasing effect.

Performance is totally contrarian in both banking groups. While the performance of cooperative banks tends to deteriorate with increasing financial expertise, savings banks' performance benefits from rising board expertise.

Further worth mentioning are bank size, loan volume growth, and efficiency. One could hypothesize that the larger the bank, the more complex its business, which requires higher expertise levels. However, only with cooperative banks does financial expertise increase with bank size. Against the odds, only in savings banks do efficiency levels benefit from higher levels of financial expertise. Savings banks with high expertise levels reveal significantly lower CIRs than low-expertise savings banks. The opposite holds for cooperative banks. With regard to loan volume growth, the analysis shows that in both groups, low-expertise banks have higher growth rates. One could assume that banks with low expertise levels are less engaged in expanding their lending activities, which might be the reason for their higher stability compared to high-expertise banks. However, the higher growth rates of low-expertise banks contradict this view. Overall, these findings are confirmed by the merger-controlled panel (see Appendix IV.6.6).

Table IV.5: Summary statistics, clustered by financial expertise, Top 200.

Dependent variables	Group	Cluster 1	Cluster 2	Cluster 3	Cluster 4	Delta Cluster 4-1
z-score	Cooperative banks	19.05	22.18	24.52	25.06	-6.01
	Savings banks	18.65	17.38	20.67	20.89	-2.25
NPL ratio (%)	Cooperative banks	3.14	2.70	2.59	2.22	0.92
	Savings banks	2.01	2.11	2.30	2.03	-0.01
ROE (%)	Cooperative banks	10.86	12.37	13.54	11.99	-1.13
	Savings banks	15.20	14.31	13.07	11.82	3.37
RORWA (%)	Cooperative banks	1.05	1.24	1.34	1.22	-0.17
	Savings banks	1.42	1.50	1.26	1.13	0.29

Bank level variables						
Financial expertise (%)	Cooperative banks	76.53	54.89	39.85	19.78	56.75
	Savings banks	86.38	71.28	58.69	43.56	42.81
Outside financial expertise (%)	Cooperative banks	72.95	53.04	36.87	18.13	54.82
	Savings banks	81.12	61.24	43.70	26.56	54.56
Board size	Cooperative banks	12.65	11.66	12.67	12.69	-0.04
	Savings banks	17.37	16.39	16.67	16.80	0.57
Bank size (ln '000s of EUR)	Cooperative banks	21.09	20.89	20.88	20.74	0.35
	Savings banks	21.74	21.87	21.68	21.84	-0.10
Bank size growth (%)	Cooperative banks	1.82	2.96	2.62	3.01	-1.19
	Savings banks	0.67	0.17	0.25	-0.07	0.73
Bank efficiency (%)	Cooperative banks	67.92	66.54	65.61	65.88	2.04
	Savings banks	64.05	64.69	65.64	66.78	-2.74
Loan growth (%)	Cooperative banks	4.08	5.26	5.03	5.54	-1.46
	Savings banks	2.46	2.28	2.69	4.02	-1.56
Claims on MFI (%)	Cooperative banks	12.06	11.97	13.06	10.47	1.59
	Savings banks	11.58	9.72	10.06	8.03	3.55
Claims on non-MFI (%)	Cooperative banks	59.73	57.06	58.46	59.44	0.29
	Savings banks	53.55	58.24	59.75	64.11	-10.56

Table IV.6 provides the significance of pairwise tests between the clusters in both groups (see Appendix IV.6.7 for the merger-controlled panel).

Table IV.6: Pairwise test of significance between expertise clusters, Top 200.

Dependent variables		Cluster 1 vs. 2	Cluster 1 vs. 3	Cluster 1 vs. 4	Cluster 2 vs. 3	Cluster 2 vs. 4	Cluster 3 vs. 4
		t (p-value)	t (p-value)	t (p-value)	t (p-value)	t (p-value)	t (p-value)
z-score	Cooperative banks	-2.9416 ***	-5.1116 ***	-5.3941 ***	-2.1057 **	-2.2044 **	-0.3978
		0.0035	0.0000	0.0000	0.0361	0.0283	0.6910
	Savings banks	1.7932 *	-2.0026 **	-2.6364 ***	-3.5476 ***	-4.6260 ***	-0.2238
		0.0740	0.0461	0.0088	0.0005	0.0000	0.8230
NPL ratio	Cooperative banks	2.9874 ***	4.0449 ***	6.0319 ***	0.5127	2.9269 ***	2.2893 **
		0.0031	0.0001	0.0000	0.6085	0.0037	0.0228
	Savings banks	-0.8212	-2.3812 **	0.0338	-1.8113 *	0.9519	2.8269 ***
		0.4122	0.0179	0.9730	0.0711	0.3419	0.0050
ROE	Cooperative banks	-2.4392 **	-4.8278 ***	-2.0750 **	-2.0154 **	0.7044	3.0085 ***
		0.0153	0.0000	0.0388	0.0448	0.4817	0.0028
	Savings banks	1.5491	2.9093 ***	6.0121 ***	1.7952 *	4.3481 ***	1.8871 *
		0.1224	0.0040	0.0000	0.0736	0.0000	0.0601
RORWA	Cooperative banks	-2.9746 ***	-5.1122 ***	-2.8960 ***	-1.7083 *	0.2822	2.2395 **
		0.0032	0.0000	0.0041	0.0886	0.7780	0.0259
	Savings banks	-1.1722	2.0085 **	4.5434 ***	2.9031 ***	4.8021 ***	1.7949 *
		0.2420	0.0455	0.0000	0.0040	0.0000	0.0737

Bank level variables

Financial expertise	Cooperative banks	36.4796 ***	62.4921 ***	107.0168 ***	31.6913 ***	58.9953 ***	35.3432 ***
		0.0000	*0.0000*	*0.0000*	*0.0000*	*0.0000*	*0.0000*
	Savings banks	38.6471 ***	72.3544 ***	97.5500 ***	31.8934 ***	61.9574 ***	32.0524 ***
		0.0000	*0.0000*	*0.0000*	*0.0000*	*0.0000*	*0.0000*
Outside financial expertise	Cooperative banks	25.2058 ***	37.7623 ***	79.3250 ***	20.1509 ***	47.0515 ***	21.5942 ***
		0.0000	*0.0000*	*0.0000*	*0.0000*	*0.0000*	*0.0000*
	Savings banks	29.4410 ***	54.4313 ***	68.7638 ***	22.6287 ***	42.3762 ***	20.1752 ***
		0.0000	*0.0000*	*0.0000*	*0.0000*	*0.0000*	*0.0000*
Bank size	Cooperative banks	4.0484 ***	3.5593 ***	6.9548 ***	0.2905	3.3427 ***	2.2812 **
		0.0001	*0.0004*	*0.0000*	*0.7716*	*0.0009*	*0.0232*
	Savings banks	-3.0146 ***	1.3804	-1.9940 **	4.2496 ***	0.7161	-2.9528 ***
		0.0028	*0.1685*	*0.0471*	*0.0000*	*0.4745*	*0.0034*
Bank efficiency	Cooperative banks	1.8552 *	3.4015 ***	3.2641 ***	1.2181	0.8768	-0.4186
		0.0645	*0.0008*	*0.0000*	*0.2241*	*0.3813*	*0.6758*
	Savings banks	-1.0181	-2.6110 ***	-4.4523 ***	-1.8035 *	-3.6803 ***	-2.1189 **
		0.3094	*0.0095*	*0.0000*	*0.0723*	*0.0003*	*0.0349*
Bank size growth	Cooperative banks	-3.3467 ***	-1.9672 *	-3.2731 ***	1.0335	-0.3325	-0.8804
		0.0009	*0.0502*	*0.0012*	*0.3023*	*0.7397*	*0.3795*
	Savings banks	1.7965 *	1.4950	2.6986 ***	-0.0661	0.9662	1.1114
		0.0735	*0.1361*	*0.0074*	*0.9473*	*0.3348*	*0.2674*
Board size	Cooperative banks	2.7820 ***	-0.0637	-0.0953	-3.5862 ***	-2.8178 ***	-0.0343
		0.0057	*0.9492*	*0.9242*	*0.0004*	*0.0052*	*0.9726*
	Savings banks	2.0786 **	1.5048	1.3134	-0.8163	-1.2133	-0.3118
		0.0385	*0.1334*	*0.1900*	*0.4150*	*0.2260*	*0.7554*
Loan growth	Cooperative banks	-2.6742 ***	-2.0712 **	-3.1177 ***	0.4078	-0.4854	-0.7861
		0.0080	*0.0393*	*0.0020*	*0.6837*	*0.6278*	*0.4325*
	Savings banks	0.3587	-0.6442	-2.2038 **	-1.0905	-2.1322 **	-1.4634
		0.7201	*0.5200*	*0.0284*	*0.2764*	*0.0338*	*0.1445*
Claims on MFI	Cooperative banks	0.1639	-1.9450 *	2.9122 ***	-1.9462 *	2.8777 ***	4.6932 ***
		0.8699	*0.0527*	*0.0039*	*0.0526*	*0.0043*	*0.0000*
	Savings banks	3.4456 ***	2.7623 ***	7.0218 ***	-0.6907	3.5515 ***	4.4932 ***
		0.0007	*0.0061*	*0.0000*	*0.4903*	*0.0000*	*0.0000*
Claims on non-MFI	Cooperative banks	2.8703 ***	1.7566 *	0.3068	-1.4140	-2.4490 **	-1.1065
		0.0044	*0.0800*	*0.7592*	*0.1584*	*0.0149*	*0.2694*
	Savings banks	-5.0788 ***	-6.2691 ***	-11.3830 ***	-1.6453	-7.3531 ***	-4.7265 ***
		0.0000	*0.0000*	*0.0000*	*0.1010*	*0.0000*	*0.0000*

Confidence level: 95%
* indicates significance at the 10% level, ** at the 5% level, and *** at the 1% level, respectively.

IV.4.2 Regression Results

Regression results show that financial experts on supervisory boards cannot contribute to more stability and less loan portfolio risk but rather lead to greater risk-taking. The results lend support to evidence from behavioural finance theory. Fellner, Güth, and Maciejovsky (2004) show that such an "illusion of expertise" can result in an overestimation of one's own abilities in trading off risks and expected returns. Hence, the calls for more expertise in supervisory boards could potentially result in a vicious circle. As Odean (1998) points out, overconfidence increases with expertise, which then might aggravate the problem. Furthermore, our finding is consistent across ownership structures and supports the results of Minton, Taillard, and Williamson (2010), who also find that higher levels of expertise are associated with higher levels of bank risk. In terms of bank performance, financial expertise only pays off for savings banks. This is remarkable because both banking groups have similar business models and operate in the same regulatory environment. Savings banks are compensated for greater risk, as their performance increases in tandem, in contrast to cooperative banks, where financial expertise reduces profitability.

All regressions with z-score and NPL ratio as dependent variables are significant at the 1% level, as indicated by the Wald chi-square test (see Table IV.7). The impact of financial expertise on stability and risk is similar in cooperative and savings banks as indicated by the financial expertise and outside financial expertise coefficients. Although at first sight the negative impact appears to be stronger at cooperative banks, the effect is only significantly different from savings banks for outside financial expertise (see Table IV.8). Thus, insiders apparently impact both banking groups differently. Since the negative effect of expertise on z-score at savings banks is stronger inclusive insiders, the statutory employee representatives do obviously not exert a favourable influence on the other financial experts. Contrary, at cooperative banks where on average much less employee representatives are on the supervisory board, insiders influence the other financial experts positively. The reason why the negative impact of financial expertise on loan portfolio risk is significant at cooperative banks in particular might be due to the different board compositions. Cooperative banks' supervisory boards include a large fraction of entrepreneurs. Although they are supposed to have a sound understanding of business risk, they might also tend to overrate their abilities more than people of different professions.

Only at first sight most bank characteristics affect both groups' z-score differently. Although except of claims on non-MFI and board size all other variables have different directions, the comparison of the coefficients does not provide evidence for highly significant different effects on both banking groups' stability through most bank characteristics. However, bank size growth and loan volume growth are significantly different between both groups. Given the much higher growth rate of cooperative banks and the negative impact of loan volume growth on stability, this indicates from a stability viewpoint that they primarily grow in more disadvantageous business than savings banks do.

In contrast to z-score, the impacts of bank characteristics on the NPL ratio have the same direction but are mainly significantly different between both groups (see Table IV.8). Bank size and bank size growth are of particular interest. The fact that both variables have a more pronounced negative impact on the NPL ratio at cooperative banks implies that they can better benefit from an increase in banks size than savings banks. Whereas savings bank can hardly further improve their loan portfolio through economies of scale, cooperative banks can catch up with savings banks which are larger in size and already better realize diversification benefits within their loan portfolio. The adverse effect of board size on both measures in both banking groups follows the theory that larger boards tend to ease free riding (Jensen, 1993). In larger boards, individuals might feel less personally responsible. As a result, this might lead to less strict decisions with regard to risk and stability.

Table IV.7: Random-effect regressions with dependent variables z-score and NPL ratio, Top 200.

Variable		z-score (RE) Financial expertise		z-score (RE) Out. fin. expertise		NPL ratio (RE) Financial expertise		NPL ratio (RE) Out. fin. expertise	
		Coeff.	SE (robust)	Coeff.	SE (robust)	Coeff.	SE (robust)	Coeff.	SE (robust)
Financial expertise	Financial expertise*C	-0.0665	0.0486			0.0124	0.0040***		
	Outside financial expertise*C			-0.0933	0.0433**			0.0129	0.0039***
	Financial expertise*S	-0.0126	0.0297			0.0083	0.0041**		
	Outside financial expertise*S			-0.0069	0.0239			0.0034	0.0033
Bank level	Savings	-109.6875	77.4025	-116.0794	79.0390	-9.5294	4.6658**	-7.4002	4.7363
	Bank size*C	-2.3704	2.8477	-2.5019	2.8979	-0.6060	0.1504***	-0.5376	0.1478***
	Bank efficiency*C	-0.0625	0.0253**	-0.0609	0.0256**	-0.0014	0.0059	-0.0014	0.0059
	Bank size growth*C	0.0479	0.0596	0.0459	0.0589	-0.1586	0.0145***	-0.1583	0.0145***
	Loan growth*C	-0.0927	0.0364**	-0.0912	0.0360**	0.0950	0.0106***	0.0946	0.0106***
	Claims on MFI*C	-0.0069	0.0751	-0.0110	0.0760	0.0331	0.0114***	0.0329	0.0113***
	Claims on Non-MFI*C	0.1864	0.1243	0.1807	0.1238	0.0320	0.0080***	0.0329	0.0081***
	Board size*C	-0.2583	0.2650	-0.2780	0.2670	0.0488	0.0190***	0.0509	0.0191***
	Bank size*S	2.4890	2.0066	2.5571	2.0101	-0.0841	0.1835	-0.0926	0.1855
	Bank efficiency*S	0.0210	0.0336	0.0211	0.0338	-0.0228	0.0083***	-0.0233	0.0084***
	Bank size growth*S	-0.1114	0.0230***	-0.1114	0.0230***	-0.0984	0.0125***	-0.0985	0.0125***
	Loan growth*S	0.0370	0.0072***	0.0366	0.0069***	0.0495	0.0062***	0.0497	0.0063***
	Claims on MFI*S	0.0278	0.0401	0.0273	0.0402	-0.0148	0.0086*	-0.0147	0.0086*
	Claims on Non-MFI*S	0.0318	0.0519	0.0331	0.0523	0.0299	0.0105***	0.0284	0.0106***
	Board size*S	-0.0093	0.0767	-0.0106	0.0774	0.0343	0.0107***	0.0305	0.0105***
Macroeconomic and structural environment	East/West	-6.4381	1.9577***	-6.3819	1.9836***	0.5403	0.3142*	0.5537	0.3150*
	GDP per capita	-0.0426	0.0762	-0.0386	0.0760	-0.0285	0.0071***	-0.0283	0.0071***
	Population	-0.7003	1.0528	-0.8073	1.0453	-0.2003	0.0677***	-0.1944	0.0677***
	constant	75.3387	66.4776	79.8147	67.7597	13.1721	3.2084***	11.6559	3.2035***
	Wald chi^2	165.02	***	164.49	***	492.88	***	493.54	***
	R-sq	0.0850		0.0880		0.2788		0.2798	
	No of observations	2,278		2,278		2,259		2,259	

* indicates significance at the 10% level, ** at the 5% level, and *** at the 1% level, respectively.
Standard errors control for clustering at the bank level.

The following Table IV.8 provides the comparison of the coefficients of the z-score and NPL ratio regressions (for the merger-controlled panel, see Appendix IV.6.11).

Table IV.8: *Coefficient comparison, random-effect regressions with dependent variables z-score and NPL ratio, Top 200.*

Variable		z-score (RE) Financial expertise		z-score (RE) Out. fin. expertise		NPL ratio (RE) Financial expertise		NPL ratio (RE) Out. fin. expertise	
		chi²	P>chi²	chi²	P>chi²	chi²	P>chi²	chi²	P>chi²
Financial expertise	Financial expertise: C vs. S	0.8800	0.3469			0.5100	0.4769		
	Outside financial expertise: C vs. S			3.0200	0.0802 *			3.5300	0.0603 *
Bank level	Bank size: C vs. S	2.1600	0.1418	2.2300	0.1353	6.8600	0.0088 ***	4.9200	0.0266 **
	Bank efficiency: C vs. S	3.9000	0.0482 **	3.7000	0.0543 *	4.4800	0.0343 **	4.6400	0.0312 **
	Bank size growth: C vs. S	6.2600	0.0124 **	6.2400	0.0125 **	9.8800	0.0017 ***	9.7700	0.0018 ***
	Board size: C vs. S	0.8500	0.3574	0.9600	0.3276	0.4500	0.5002	0.4500	0.5015
	Loan growth: C vs. S	12.1100	0.0050 ***	12.0500	0.0005 ***	13.6700	0.0002 ***	13.3100	0.0003 ***
	Claims on MFI: C vs. S	0.1600	0.6870	0.2000	0.6584	11.2200	0.0008 ***	11.0500	0.0009 ***
	Claims on Non-MFI: C vs. S	1.5000	0.2202	1.3900	0.2386	0.0300	0.8742	0.1200	0.7310

* indicates significance at the 10% level, ** at the 5% level, and *** at the 1% level, respectively.

All regression models with RORWA and ROE as dependent variables are significant at the 1% level as well (see Table IV.9). The expertise coefficients show that the impact on cooperative banks is opposite to that on savings banks. While savings banks' performance is improved, cooperative banks are affected negatively. This finding on cooperative banks is contradictory to the corporate finance theory predicting compensation for risk according to the risk-return trade-off. We hypothesize that experts at cooperative banks are overly enthusiastic on growth and business development and therefore disregard the inherent risks of growing by neglecting a careful business risk selection. Similar to loan portfolio risk and stability, insiders hardly make a difference. Overall, banks without merger activities confirm these results (see Appendix IV.6.12).

In contrast to the expertise coefficients most other bank level variables have the same direction. However, the comparisons of the coefficients suggest that both banking groups are affected significantly different (see Table IV.10). The negative impact of bank size in both groups might be due to the limited number of highly profitable projects within each area. Thus, we conclude that larger banks have to switch to more projects with lower profitability and suffer from sinking returns. For this reason it seems logical that bank size growth reduces profitability, as well. Given the coefficients, cooperative banks apparently suffer more from this "switching-effect" than savings banks. The expansion of the loan portfolio has a highly significant positive impact in both banking groups what implies that for all banks in the sample, it is beneficial to expand their traditional core business as this still boosts their performance. Whereas cooperative banks' higher loan volume growth rate impacts stability negatively, it pays off for their performance at least.

Board size reveals an ambiguous relationship with performance. Whereas it is positively related to performance at cooperative banks, it reduces performance at savings banks. Since both banking groups have significantly different board sizes, this suggests that the optimal board size for performance lies in between. However, the question remains unanswered whether cooperative banks' supervisory boards should be staffed with more financial or with non-financial experts and who should be removed from savings banks' supervisory boards.

Table IV.9: Random-effect regressions with dependent variables RORWA and ROE, Top 200.

Variable		RORWA (RE) Financial expertise		RORWA (RE) Out. fin. expertise		ROE (RE) Financial expertise		ROE (RE) Out. fin. expertise	
		Coeff.	SE (robust)	Coeff.	SE (robust)	Coeff.	SE (robust)	Coeff.	SE (robust)
Financial expertise	Financial expertise*C	-0.0011	0.0013			-0.0038	0.0135		
	Outside financial expertise*C			-0.0013	0.0012			-0.0067	0.0133
	Financial expertise*S	0.0014	0.0017			0.0309	0.0169*		
	Outside financial expertise*S			0.0017	0.0013			0.0290	0.0126**
Bank level	Savings	-2.5366	1.5852	-2.7989	1.5820*	-9.3458	17.8275	-10.6689	17.5873
	Bank size*C	-0.2604	0.0555***	-0.2660	0.0534***	-1.8690	0.6220***	-1.8773	0.5917***
	Bank efficiency*C	-0.0268	0.0033***	-0.0268	0.0033***	-0.2728	0.0335***	-0.2722	0.0336***
	Bank size growth*C	-0.0411	0.0072***	-0.0412	0.0072***	-0.2486	0.0688***	-0.2495	0.0688***
	Loan growth*C	0.0433	0.0041***	0.0434	0.0041***	0.2667	0.0331***	0.2670	0.0330***
	Claims on MFI*C	-0.0082	0.0048*	-0.0081	0.0048*	-0.1275	0.0448***	-0.1268	0.0449***
	Claims on Non-MFI*C	-0.0129	0.0027***	-0.0129	0.0027***	-0.0625	0.0292**	-0.0620	0.0291**
	Board size*C	0.0073	0.0069	0.0069	0.0069	0.0797	0.0655	0.0770	0.0660
	Bank size*S	-0.0147	0.0680	-0.0104	0.0683	-0.5022	0.6934	-0.4515	0.6962
	Bank efficiency*S	-0.0473	0.0055***	-0.0471	0.0055***	-0.4785	0.0569***	-0.4775	0.0570***
	Bank size growth*S	-0.0126	0.0105	-0.0128	0.0105	-0.0400	0.0828	-0.0436	0.0826
	Loan growth*S	0.0186	0.0029***	0.0188	0.0029***	0.0898	0.0209***	0.0924	0.0213***
	Claims on MFI*S	-0.0161	0.0049***	-0.0163	0.0049***	-0.1347	0.0437***	-0.1367	0.0439***
	Claims on Non-MFI*S	-0.0263	0.0040***	-0.0259	0.0040***	-0.1231	0.0334***	-0.1198	0.0332***
	Board size*S	-0.0191	0.0057***	-0.0186	0.0056***	-0.1099	0.0546**	-0.1100	0.0534*
Macroeconomic and structural environment	East/West	0.1562	0.1337	0.1666	0.1336	1.1746	1.1299	1.3376	1.1400
	GDP per capita	-0.0029	0.0027	-0.0031	0.0027	-0.0674	0.0321**	-0.0700	0.0322**
	Population	0.0032	0.0287	0.0031	0.0286	0.0120	0.2551	0.0142	0.2541
	constant	9.2151	1.0695***	9.3479	1.0314***	74.9554	12.6401***	75.2761	12.0385***
	Wald chi^2	439.16	***	441.53	***	464.54	***	464.13	***
	R-sq	0.3129		0.3135		0.2383		0.2393	
	No of observations	2,278		2,278		2,278		2,278	

* indicates significance at the 10% level, ** at the 5% level, and *** at the 1% level, respectively.
Standard errors control for clustering at the bank level.

The following Table IV.10 provides the comparison of the coefficients of the RORWA and ROE regressions (for the merger-controlled panel, see Appendix IV.6.13).

Table IV.10: Coefficient comparison, random-effect regressions with dependent variables RORWA and ROE, Top 200.

Variable		RORWA (RE) Financial expertise		RORWA (RE) Out. fin. expertise		ROE (RE) Financial expertise		ROE (RE) Out. fin. expertise	
		chi^2	$P>chi^2$	chi^2	$P>chi^2$	chi^2	$P>chi^2$	chi^2	$P>chi^2$
Financial expertise	Financial expertise: C vs. S	1.3900	0.2385			2.5100	0.1132		
	Outside financial expertise: C vs. S			2.7500	0.0975 *			3.7200	0.0539 *
Bank level	Bank size: C vs. S	11.8000	0.0006 ***	13.0200	0.0003 ***	3.2500	0.0716 *	3.6700	0.0556 *
	Bank efficiency: C vs. S	10.3800	0.0013 ***	10.1600	0.0014 ***	9.7500	0.0018 ***	9.6800	0.0019 ***
	Bank size growth: C vs. S	5.0700	0.0244 **	5.0100	0.0252 **	3.7800	0.0519 *	3.7000	0.0545 *
	Board size: C vs. S	8.7200	0.0031 ***	8.2800	0.0040 ***	4.9400	0.0263 **	4.3300	0.0375 **
	Loan growth: C vs. S	24.5300	0.0000 ***	24.2300	0.0000 ***	20.2900	0.0000 ***	19.6400	0.0000 ***
	Claims on MFI: C vs. S	1.3200	0.2501	1.4000	0.2374	0.0100	0.9092	0.0200	0.8753
	Claims on Non-MFI: C vs. S	8.7600	0.0031 ***	8.1100	0.0044 ***	2.2800	0.1314	2.1000	0.1472

* indicates significance at the 10% level, ** at the 5% level, and *** at the 1% level, respectively.

IV.4.3   Robustness Checks

To validate the robustness of the results, both panels are adjusted in two ways. All variables are truncated, except for the binary variable (East/West) and the index variable on population. First, all observations lower than the 1st percentile of the distribution are set to the value of the 1st percentile. Observations higher than the 99th percentile are set to the value of the 99th percentile. Second, all observations lower than the 5th percentile of the distribution are set to the value of the 5th percentile, and observations higher than the 95th percentile are set to the value of the 95th percentile. The adjustments are made for both banking groups independently.

In general, both outlier-corrected datasets provide the same results as in the original analyses, but lead to increased explanatory power, as indicated by the higher R-squared. This proves the robustness of the findings outlined above. Furthermore, the performance regressions with the outlier-corrected samples provide financial expertise coefficients with higher significance for savings banks. Similarly, the significance of the financial expertise coefficients of cooperative banks increases in the risk regressions.

With regard to risk, the outlier-corrected regressions confirm the base regressions (see Appendices IV.6.14, IV.6.15, IV.6.18, IV.6.19, IV.6.22, IV.6.23, IV.6.26, and IV.6.27). On the one hand, the financial expertise coefficients of cooperative banks in the regression with the NPL ratio retain the 1% level of significance. On the other hand, savings banks' coefficients remain insignificant.

Regarding ROE performance, the 5% outlier-corrected dataset results in significance at the 1% level for the (outside) financial expertise of savings banks. The expertise coefficients of savings banks in the RORWA regression become significant at the 10% (total supervisory board expertise) and 5% (outside financial expertise) levels. The cooperative banks' coefficients remain insignificant (see Appendices IV.6.16, IV.6.17, IV.6.20, IV.6.21, IV.6.24, IV.6.25, IV.6.28, and IV.6.29).

Comparing the coefficients with outlier-corrected data backs the initial hypotheses. Whereas risk and stability are affected similarly across the two banking groups, financial expertise influences performance differently in both groups.

IV.5   Conclusion

The present study explores the impact of supervisory board financial expertise on bank risk, stability, and (risk-adjusted) performance. It further tests the hypothesis of whether the effects are equal across different ownership types and banking groups with differently staffed supervisory boards.

We find that financial experts cannot contribute to more stability and less risk. Despite calls for more expertise in internal bank governance, the study does not provide evidence that this is beneficial to stability and risk. This result is consistent across bank groups with different ownership types, underlining the explanatory power of this finding. The reason for the disadvantageous impact of financial expertise might be overconfidence (e.g., Fischhoff, Slovic, and Lichtenstein, 1977; Moore and Healy, 2007). When it comes to assessing bank risks, financial experts may overestimate their individual competences and, consequently, overrate their risk assessment based on their private information (Chuang and Lee, 2006; Fellner, Güth, and Maciejovsky, 2004). Odean (1998) shows that overconfidence rises with increasing expertise. Thus, more financial experts on the boards do not lead to an improvement but could even weaken banks' stability as they eventually advocate risky business.

Concerning (risk-adjusted) performance, financial expertise affects both banking groups differently as shown by the robustness checks in particular. The risk-return trade-off apparently works for savings banks, but it does not work for cooperative banks. Whereas financial experts on the supervisory boards of savings banks lead to a compensation for the increase in risk, cooperative banks cannot benefit from financial experts either way. For the sake of growing their bank size and loan volume, cooperative banks' supervisory board members obviously do not put enough emphasis on profitable business development. Contrary, supervisory board members in savings banks make the banks' management to follow a more selective strategy, at least as regards profitability.

The analysis of the composition of the supervisory boards shows that employed people dominate savings banks' supervisory boards, and at the same time self-employed people play a minor role. This is different at cooperative banks, where both employed and self-employed people are comparably important. The large fraction of self-employed people at cooperative banks might be one reason for the twofold adverse effect of financial expertise. Cooper, Woo, and Dunkelberg (1988) provide a background for this finding. They point out that entrepreneurs generally display a high degree of optimism and overrate their abilities to determine their destiny on their own. This might result in a considerable misestimation of bank risks and profitability since cooperative banks' loan portfolio risk is higher and profitability is lower compared to savings banks. As the results suggest, cooperative banks accept prices at which no other bank would underwrite a business. Similar to entrepreneurs at cooperative banks, insiders at savings banks do not exert a beneficial influence, although they are supposed to understand banking business best. The analysis further points out that not only the composition matters, but that the board size is another relevant factor. The comparison of both banking groups suggests that only up to a certain board size threshold, stability, risk, and performance are impacted beneficially. Hence, banks should not only focus on the individuals and their characteristics but also on the board as a whole.

In summary, all banks in our sample suffer from adverse impacts from financial expertise. The findings of the present study question the effectiveness of more required universal financial expertise of supervisory board members. First, the present study does not document a consistent risk-decreasing or stability-enhancing effect across banking sectors. Second, in the case of cooperative banks, financial expertise is even detrimental to performance. Instead of aspiring to have supervisory boards with 100% financial experts whose competences are only broadly defined, it may be better to increase supervisory board knowledge in specific areas. Regulators could think of key areas to be monitored. These areas should be the core responsibilities for which the supervisory boards are fully accountable. Authorities could then force supervisory boards to have experts in all of these core areas. This would ensure that expertise in clearly defined areas is present on the supervisory board.

Assessing financial expertise on the basis of more detailed information is an avenue for future research that can contribute significantly to the regulation and supervision of banks. In addition, the issue remains open on whether regulation should prescribe the adequacy of individuals or the composition of bank supervisory boards in order to balance various interests. The tasks the supervisory board has to fulfill and how these tasks can be accomplished by its members or experts in specific areas must be clearly stated.

IV.6   Appendix

Appendix IV.6.1:   Underlying assumptions and definition of local and regional politicians

The following assumptions have been applied for the present analysis:

- For the information merchant, we assume a merchant in terms of § 1, German Commercial Code (HGB).
- For information entrepreneurs, we assume that the person is a managing partner/owner of a company.
- A farmer is treated as self-employed if not otherwise explicitly stated.
- In cases of jobs based on apprenticeships, which could suggest both self-employed and employed, employed is assumed if no further information is available.
- If the academic title is the only available information, no classification is attributed (others).

For the determination of board size, as well as for further analysis, we do not consider the following board members:

- Advisory members
- Honorary members
- Members with tenures of less than half a year.

Ministers, state secretaries, and members of parliament at the federal and federal-state level are federal politicians or federal-state politicians, respectively. The number of members of the European parliament is not material for the dataset, and these members are classified as federal politicians. For the identification of politicians at the regional and local levels, a two-step approach has been applied to differentiate between politicians in the strict sense and holders of political electoral office. This is necessary due to the multitude of administrative bodies at the regional and local levels and the heterogeneity of different federal states.

First, given the difference between full-time and voluntary electoral offices, individuals officiating voluntarily in political electoral offices are not considered politicians. These offices include honorary county councils, city councils, and municipal councils. Second, the hierarchical level of the function is considered. In our analysis, we classify the concerned person as a politician if he or she is the head of the administration. This selection step assures that politicians in our dataset are directly elected, with the exception of county administrators in Baden-Wuerttemberg.

Persons who are subject to directives and who have to report to the head of the administration do not count as politicians in the present analysis. Subsequently, district administrators, lord mayors, and mayors are consistently counted nationwide as politicians. There are a few federal states in which city directors, presidents of regional committees, presidents of local committees, and presidents of regional committees are counted as politicians if all the criteria outlined above are satisfied. Other holders of state-specific functions are not counted as politicians even though they are directly or indirectly elected and represent a political position and/or party, such as full-time city councilors in Bavaria, magistrates in Hessen, and (county) deputies in several federal states. All these persons violate the criterion regarding heading the administration. If the function is exercised full-time, the office holders are typically responsible for particular divisions or departments.

Appendix IV.6.2: Supervisory board composition, Top 150

Variables		Mean	Std. Dev.	Coeff. of Variation	Min	Max
Insider (%)	Cooperative banks	2.94	9.19	313.05	0.00	52.94
	Savings banks	24.58	12.16	49.46	0.00	41.67
Outsider (%)	Cooperative banks	97.06	9.19	9.47	47.06	100.00
	Savings banks	75.42	12.16	16.12	58.33	100.00
Employment						
Employed individuals (%)	Cooperative banks	49.61	23.89	48.16	0.00	100.00
	Savings banks	72.50	12.21	16.84	36.36	100.00
Self-employed individuals (%)	Cooperative banks	39.70	25.43	64.05	0.00	90.91
	Savings banks	13.52	9.91	73.32	0.00	47.37
Retired individuals (%)	Cooperative banks	9.74	12.06	123.79	0.00	77.78
	Savings banks	12.64	10.27	81.21	0.00	55.56
Other (%)	Cooperative banks	0.95	2.91	307.03	0.00	16.67
	Savings banks	1.34	2.82	209.61	0.00	12.50
Politicians (officiating)						
Federal politicians (%)	Cooperative banks	0.26	1.52	591.71	0.00	11.11
	Savings banks	0.74	2.37	320.61	0.00	15.38
Federal state politicians (%)	Cooperative banks	0.15	1.18	771.01	0.00	11.11
	Savings banks	2.64	4.36	164.99	0.00	23.08
Regional politicans (%)	Cooperative banks	0.00	0.00	0.00	0.00	0.00
	Savings banks	5.52	4.09	74.14	0.00	20.00
Local politicians (%)	Cooperative banks	1.85	4.44	239.60	0.00	25.00
	Savings banks	15.78	12.86	81.50	0.00	66.67
Officiating and retired politicians (%)	Cooperative banks	3.22	6.31	195.77	0.00	35.29
	Savings banks	28.64	15.39	53.73	0.00	75.00

Appendix IV.6.3: Mean comparison cooperative vs. savings banks, t-test, Top 200

Dependent variables	Group	Mean	Std. error	t	df
z-score	Cooperative banks	22.7075	0.4285	6.2873	2157.6500
	Savings banks	19.4006	0.3050		
NPL ratio	Cooperative banks	2.6616	0.0573	7.6087	2219.4500
	Savings banks	2.1136	0.0437		
ROE	Cooperative banks	12.1898	0.2183	-4.3042	2369.3400
	Savings banks	13.5984	0.2438		
RORWA	Cooperative banks	1.2118	0.0230	-3.2372	2296.5300
	Savings banks	1.3301	0.0284		
Bank level variables					
Financial expertise	Cooperative banks	47.7642	0.6602	-20.8182	2229.7100
	Savings banks	64.9789	0.4980		
Outside financial expertise	Cooperative banks	45.2461	0.6705	-8.4056	2397.3900
	Savings banks	53.1539	0.6599		
Board size	Cooperative banks	12.4175	0.1282	-22.0161	2328.3300
	Savings banks	16.8058	0.1526		
Bank size	Cooperative banks	20.9000	0.0198	-33.4650	2359.7700
	Savings banks	21.7833	0.0174		
Bank size growth	Cooperative banks	2.6078	0.1380	13.9148	2028.4600
	Savings banks	0.2526	0.0980		
Bank efficiency	Cooperative banks	66.4850	0.2757	3.4443	2245.4700
	Savings banks	65.2888	0.2112		
Loan growth	Cooperative banks	4.9788	0.2228	5.8245	2162.4000
	Savings banks	2.8602	0.2875		
Claims on MFI	Cooperative banks	11.8889	0.1904	7.6137	2397.9100
	Savings banks	9.8452	0.1892		
Claims on non-MFI	Cooperative banks	58.6740	0.3287	-0.5022	2391.4400
	Savings banks	58.9138	0.3464		

Confidence level: 95%

Appendix IV.6.4:   Summary statistics, Top 150

Dependent variables	Group	Mean	Std. Dev.	Coeff. of Variation	Min	Max
z-score	Cooperative banks	17.69	8.48	47.95	3.95	66.43
	Savings banks	19.16	9.76	50.94	3.02	77.02
NPL ratio (%)	Cooperative banks	2.69	2.10	77.95	0.00	13.47
	Savings banks	2.08	1.46	70.08	0.04	11.56
ROE (%)	Cooperative banks	12.27	8.10	66.03	-21.43	55.21
	Savings banks	14.15	7.61	53.74	-28.36	67.79
RORWA (%)	Cooperative banks	1.20	0.82	68.27	-1.67	6.27
	Savings banks	1.39	0.94	67.68	-2.92	8.34

Bank level variables						
Financial expertise (%)	Cooperative banks	47.53	22.74	47.85	0.00	100.00
	Savings banks	65.46	17.22	26.30	20.00	100.00
Outside financial expertise (%)	Cooperative banks	45.81	23.65	51.63	0.00	100.00
	Savings banks	53.84	22.96	42.64	0.00	100.00
Board size	Cooperative banks	10.81	3.66	33.88	4.00	33.00
	Savings banks	15.89	4.12	25.96	7.00	33.00
Bank size (ln '000 EUR)	Cooperative banks	20.61	0.72	3.50	19.30	24.45
	Savings banks	21.69	0.54	2.47	20.89	23.47
Bank size growth (%)	Cooperative banks	2.52	4.62	183.63	-19.46	30.61
	Savings banks	0.30	3.25	1,074.99	-16.29	14.74
Bank efficiency (%)	Cooperative banks	66.51	9.95	14.96	15.98	112.92
	Savings banks	64.55	7.29	11.29	36.00	90.25
Loan growth (%)	Cooperative banks	4.90	7.18	146.63	-12.36	39.29
	Savings banks	2.76	9.58	347.08	-14.70	104.87
Claims on MFI (%)	Cooperative banks	12.09	6.66	55.07	0.06	37.92
	Savings banks	9.86	6.56	66.55	0.00	44.37
Claims on non-MFI (%)	Cooperative banks	58.57	11.26	19.22	11.17	82.75
	Savings banks	59.79	11.03	18.44	24.21	85.36

Macroeconomic and structural variables						
East/West	Cooperative banks	0.03	0.16	604.49	0.00	1.00
	Savings banks	0.09	0.29	311.85	0.00	1.00
GDP per capita ('000 EUR)	Cooperative banks	28.42	10.13	35.63	14.76	231.16
	Savings banks	27.83	7.70	27.66	14.16	72.20
Population	Cooperative banks	2.49	1.41	56.73	1.00	5.00
	Savings banks	1.56	0.74	47.39	1.00	5.00

Appendix IV.6.5: Mean comparison cooperative vs. savings banks, t-test, Top 150

Dependent variables	Group	Mean	Std. error	t	df
z-score	Cooperative banks	17.6920	0.2828	-3.4061	1763.7600
	Savings banks	19.1602	0.3253		
NPL ratio	Cooperative banks	2.6882	0.0703	7.0774	1584.4500
	Savings banks	2.0828	0.0488		
ROE	Cooperative banks	12.2717	0.2701	-5.0743	1790.8300
	Savings banks	14.1514	0.2535		
RORWA	Cooperative banks	1.1960	0.0272	-4.5651	1764.7400
	Savings banks	1.3851	0.0312		
Bank level variables					
Financial expertise	Cooperative banks	47.5350	0.7581	-18.8507	1674.5600
	Savings banks	65.4584	0.5738		
Outside financial expertise	Cooperative banks	45.8105	0.7883	-7.3056	1796.4100
	Savings banks	53.8369	0.7652		
Board size	Cooperative banks	10.8133	0.1221	-27.5990	1773.3800
	Savings banks	15.8878	0.1375		
Bank size	Cooperative banks	20.6116	0.0240	-36.1164	1661.5400
	Savings banks	21.6936	0.0179		
Bank size growth	Cooperative banks	2.5163	0.1544	11.7446	1605.1500
	Savings banks	0.3021	0.1082		
Bank efficiency	Cooperative banks	66.5056	0.3316	4.7512	1647.9000
	Savings banks	64.5529	0.2428		
Loan growth	Cooperative banks	4.8971	0.2399	5.3517	1666.8700
	Savings banks	2.7598	0.3193		
Claims on MFI	Cooperative banks	12.0907	0.2219	7.1625	1797.6100
	Savings banks	9.8588	0.2187		
Claims on non-MFI	Cooperative banks	58.5717	0.3752	-2.3106	1797.2300
	Savings banks	59.7853	0.3675		

Confidence level: 95%

Appendix IV.6.6: Cluster analysis, clustered by financial expertise, Top 150

Dependent variables	Group	Cluster 1	Cluster 2	Cluster 3	Delta Cluster 1-3
z-score	Cooperative banks	15.62	17.85	19.61	-3.99
	Savings banks	19.76	18.23	19.49	0.27
NPL ratio (%)	Cooperative banks	3.20	2.58	2.29	0.91
	Savings banks	1.97	2.07	2.21	-0.24
ROE (%)	Cooperative banks	11.59	13.23	11.99	-0.40
	Savings banks	15.85	13.95	12.65	3.21
RORWA (%)	Cooperative banks	1.15	1.25	1.18	-0.03
	Savings banks	1.58	1.36	1.22	0.36

Bank level variables					
Financial expertise (%)	Cooperative banks	71.74	47.16	23.70	48.03
	Savings banks	83.78	65.96	46.64	37.14
Outside financial expertise (%)	Cooperative banks	70.55	44.60	22.28	48.27
	Savings banks	77.32	54.81	29.38	47.95
Board size	Cooperative banks	10.52	10.91	11.02	-0.50
	Savings banks	16.01	16.25	15.41	0.60
Bank size (ln '000 EUR)	Cooperative banks	20.63	20.69	20.51	0.11
	Savings banks	21.69	21.75	21.64	0.06
Bank size growth (%)	Cooperative banks	1.87	2.97	2.71	-0.84
	Savings banks	0.58	0.18	0.14	0.43
Bank efficiency (%)	Cooperative banks	67.17	65.93	66.42	0.75
	Savings banks	62.34	65.54	65.78	-3.44
Loan growth (%)	Cooperative banks	4.12	5.37	5.21	-1.09
	Savings banks	2.35	2.03	3.89	-1.54
Claims on MFI (%)	Cooperative banks	12.11	12.66	11.50	0.62
	Savings banks	10.63	10.65	8.30	2.33
Claims on non-MFI (%)	Cooperative banks	56.93	58.86	59.92	-2.99
	Savings banks	56.82	59.14	63.39	-6.57

Appendix IV.6.7: Pairwise test of significance between expertise clusters, Top 150

Dependent variables		Cluster 1 vs. 2 t (*p-value*)	Cluster 1 vs. 3 t (*p-value*)	Cluster 2 vs. 3 t (*p-value*)
z-score	Cooperative banks	-3.8227 *** *0.0002*	-5.2972 *** *0.0000*	-2.5639 ** *0.0108*
	Savings banks	2.1519 ** *0.0322*	0.2783 *0.7810*	-1.5821 *0.1147*
NPL ratio	Cooperative banks	4.3753 *** *0.0000*	6.0238 *** *0.0000*	2.1036 ** *0.0363*
	Savings banks	-1.0372 *0.3005*	-2.1583 ** *0.0317*	-1.2316 *0.2191*
ROE	Cooperative banks	-2.5850 ** *0.0102*	-0.6422 *0.5213*	2.1633 ** *0.0313*
	Savings banks	3.2540 *** *0.0013*	6.2159 *** *0.0000*	2.3510 ** *0.0194*
RORWA	Cooperative banks	-1.5285 *0.1275*	-0.4669 *0.6409*	1.1298 *0.2595*
	Savings banks	2.9212 *** *0.0038*	5.1308 *** *0.0000*	2.0891 ** *0.0375*

Bank level variables				
Financial expertise	Cooperative banks	42.2232 *** *0.0000*	75.5214 *** *0.0000*	41.0016 *** *0.0000*
	Savings banks	50.1895 *** *0.0000*	96.1220 *** *0.0000*	44.0866 *** *0.0000*
Outside financial expertise	Cooperative banks	32.4137 *** *0.0000*	70.3125 *** *0.0000*	26.9993 *** *0.0000*
	Savings banks	35.2981 *** *0.0000*	67.3601 *** *0.0000*	29.7499 *** *0.0000*
Bank size	Cooperative banks	-1.0340 *0.3020*	2.2612 ** *0.0245*	2.8167 *** *0.0052*
	Savings banks	-1.2410 *0.2156*	1.4256 *0.1550*	2.4038 ** *0.0168*
Bank efficiency	Cooperative banks	1.5473 *0.1229*	0.9486 *0.3436*	-0.6065 *0.5446*
	Savings banks	-5.1310 *** *0.0000*	-5.8860 *** *0.0000*	-0.4735 *0.6362*
Bank size growth	Cooperative banks	-2.9847 *** *0.0031*	-2.3450 ** *0.0197*	0.8224 *0.4115*
	Savings banks	1.5352 *0.1258*	1.7050 * *0.0892*	0.1416 *0.8875*
Board size	Cooperative banks	-1.6942 * *0.0913*	-1.6502 * *0.1000*	-0.3398 *0.7342*
	Savings banks	-0.6500 *0.5162*	1.6842 * *0.0932*	2.6486 *** *0.0085*
Loan growth	Cooperative banks	-3.1168 *** *0.0020*	-2.5868 ** *0.0102*	0.4502 *0.6529*
	Savings banks	0.5969 *0.5510*	-2.3829 ** *0.0178*	-2.2693 ** *0.0240*

Claims on MFI	Cooperative banks	-1.0752	1.1601	2.3587 **
		0.2832	0.2469	0.0190
	Savings banks	-0.0377	4.4976 ***	5.0412 ***
		0.9700	0.0000	0.0000
Claims on non-MFI	Cooperative banks	-2.1078 **	-3.5104 ***	-1.0176
		0.0359	0.0005	0.3097
	Savings banks	-2.7057 ***	-7.0374 ***	-5.0723 ***
		0.0072	0.0000	0.0000

Confidence level: 95%
* indicates significance at the 10% level, ** at the 5% level, and *** at the 1% level, respectively.

Appendix IV.6.8:   Correlation matrix, Top 200

	RORWA	ROE	z-score	NPL ratio	FinExp*C	OutFin Exp*C	Bank size*C
RORWA	1.0000						
ROE	0.8827*	1.0000					
z-score	0.0957*	0.0290	1.0000				
NPL ratio	-0.0558*	-0.0725*	-0.0106	1.0000			
FinExp*C	-0.0901*	-0.0996*	0.0366	0.2049*	1.0000		
OutFinExp*C	-0.0829*	-0.0954*	0.0354	0.2346*	0.9855*	1.0000	
Bank size*C	-0.0682	-0.089*	0.1234*	0.1439*	0.8325*	0.8087*	1.0000
Bank efficiency *C	-0.1051*	-0.1310*	0.1212*	0.1725*	0.8228*	0.8075*	0.9772*
Bank size growth*C	-0.0026	-0.0076	0.0004	-0.1406*	0.2637*	0.2438*	0.3789*
Loan growth*C	0.1205*	0.0706*	-0.0052	0.0599*	0.3306*	0.3110*	0.4368*
Claims on MFI*C	-0.0747*	-0.1216*	0.0354	0.1045*	0.6624*	0.6509*	0.7878*
Claims on nonMFI*C	-0.0900*	-0.0956*	0.1850*	0.1899*	0.7978*	0.7801*	0.9609*
Board size*C	-0.0662*	-0.0766*	0.1782*	0.1590*	0.7365*	0.7013*	0.8961*
FinExp*S	0.1001*	0.1228*	-0.1380*	-0.1447*	-0.7754*	-0.7577*	-0.9352*
OutFinExp*S	0.1108*	0.1342*	-0.1137*	-0.1526*	-0.7076*	-0.6916*	-0.8536*
Bank size *S	0.0637*	0.0856*	-0.1263*	-0.1561*	-0.8275*	-0.8087*	-0.9982*
Bank efficiency*S	0.0122	0.0342	-0.1316*	-0.1587*	-0.8180*	-0.7994*	-0.9866*
Bank size growth*S	0.0586*	0.0612*	-0.0130	-0.1405*	-0.0439*	-0.0429*	-0.0528*
Loan growth*S	0.1592*	0.1074*	-0.0339	0.1304*	-0.1664*	-0.1624*	-0.2000*
Claims on MFI*S	0.0658*	0.0694*	-0.1388*	-0.1654*	-0.6031*	-0.5894*	-0.7274*
Claims on nonMFI*S	-0.0179	0.0290	-0.0749*	-0.1238*	-0.7958*	-0.7777*	-0.9599*
Board size*S	0.0016	0.0335	-0.1201*	-0.1155*	-0.7567*	-0.7395*	-0.9127*
GDP per capita	-0.0808*	-0.0984*	-0.0075	-0.1071*	0.0643*	0.0486*	0.0467*
Population	-0.0512*	-0.0701*	-0.0518*	-0.1922*	0.3025*	0.2386*	0.3942*
East/West	0.2480*	0.1853*	-0.1749*	-0.0188	-0.1614*	-0.1537*	-0.2108*

* indicates significance at the 5% level

	Bank effic.*C	Bank size growth*C	Loan growth*C	Claims on MFI*C	Claims on non-MFI*C	Board size*C
RORWA						
ROE						
z-score						
NPL ratio						
FinExp*C						
OutFinExp*C						
Bank size*C						
Bank efficiency *C	1.0000					
Bank size growth*C	0.3476*	1.0000				
Loan growth*C	0.4111*	0.6774*	1.0000			
Claims on MFI*C	0.7835*	0.3505*	0.3423*	1.0000		
Claims on nonMFI*C	0.9497*	0.3229*	0.3780*	0.6929*	1.0000	
Board size*C	0.8728*	0.3273*	0.3697*	0.6666*	0.8716*	1.0000
FinExp*S	-0.9175	-0.3505*	-0.4032*	-0.7367*	-0.9029*	-0.8356*
OutFinExp*S	-0.8374*	-0.3194*	-0.3675*	-0.6724*	-0.8240*	-0.7626*
Bank size *S	-0.9792*	-0.3745*	-0.4309*	-0.7863*	-0.9636*	-0.8918*
Bank efficiency*S	-0.9679*	-0.3701*	-0.4258*	-0.7772*	-0.9525*	-0.8815*
Bank size growth*S	-0.0518*	-0.0198	-0.0228	-0.0416*	-0.0509*	-0.0475*
Loan growth*S	-0.1962*	-0.0750*	-0.0863*	-0.1576*	-0.1930*	-0.1799*
Claims on MFI*S	-0.7136*	-0.2717*	-0.3126*	-0.5730*	-0.7022*	-0.6499*
Claims on nonMFI*S	-0.9417*	-0.3604*	-0.4146*	-0.7562*	-0.9267*	-0.8576*
Board size*S	-0.8954*	-0.3424*	-0.3939*	-0.7190*	-0.8811*	-0.8154*
GDP per capita	0.0375	0.0676*	0.0629*	0.1118*	0.0171	-0.0033
Population	0.3345*	0.2314*	0.2319*	0.3593*	0.3000*	0.3315*
East/West	-0.1983*	-0.0833*	-0.0936*	-0.1504*	-0.2295*	-0.1925*

* indicates significance at the 5% level

118

	FinExp*S	OutFin Exp*S	Bank size*S	Bank effic.*S	Bank size growth*S	Loan growth*S	Claims on MFI*S
RORWA							
ROE							
z-score							
NPL ratio							
FinExp*C							
OutFinExp*C							
Bank size*C							
Bank efficiency *C							
Bank size growth*C							
Loan growth*C							
Claims on MFI*C							
Claims on nonMFI*C							
Board size*C							
FinExp*S	1.0000						
OutFinExp*S	0.9709*	1.0000					
Bank size *S	0.9350*	0.8518*	1.0000				
Bank efficiency*S	0.9172*	0.8341*	0.9864*	1.0000			
Bank size growth*S	0.0752*	0.0972*	0.0526*	0.0389	1.0000		
Loan growth*S	0.1712*	0.1237*	0.2016*	0.1882*	0.2411*	1.0000	
Claims on MFI*S	0.7277*	0.6909*	0.7298*	0.7210*	0.1237*	0.1066*	1.0000
Claims on nonMFI*S	0.8695*	0.7821*	0.9609*	0.9554*	0.0198	0.1901*	0.6150*
Board size*S	0.8619*	0.7683*	0.9203*	0.9075*	0.0213	0.1834*	0.6684*
GDP per capita	-0.0133	0.0182	-0.0279	-0.0324	0.0547*	-0.0090	0.0075
Population	-0.3515*	-0.3464*	-0.3573*	-0.3668*	-0.0437*	-0.0634*	-0.2596*
East/West	0.2404*	0.2111*	0.2039*	0.1916*	-0.0468*	0.0042	0.2479*

* indicates significance at the 5% level

	Claims on non-MFI*S	Board size*S	GDP per capita	Population	East/West
RORWA					
ROE					
z-score					
NPL ratio					
FinExp*C					
OutFinExp*C					
Bank size*C					
Bank efficiency *C					
Bank size growth*C					
Loan growth*C					
Claims on MFI*C					
Claims on nonMFI*C					
Board size*C					
FinExp*S					
OutFinExp*S					
Bank size *S					
Bank efficiency*S					
Bank size growth*S					
Loan growth*S					
Claims on MFI*S					
Claims on nonMFI*S	1.0000				
Board size*S	0.8859*	1.0000			
GDP per capita	-0.0149	-0.0335	1.0000		
Population	-0.3634*	-0.2517	0.256*	1.0000	
East/West	0.0291	0.1432*	-0.2363*	-0.0706*	1.0000

* indicates significance at the 5% level

119

Appendix IV.6.9: Correlation matrix, Top 150

	RORWA	ROE	z-score	NPL ratio	FinExp*C	OutFinExp*C	Bank size*C
RORWA	1.0000						
ROE	0.8804*	1.0000					
z-score	0.0791*	0.0041	1.0000				
NPL ratio	-0.0884*	-0.1021*	-0.0636*	1.0000			
FinExp*C	-0.1062*	-0.1222*	-0.1213*	0.2421*	1.0000		
OutFinExp*C	-0.1020*	-0.1220*	-0.1163*	0.2682*	0.9879*	1.0000	
Bank size*C	-0.1076*	-0.1181*	-0.0857*	0.1527*	0.8294*	0.8042*	1.0000
Bank efficiency *C	-0.1549*	-0.1731*	-0.0776*	0.1851*	0.8174*	0.8009*	0.9753*
Bank size growth*C	-0.0127	0.0056	-0.0935*	-0.1768*	0.2449*	0.2184*	0.3654*
Loan growth*C	0.0980*	0.0743*	-0.0792*	0.0442	0.3393*	0.3174*	0.4407*
Claims on MFI*C	-0.1172*	-0.1553*	-0.1368*	0.0996*	0.6671*	0.6512*	0.7887*
Claims on nonMFI*C	-0.1301*	-0.1274*	-0.0298	0.2052*	0.7873*	0.7684*	0.9607*
Board size*C	-0.1066*	-0.1042*	-0.0154	0.1688*	0.7300*	0.6962*	0.9054*
FinExp*S	0.1377*	0.1475*	0.0699*	-0.1587*	-0.7765*	-0.7572*	-0.9362*
OutFinExp*S	0.1387*	0.1521*	0.0800*	-0.1651*	-0.7095*	-0.6919*	-0.8554*
Bank size *S	0.1066*	0.1189*	0.0822*	-0.1674*	-0.8279*	-0.8073*	-0.9982*
Bank efficiency*S	0.0520*	0.0679*	0.0702*	-0.1721*	-0.8180*	-0.7977*	-0.9863*
Bank size growth*S	0.0545*	0.0495*	-0.0096	-0.1282*	-0.0544*	-0.0530*	-0.0655*
Loan growth*S	0.1547*	0.1027*	0.0056	0.1171*	-0.1654*	-0.1613*	-0.1993*
Claims on MFI*S	0.0896*	0.0957*	-0.0021	-0.1886*	-0.6034*	-0.5884*	-0.7275*
Claims on nonMFI*S	0.0266	0.0686*	0.1367*	-0.1347*	-0.8016*	-0.7817*	-0.9665*
Board size*S	0.0661*	0.0903*	0.0772*	-0.1365*	-0.7777*	-0.7584*	-0.9377*
GDP per capita	-0.0306	-0.0192	-0.0376	-0.0957*	0.0196	0.0108	0.0370
Population	0.0193	0.0013	-0.1204*	-0.2444*	0.2672*	0.2074*	0.4044*
East/West	0.2743*	0.1872*	-0.1466*	0.0047	-0.1009*	-0.0944*	-0.1425*

* indicates significance at the 5% level

	Bank size growth*C	Loan growth*C	Claims on MFI*C	Claims on non-MFI*C	Board size*C
RORWA					
ROE					
z-score					
NPL ratio					
FinExp*C					
OutFinExp*C					
Bank size*C					
Bank efficiency *C					
Bank size growth*C	1.0000				
Loan growth*C	0.6777*	1.0000			
Claims on MFI*C	0.3393*	0.3353*	1.0000		
Claims on nonMFI*C	0.3040*	0.3825*	0.7020*	1.0000	
Board size*C	0.3041*	0.3639*	0.6802*	0.8821*	1.0000
FinExp*S	-0.3373*	-0.4077*	-0.7397*	-0.9046*	-0.8454*
OutFinExp*S	-0.3081*	-0.3724*	-0.6759*	-0.8265*	-0.7725*
Bank size *S	-0.3597*	-0.4347*	-0.7886*	-0.9644*	-0.9014*
Bank efficiency*S	-0.3554*	-0.4295*	-0.7793*	-0.9530*	-0.8907*
Bank size growth*S	-0.0236	-0.0285	-0.0518*	-0.0633*	-0.0592*
Loan growth*S	-0.0718*	-0.0868*	-0.1574*	-0.1925*	-0.1799*
Claims on MFI*S	-0.2620*	-0.3167*	-0.5748*	-0.7029*	-0.6569*
Claims on nonMFI*S	-0.3482*	-0.4209*	-0.7636*	-0.9338*	-0.8728*
Board size*S	-0.3378*	-0.4083*	-0.7408*	-0.9060*	-0.8467*
GDP per capita	0.0722*	0.0618*	0.0945*	0.0228	0.0077
Population	0.2520*	0.2323*	0.3757*	0.2997*	0.3392*
East/West	-0.0530*	-0.0671*	-0.1064*	-0.1639*	-0.1397*

* indicates significance at the 5% level

	FinExp *S	OutFin Exp*S	Bank size*S	Bank effic.*S	Bank size growth*S	Loan_ growth*S	Claims on MFI*S
RORWA							
ROE							
z-score							
NPL ratio							
FinExp*C							
OutFinExp*C							
Bank size*C							
Bank efficiency *C							
Bank size growth*C							
Loan growth*C							
Claims on MFI*C							
Claims on nonMFI*C							
Board size*C							
FinExp*S	1.0000						
OutFinExp*S	0.9721*	1.0000					
Bank size *S	0.9369*	0.8557*	1.0000				
Bank efficiency*S	0.9166*	0.8359*	0.9860*	1.0000			
Bank size growth*S	0.0789*	0.0937*	0.0663*	0.0534*	1.0000		
Loan growth*S	0.1709*	0.1247*	0.2000*	0.1873*	0.2496*	1.0000	
Claims on MFI*S	0.7234*	0.6844*	0.7323*	0.7233*	0.1408*	0.1063*	1.0000
Claims on nonMFI*S	0.8821*	0.7976*	0.9672*	0.9614*	0.0398	0.1881*	0.6313*
Board size*S	0.8907*	0.8059*	0.9422*	0.9284*	0.0464*	0.1889*	0.6984*
GDP per capita	-0.0133	0.0188	-0.0226	-0.0300	0.0516*	-0.0082	0.0270
Population	-0.3498*	-0.3239*	-0.3699*	-0.3804*	-0.0289	-0.0705*	-0.2514*
East/West	0.1542*	0.1258*	0.1348*	0.1211*	-0.0927*	-0.0211	0.1409*

* indicates significance at the 5% level

	Claims on non-MFI*S	Board size*S	GDP per capita	Population	East/West
RORWA					
ROE					
z-score					
NPL ratio					
FinExp*C					
OutFinExp*C					
Bank size*C					
Bank efficiency *C					
Bank size growth*C					
Loan growth*C					
Claims on MFI*C					
Claims on nonMFI*C					
Board size*C					
FinExp*S					
OutFinExp*S					
Bank size *S					
Bank efficiency*S					
Bank size growth*S					
Loan growth*S					
Claims on MFI*S					
Claims on nonMFI*S	1.0000				
Board size*S	0.9104*	1.0000			
GDP per capita	-0.0256	-0.0269	1.0000		
Population	-0.3750*	-0.3062*	0.2241*	1.0000	
East/West	0.0025	0.0907*	-0.1758*	-0.0918*	1.0000

* indicates significance at the 5% level

Appendix IV.6.10: Random-effect regressions with dependent variables z-score and NPL ratio, Top 150 banks

Variable		z-score (RE) Financial expertise		z-score (RE) Out. fin. expertise		NPL ratio (RE) Financial expertise		NPL ratio (RE) Out. fin. expertise	
		Coeff.	SE (robust)	Coeff.	SE (robust)	Coeff.	SE (robust)	Coeff.	SE (robust)
Financial expertise	Financial expertise*C	-0.0193	0.0235			0.0125	0.0043***		
	Out. financial expertise*C			-0.0238	0.0232			0.0125	0.0042***
	Financial expertise*S	0.0173	0.0117			0.0046	0.0040		
	Out. financial expertise*S			0.0099	0.0106			0.0010	0.0033
Bank level	Savings	-83.1116	37.1565**	-84.1552	37.4078**	-11.4575	4.2121***	-9.7527	4.3303**
	Bank size*C	-4.4277	1.6046***	-4.4225	1.6222***	-0.5308	0.1501***	-0.4723	0.1537***
	Bank efficiency*C	-0.0138	0.0082*	-0.0135	0.0083	-0.0020	0.0065	-0.0021	0.0065
	Bank size growth*C	-0.0595	0.0168***	-0.0598	0.0168***	-0.1639	0.0161***	-0.1636	0.0161***
	Loan growth*C	0.0052	0.0135	0.0055	0.0135	0.0951	0.0112***	0.0949	0.0112***
	Claims on MFI*C	-0.0320	0.0197	-0.0330	0.0196*	0.0174	0.0123	0.0177	0.0123
	Claims on non-MFI*C	0.0367	0.0282	0.0365	0.0280	0.0362	0.0089***	0.0369	0.0089***
	Board size*C	0.1177	0.1655	0.1114	0.1646	0.0695	0.0301**	0.0716	0.0301**
	Bank size*S	-0.2154	1.2117	-0.1546	1.2045	0.1036	0.1579	0.0977	0.1592
	Bank efficiency*S	-0.0162	0.0180	-0.0163	0.0180	-0.0265	0.0078***	-0.0270	0.0079***
	Bank size growth*S	-0.1143	0.0162***	-0.1144	0.0162***	-0.0911	0.0125***	-0.0911	0.0125***
	Loan growth*S	0.0391	0.0066***	0.0394	0.0067***	0.0475	0.0075***	0.0475	0.0075***
	Claims on MFI*S	0.0166	0.0272	0.0164	0.0271	-0.0179	0.0088**	-0.0178	0.0088**
	Claims on non-MFI*S	0.0216	0.0335	0.0213	0.0333	0.0284	0.0102***	0.0270	0.0101***
	Board size*S	-0.0773	0.0486	-0.0662	0.0513	0.0444	0.0174***	0.0460	0.0173***
Macroeconomic and structural environment	East/West	-6.0046	1.7353***	-5.9156	1.7234***	0.6730	0.3254**	0.6680	0.3269**
	GDP per capita	0.0340	0.0187*	0.0341	0.0189*	-0.0123	0.0045***	-0.0124	0.0045***
	Population	0.9923	0.4704**	0.9648	0.4630**	-0.3270	0.0790***	-0.3223	0.0792***
	constant	104.6185	32.2748***	104.8236	32.6349***	11.1637	3.2571***	9.9083	3.3738***
	Wald Chi^2	317.88	***	311.62	***	448.70	***	450.29	***
	R-sq	0.0548		0.0572		0.3184		0.3184	
	No of observations	1,796		1,796		1,781		1,781	

* indicates significance at the 10% level, ** at the 5% level, and *** at the 1% level, respectively.
Standard errors control for clustering at the bank level.

Appendix IV.6.11: Comparison coefficients with dependent variables z-score and NPL ratio, Top 150 banks

Variable		z-score (RE) Financial expertise		z-score (RE) Out. fin. expertise		NPL ratio (RE) Financial expertise		NPL ratio (RE) Out. fin. expertise	
		chi^2	P>chi^2	chi^2	P>chi^2	chi^2	P>chi^2	chi^2	P>chi^2
Financial expertise	Financial expertise: C vs. S	1.9300	0.1649			1.7500	0.1853		
	Out. financial expertise: C vs. S			1.7400	0.1870			4.6200	0.0316**
Bank level	Bank size: C vs. S	5.6500	0.0175**	5.7300	0.0167**	11.6800	0.0006***	9.0200	0.0027***
	Bank efficiency: C vs. S	0.0200	0.9012	0.0200	0.8887	5.8300	0.0157**	5.9400	0.0148**
	Bank size growth: C vs. S	5.6200	0.0177**	5.5700	0.0183**	12.7200	0.0004***	12.5800	0.0004***
	Board size: C vs. S	1.2800	0.2579	1.0600	0.3025	0.5300	0.4674	0.5500	0.4582
	Loan growth: C vs. S	5.1800	0.0228***	5.1600	0.0231**	12.4400	0.0004***	12.3100	0.0005***
	Claims on MFI: C vs. S	2.1100	0.1467	2.1900	0.1389	5.3700	0.0204**	5.3800	0.0203**
	Claims on non-MFI: C vs. S	0.1200	0.7288	0.1200	0.7251	0.3300	0.5641	0.5300	0.4648

* indicates significance at the 10% level, ** at the 5% level, and *** at the 1% level, respectively.

Appendix IV.6.12: Random-effect regressions with dependent variables RORWA and ROE, Top 150 banks

Variable		RORWA (RE) Financial expertise		RORWA (RE) Out. fin. expertise		ROE (RE) Financial expertise		ROE (RE) Out. fin. expertise	
		Coeff.	SE (robust)	Coeff.	SE (robust)	Coeff.	SE (robust)	Coeff.	SE (robust)
Financial expertise	Financial expertise*C	-0.0009	0.0015			-0.0122	0.0166		
	Out. financial expertise*C			-0.0011	0.0014			-0.0144	0.0162
	Financial expertise*S	0.0011	0.0019			0.0218	0.0161		
	Out. financial expertise*S			0.0012	0.0015			0.0229	0.0125 *
Bank level	Savings	-1.1028	1.7216	-1.2652	1.7123	-0.1938	17.2103	-2.3867	17.1005
	Bank size*C	-0.2679	0.0603 ***	-0.2713	0.0583 ***	-1.7035	0.6555 ***	-1.7507	0.6324 ***
	Bank efficiency*C	-0.0286	0.0037 ***	-0.0286	0.0037 ***	-0.3032	0.0379 ***	-0.3029	0.0380 ***
	Bank size growth*C	-0.0433	0.0078 ***	-0.0435	0.0078 ***	-0.2704	0.0732 ***	-0.2717	0.0732 ***
	Loan growth*C	0.0413	0.0044 ***	0.0413	0.0044 ***	0.2669	0.0398 ***	0.2674	0.0398 ***
	Claims on MFI*C	-0.0125	0.0052 **	-0.0125	0.0052 **	-0.1752	0.0520 ***	-0.1749	0.0520 ***
	Claims on non-MFI*C	-0.0135	0.0031 ***	-0.0136	0.0031 ***	-0.0601	0.0345 *	-0.0610	0.0345 *
	Board size*C	0.0083	0.0096	0.0080	0.0097	0.1351	0.1049	0.1308	0.1056
	Bank size*S	-0.0816	0.0674	-0.0788	0.0674	-0.9154	0.6963	-0.8742	0.6957
	Bank efficiency*S	-0.0475	0.0058 ***	-0.0474	0.0059 ***	-0.4640	0.0547 ***	-0.4634	0.0549 ***
	Bank size growth*S	-0.0121	0.0078	-0.0122	0.0079	-0.0763	0.0648	-0.0782	0.0645
	Loan growth*S	0.0169	0.0029 ***	0.0170	0.0029 ***	0.0797	0.0207 ***	0.0815	0.0209 ***
	Claims on MFI*S	-0.0140	0.0046 ***	-0.0141	0.0046 ***	-0.0924	0.0440 **	-0.0941	0.0443 **
	Claims on non-MFI*S	-0.0286	0.0045 ***	-0.0284	0.0045 ***	-0.1148	0.0355 ***	-0.1117	0.0350 ***
	Board size*S	-0.0206	0.0069 ***	-0.0202	0.0068 ***	-0.0726	0.0684	-0.0646	0.0680
Macroeconomic and structural environment	East/West	0.2654	0.1808	0.2724	0.1812	1.9599	1.3122	2.0866	1.3117
	GDP per capita	0.0003	0.0025	0.0002	0.0025	-0.0002	0.0353	-0.0016	0.0361
	Population	0.0645	0.0336 *	0.0632	0.0336 *	0.3658	0.3418	0.3538	0.3432
	constant	9.2457	1.1455 ***	9.3397	1.1239 ***	70.7073	12.7437 ***	71.9070	12.4292 ***
	Wald Chi^2	405.5	***	403.06	***	414.17	***	415.34	***
	R-sq	0.3371		0.3375		0.2459		0.2472	
	No of observations	1,796		1,796		1,796		1,796	

* indicates significance at the 10% level, ** at the 5% level, and *** at the 1% level, respectively.
Standard errors control for clustering at the bank level.

Appendix IV.6.13: Comparison coefficients with dependent variables RORWA and ROE, Top 150 banks

Variable		RORWA (RE) Financial expertise		RORWA (RE) Out. fin. expertise		ROE (RE) Financial expertise		ROE (RE) Out. fin. expertise	
		chi^2	P>chi^2	chi^2	P>chi^2	chi^2	P>chi^2	chi^2	P>chi^2
Financial expertise	Financial expertise: C vs. S	0.6900	0.4060			2.1100	0.1459		
	Out. financial expertise: C vs. S			1.2700	0.2592			3.2400	0.0719 *
Bank level	Bank size: C vs. S	5.6400	0.0176 **	6.1700	0.0130 **	1.0200	0.3124	1.3000	0.2534
	Bank efficiency: C vs. S	7.4300	0.0064 ***	7.3700	0.0066 ***	5.8900	0.0152 **	5.8300	0.0158 **
	Bank size growth: C vs. S	8.0300	0.0046 ***	7.9800	0.0047 ***	3.9700	0.0463 **	3.9500	0.0467 **
	Board size: C vs. S	5.8100	0.0159 **	5.5300	0.0187 **	2.7200	0.0992 *	2.3900	0.1222
	Loan growth: C vs. S	21.1100	0.0000 ***	20.9900	0.0000 ***	17.4300	0.0000 ***	17.1400	0.0000 ***
	Claims on MFI: C vs. S	0.0500	0.8282	0.0500	0.8170	1.4500	0.2292	1.3700	0.2410
	Claims on non-MFI: C vs. S	8.5100	0.0035 ***	8.1500	0.0043 ***	1.4700	0.2260	1.2800	0.2572

* indicates significance at the 10% level, ** at the 5% level, and *** at the 1% level, respectively.

Appendix IV.6.14: Random-effect regressions with dependent variables z-score and NPL ratio, Top 200 banks, 1% outlier correction

Variable		z-score (RE) Financial expertise		z-score (RE) Out. fin. expertise		NPL ratio (RE) Financial expertise		NPL ratio (RE) Out. fin. expertise	
		Coeff.	SE (robust)	Coeff.	SE (robust)	Coeff.	SE (robust)	Coeff.	SE (robust)
Financial expertise	Financial expertise*C	-0.0613	0.0450			0.0122	0.0040***		
	Out. financial expertise*C			-0.0836	0.0402**			0.0127	0.0038***
	Financial expertise*S	-0.0148	0.0296			0.0074	0.0037**		
	Out. financial expertise*S			-0.0091	0.0239			0.0028	0.0029
Bank level	Savings	-116.8259	77.6643	-122.1647	78.3245	-9.6770	4.6872**	-7.6533	4.7105
	Bank size*C	-3.2622	3.2207	-3.3643	3.2199	-0.6632	0.1605***	-0.6605	0.1543***
	Bank efficiency*C	-0.0715	0.0285**	-0.0701	0.0286**	-0.0041	0.0063	-0.0041	0.0063
	Bank size growth*C	0.0206	0.0549	0.0187	0.0543	-0.1674	0.0137***	-0.1671	0.0137***
	Loan growth*C	-0.0852	0.0335**	-0.0841	0.0334**	0.1023	0.0098***	0.1019	0.0098***
	Claims on MFI*C	0.0177	0.0721	0.0141	0.0727	0.0335	0.0108***	0.0333	0.0108***
	Claims on non-MFI*C	0.1549	0.1091	0.1501	0.1084	0.0325	0.0082***	0.0333	0.0083***
	Board size*C	-0.1672	0.2326	-0.1863	0.2340	0.0466	0.0194**	0.0491	0.0195**
	Bank size*S	1.9323	2.0587	1.9931	2.0641	-0.1210	0.1793	-0.1320	0.1807
	Bank efficiency*S	0.0235	0.0345	0.0235	0.0347	-0.0242	0.0074***	-0.0242	0.0075***
	Bank size growth*S	-0.1162	0.0249***	-0.1162	0.0249***	-0.1087	0.0119***	-0.1086	0.0120***
	Loan growth*S	0.0449	0.0079***	0.0443	0.0076***	0.0580	0.0053***	0.0581	0.0053***
	Claims on MFI*S	0.0283	0.0416	0.0279	0.0418	-0.0188	0.0084**	-0.0186	0.0084**
	Claims on non-MFI*S	0.0322	0.0520	0.0331	0.0524	0.0247	0.0096***	0.0233	0.0096**
	Board size*S	-0.0021	0.1028	-0.0053	0.1042	0.0378	0.0121***	0.0400	0.0119***
Macroeconomic and structural environment	East/West	-6.4073	1.9334***	-6.3765	1.9536***	0.4057	0.3040	0.4170	0.3042
	GDP per capita	-0.0151	0.0786	-0.0116	0.0784	-0.0324	0.0077***	-0.1763	0.0667***
	Population	-0.4519	0.9878	-0.5489	0.9811	-0.1833	0.0668***	-0.0321	0.0076***
	constant	93.1832	71.5405	96.7972	71.7857	14.5980	3.4664***	13.1956	3.3843***
	Wald Chi²	182.68	***	183.24	***	682.72	***	680.89	***
	R-sq	0.0875		0.0897		0.2915		0.2931	
	No of observations	2,278		2,278		2,259		2,259	

* indicates significance at the 10% level, ** at the 5% level, and *** at the 1% level, respectively.
Standard errors control for clustering at the bank level.

Appendix IV.6.15: Comparison coefficients with dependent variables z-score and NPL ratio, Top 200 banks, 1% outlier correction

Variable		z-score (RE) Financial expertise		z-score (RE) Out. fin. expertise		NPL ratio (RE) Financial expertise		NPL ratio (RE) Out. fin. expertise	
		chi²	P>chi²	chi²	P>chi²	chi²	P>chi²	chi²	P>chi²
Financial expertise	Financial expertise: C vs. S	0.7400	0.3893			0.7800	0.3784		
	Out. financial expertise: C vs. S			2.5300	0.1120			4.2900	0.0383 **
Bank level	Bank size: C vs. S	2.2900	0.1300	2.4000	0.1213	7.1800	0.0074 ***	5.4200	0.0199 **
	Bank efficiency: C vs. S	4.6200	0.0316 **	4.4400	0.0350 **	4.1300	0.0421 **	4.2800	0.0386 **
	Bank size growth: C vs. S	5.2000	0.0226 **	5.1400	0.0233 **	10.4800	0.0012 ***	10.3600	0.0013 ***
	Board size: C vs. S	0.4500	0.5045	0.5300	0.4685	0.1500	0.6959	0.1600	0.6866
	Loan growth: C vs. S	14.1700	0.0002 ***	14.0200	0.0002 ***	15.8600	0.0001 ***	15.4500	0.0001 ***
	Claims on MFI: C vs. S	0.0200	0.8994	0.0300	0.8694	14.5900	0.0001 ***	14.4000	0.0001 ***
	Claims on non-MFI: C vs. S	1.1800	0.2766	1.0900	0.2964	0.3900	0.5308	0.6500	0.4191

* indicates significance at the 10% level, ** at the 5% level, and *** at the 1% level, respectively.

Variable		RORWA (RE) Financial expertise		RORWA (RE) Out. fin. expertise		ROE (RE) Financial expertise		ROE (RE) Out. fin. expertise	
		Coeff.	SE (robust)	Coeff.	SE (robust)	Coeff.	SE (robust)	Coeff.	SE (robust)
Financial expertise	Financial expertise*C	-0.0010	0.0012			-0.0039	0.0131		
	Out. financial expertise*C			-0.0013	0.0012			-0.0064	0.0128
	Financial expertise*S	0.0020	0.0016			0.0374	0.0149**		
	Out. financial expertise*S			0.0022	0.0012*			0.0337	0.0111***
Bank level	Savings	-2.5350	1.5845	-2.7708	1.5757*	-12.0046	16.6273	-13.1084	16.3341
	Bank size*C	-0.2778	0.0582***	-0.2823	0.0561***	-1.9017	0.6549***	-1.9086	0.6268***
	Bank efficiency*C	-0.0250	0.0032***	-0.0250	0.0032***	-0.2618	0.0307***	-0.2612	0.0307***
	Bank size growth*C	-0.0435	0.0072***	-0.0436	0.0072***	-0.2641	0.0694***	-0.2649	0.0694***
	Loan growth*C	0.0452	0.0038***	0.0453	0.0038***	0.2748	0.0340***	0.2752	0.0339***
	Claims on MFI*C	-0.0075	0.0048	-0.0074	0.0048	-0.1196	0.0444***	-0.1189	0.0445***
	Claims on non-MFI*C	-0.0118	0.0027***	-0.0118	0.0027***	-0.0519	0.0289*	-0.0512	0.0288*
	Board size*C	0.0063	0.0064	0.0059	0.0064	0.0876	0.0645	0.0848	0.0650
	Bank size*S	-0.0382	0.0672	-0.0334	0.0675	-0.4193	0.6266	-0.3695	0.6275
	Bank efficiency*S	-0.0250	0.0045***	-0.0456	0.0045***	-0.4727	0.0452***	-0.4720	0.0453***
	Bank size growth*S	-0.0120	0.0074	-0.0123	0.0074*	-0.0378	0.0628	-0.0417	0.0624
	Loan growth*S	0.0220	0.0026***	0.0222	0.0026***	0.1035	0.0206***	0.1066	0.0208***
	Claims on MFI*S	-0.0146	0.0048***	-0.0147	0.0048***	-0.1377	0.0456***	-0.1140	0.0458***
	Claims on non-MFI*S	-0.0236	0.0033***	-0.0232	0.0033***	-0.1074	0.0301***	-0.1042	0.0299***
	Board size*S	-0.0177	0.0057***	-0.0169	0.0056***	-0.1103	0.0550**	-0.0971	0.0545*
Macroeconomic and structural environment	East/West	0.1155	0.1220	0.1285	0.1215	1.0523	1.0904	1.2370	1.0958
	GDP per capita	-0.0039	0.0028	-0.0041	0.0028	-0.0884	0.0317***	-0.0912	0.0319***
	Population	0.0098	0.0274	0.0097	0.0273	0.0168	0.2365	0.0209	0.2363
	constant	9.3987	1.1262***	9.5061	1.0898***	74.6851	13.2673***	74.9441	12.7012***
	Wald Chi^2	613.62	***	616.48	***	536.74	***	534.78	***
	R-sq	0.3263		0.3272		0.2447		0.2458	
	No of observations	2,278		2,278		2,278		2,278	

* indicates significance at the 10% level, ** at the 5% level, and *** at the 1% level, respectively.
Standard errors control for clustering at the bank level.

Variable		RORWA (RE) Financial expertise		RORWA (RE) Out. fin. expertise		ROE (RE) Financial expertise		ROE (RE) Out. fin. expertise	
		chi^2	P>chi^2	chi^2	P>chi^2	chi^2	P>chi^2	chi^2	P>chi^2
Financial expertise	Financial expertise: C vs. S	2.2700	0.1318			4.3000	0.0381 **		
	Out. financial expertise: C vs. S			3.9700	0.0462 **			5.5800	0.0182 **
Bank level	Bank size: C vs. S	10.7500	0.0010 ***	11.8800	0.0006 **	3.8500	0.0498 **	4.3600	0.0367 **
	Bank efficiency: C vs. S	14.5800	0.0001 **	14.3500	0.0002 ***	15.1000	0.0001 ***	15.0100	0.0001 ***
	Bank size growth: C vs. S	9.3500	0.0022 ***	9.2200	0.0024 ***	5.8900	0.0152 **	5.7700	0.0163 **
	Board size: C vs. S	7.7400	0.0054 ***	7.0800	0.0078 ***	5.4000	0.0201 **	4.5500	0.0329 **
	Loan growth: C vs. S	25.1600	0.0000 ***	24.7800	0.0000 ***	18.5000	0.0000 ***	17.8500	0.0000 ***
	Claims on MFI: C vs. S	1.0900	0.2955	1.1700	0.2797	0.0800	0.7762	0.1100	0.7425
	Claims on non-MFI: C vs. S	9.3000	0.0023 ***	8.6100	0.0033 ***	2.1700	0.1403	2.0100	0.1565

* indicates significance at the 10% level, ** at the 5% level, and *** at the 1% level, respectively.

125

Appendix IV.6.18: Random-effect regressions with dependent variables z-score and NPL ratio, Top 150 banks, 1% outlier correction

Variable		z-score (RE) Financial expertise		z-score (RE) Out. fin. expertise		NPL ratio (RE) Financial expertise		NPL ratio (RE) Out. fin. expertise	
		Coeff.	SE (robust)	Coeff.	SE (robust)	Coeff.	SE (robust)	Coeff.	SE (robust)
Financial expertise	Financial expertise*C	-0.0160	0.0173			0.0121	0.0044***		
	Out. financial expertise*C			-0.0209	0.0168			0.0122	0.0043***
	Financial expertise*S	0.0147	0.0110			0.0055	0.0040		
	Out. financial expertise*S			0.0089	0.0100			0.0024	0.0031
Bank level	Savings	-68.8123	34.9631**	-69.3353	34.8976**	-14.2733	4.4148***	-12.7481	4.4770***
	Bank size*C	-5.1143	1.5692***	-5.1056	1.5670***	-0.5785	0.1626***	-0.5274	0.1613***
	Bank efficiency*C	-0.0215	0.0095**	-0.0213	0.0095**	-0.0036	0.0071	-0.0037	0.0071
	Bank size growth*C	-0.0770	0.0168***	-0.0774	0.0167***	-0.1703	0.0164***	-0.1700	0.0164***
	Loan growth*C	0.0017	0.0129	0.0019	0.0129	0.0991	0.0111***	0.0990	0.0111***
	Claims on MFI*C	-0.0408	0.0205**	-0.0420	0.0205**	0.0204	0.0122*	0.0206	0.0122*
	Claims on non-MFI*C	0.0279	0.0303	0.0276	0.0299	0.0386	0.0092***	0.0393	0.0092***
	Board size*C	-0.0001	0.1146	-0.0063	0.1133	0.0588	0.0310*	0.0617	0.0312**
	Bank size*S	-1.6599	1.1577	-1.6259	1.1509	0.1855	0.1672	0.1797	0.1687
	Bank efficiency*S	-0.0251	0.0167	-0.0252	0.0168	-0.0230	0.0072***	-0.0234	0.0073***
	Bank size growth*S	-0.1143	0.0162***	-0.1143	0.0162***	-0.1037	0.0129***	-0.1038	0.0129***
	Loan growth*S	0.0481	0.0059***	0.0484	0.0059***	0.0593	0.0063***	0.0594	0.0063***
	Claims on MFI*S	0.0093	0.0238	0.0090	0.0237	-0.0183	0.0092**	-0.0182	0.0092**
	Claims on non-MFI*S	0.0369	0.0333	0.0368	0.0330	0.0256	0.0096***	0.0246	0.0096***
	Board size*S	-0.0447	0.0472	-0.0346	0.0492	0.0383	0.0175***	0.0404	0.0173**
Macroeconomic and structural environment	East/West	-5.1094	1.6725***	-5.0207	1.6607***	0.5393	0.3378	0.5426	0.3386
	GDP per capita	0.1675	0.0374***	0.1691	0.0375***	-0.0302	0.0081***	-0.0303	0.0081***
	Population	0.9751	0.3582***	0.9568	0.3570***	-0.2775	0.0759***	-0.2708	0.0757***
	constant	117.2101	31.8826***	117.3096	31.8375***	12.5795	3.5411***	11.4590	3.5525***
	Wald Chi^2	342.02	***	336.14	***	543.77	***	543.45	***
	R-sq	0.0375		0.0390		0.3179		0.3183	
	No of observations	1,796		1,796		1,781		1,781	

* indicates significance at the 10% level, ** at the 5% level, and *** at the 1% level, respectively.
Standard errors control for clustering at the bank level.

Appendix IV.6.19: Comparison coefficients with dependent variables z-score and NPL ratio, Top 150 banks, 1% outlier correction

Variable		z-score (RE) Financial expertise		z-score (RE) Out. fin. expertise		NPL ratio (RE) Financial expertise		NPL ratio (RE) Out. fin. expertise	
		chi^2	P>chi^2	chi^2	P>chi^2	chi^2	P>chi^2	chi^2	P>chi^2
Financial expertise	Financial expertise: C vs. S	2.2700	0.1315			1.2100	0.2704		
	Out. financial expertise: C vs. S			2.3300	0.1267			3.5300	0.0602 **
Bank level	Bank size: C vs. S	4.4500	0.0350 **	4.5300	0.0333 **	15.3000	0.0001 ***	12.9600	0.0003 ***
	Bank efficiency: C vs. S	0.0300	0.8561	0.0400	0.8456	3.6800	0.0550 *	3.7600	0.0525 *
	Bank size growth: C vs. S	2.5300	0.1119 *	2.4800	0.1153 *	10.1800	0.0014 ***	10.0300	0.0015 ***
	Board size: C vs. S	0.1300	0.7166	0.0500	0.8181	0.3400	0.5579	0.3700	0.5436
	Loan growth: C vs. S	10.6300	0.0011 ***	10.7000	0.0011 ***	9.7600	0.0018 ***	9.6300	0.0019 ***
	Claims on MFI: C vs. S	2.6100	0.1063	2.7100	0.0999	6.2900	0.0121 **	6.3300	0.0119 **
	Claims on non-MFI: C vs. S	0.0400	0.8406	0.0400	0.8362	0.9500	0.3288	1.2300	0.2665

* indicates significance at the 10% level, ** at the 5% level, and *** at the 1% level, respectively.

Variable		RORWA (RE) Financial expertise		RORWA (RE) Out. fin. expertise		ROE (RE) Financial expertise		ROE (RE) Out. fin. expertise	
		Coeff.	SE (robust)	Coeff.	SE (robust)	Coeff.	SE (robust)	Coeff.	SE (robust)
Financial expertise	Financial expertise*C	-0.0009	0.0015			-0.0112	0.0161		
	Out. financial expertise*C			-0.0011	0.0014			-0.0127	0.0158
	Financial expertise*S	0.0018	0.0018			0.0274	0.0156*		
	Out. financial expertise*S			0.0018	0.0014			0.0276	0.0119**
Bank level	Savings	-1.9979	1.7968	-2.1549	1.7755	-10.7607	17.8966	-12.8457	17.6497
	Bank size*C	-0.2915	0.0659***	-0.2943	0.0643***	-1.9041	0.7413***	-1.9370	0.7224***
	Bank efficiency*C	-0.0276	0.0037***	-0.0276	0.0037***	-0.3027	0.0360***	-0.3023	0.0360***
	Bank size growth*C	-0.0438	0.0081***	-0.0440	0.0081***	-0.2678	0.0778***	-0.2688	0.0779***
	Loan growth*C	0.0417	0.0044***	0.0418	0.0044***	0.2662	0.0397***	0.2666	0.0396***
	Claims on MFI*C	-0.0119	0.0052**	-0.0119	0.0052**	-0.1656	0.0511***	-0.1650	0.0511***
	Claims on non-MFI*C	-0.0125	0.0034***	-0.0126	0.0034***	-0.0481	0.0358	-0.0486	0.0358
	Board size*C	0.0088	0.0097	0.0084	0.0098	0.1449	0.1012	0.1400	0.1024
	Bank size*S	-0.0705	0.0651	-0.0667	0.0652	-0.6298	0.6929	-0.5731	0.6934
	Bank efficiency*S	-0.0456	0.0051***	-0.0456	0.0051***	-0.4534	0.0489***	-0.4527	0.0490***
	Bank size growth*S	-0.0135	0.0075*	-0.0137	0.0075*	-0.0747	0.0633	-0.0774	0.0631
	Loan growth*S	0.0214	0.0025***	0.0216	0.0025***	0.0917	0.0212***	0.0942	0.0214***
	Claims on MFI*S	-0.0123	0.0047***	-0.0124	0.0047***	-0.0912	0.0460**	-0.0929	0.0462
	Claims on non-MFI*S	-0.0264	0.0038***	-0.0262	0.0038***	-0.1059	0.0331***	-0.1030	0.0324***
	Board size*S	-0.0208	0.0068***	-0.0201	0.0067***	-0.0889	0.0688	-0.0789	0.0684
Macroeconomic and structural environment	East/West	0.2090	0.1723	0.2176	0.1720	1.3214	1.3312	1.4572	1.3251
	GDP per capita	-0.0036	0.0033	-0.0038	0.0033	-0.0635	0.0409	-0.0667	0.0413
	Population	0.0720	0.0343***	0.0710	0.0344	0.4667	0.3432	0.4570	0.3450
	constant	9.6835	1.2651***	9.7611	1.2431***	75.3750	14.3722***	76.2650	14.0815***
	Wald Chi^2	513.29	***	512.77	***	483.35	***	485.09	***
	R-sq	0.3425		0.3432		0.2434		0.2449	
	No of observations	1,796		1,796		1,796		1,796	

* indicates significance at the 10% level, ** at the 5% level, and *** at the 1% level, respectively.
Standard errors control for clustering at the bank level.

Appendix IV.6.21: Comparison coefficients with dependent variables RORWA and ROE, Top 150 banks, 1% outlier correction

Variable		RORWA (RE) Financial expertise		RORWA (RE) Out. fin. expertise		ROE (RE) Financial expertise		ROE (RE) Out. fin. expertise	
		chi^2	P>chi^2	chi^2	P>chi^2	chi^2	P>chi^2	chi^2	P>chi^2
Financial expertise	Financial expertise: C vs. S	1.3000	0.2535			2.9400	0.0864 *		
	Out. financial expertise: C vs. S			1.9800	0.1596 *			4.1200	0.0424 **
Bank level	Bank size: C vs. S	7.0900	0.0078 ***	7.7800	0.0053 *	2.4200	0.1201	2.9000	0.0888 *
	Bank efficiency: C vs. S	8.3500	0.0039 ***	8.3200	0.0039 ***	6.3100	0.0120 **	6.2700	0.0123 **
	Bank size growth: C vs. S	7.6400	0.0057 ***	7.5400	0.0060 ***	3.7300	0.0536 *	3.6700	0.0555 *
	Board size: C vs. S	6.1100	0.0134 **	5.6900	0.0171 **	3.5800	0.0583 *	3.1000	0.0785 *
	Loan growth: C vs. S	15.9800	0.0001 ***	15.8000	0.0001 ***	15.0500	0.0001 ***	14.6600	0.0001 ***
	Claims on MFI: C vs. S	0.0000	0.9542	0.0100	0.9382	1.1600	0.2821	1.0800	0.2982
	Claims on non-MFI: C vs. S	8.6600	0.0033 ***	8.4000	0.0038 ***	1.6800	0.1952	1.5200	0.2171

* indicates significance at the 10% level, ** at the 5% level, and *** at the 1% level, respectively.

Appendix IV.6.22: Random-effect regressions with dependent variables z-score and NPL ratio, Top 200 banks, 5% outlier correction

Variable		z-score (RE) Financial expertise		z-score (RE) Out. fin. expertise		NPL ratio (RE) Financial expertise		NPL ratio (RE) Out. fin. expertise	
		Coeff.	SE (robust)	Coeff.	SE (robust)	Coeff.	SE (robust)	Coeff.	SE (robust)
Financial expertise	Financial expertise*C	-0.0497	0.0400			0.0124	0.0037***		
	Out. financial expertise*C			-0.0689	0.0368*			0.0129	0.0035***
	Financial expertise*S	-0.0149	0.0228			0.0044	0.0034		
	Out. financial expertise*S			-0.0132	0.0205			0.0007	0.0026
Bank level	Savings	-63.1907	66.8176	-65.7156	67.2402	-9.5436	4.4046**	-7.7266	4.3933*
	Bank size*C	-2.0985	2.8577	-2.1198	2.8643	-0.7135	0.1750***	-0.6586	0.1696***
	Bank efficiency*C	-0.0919	0.0290***	-0.0896	0.0291***	-0.0090	0.0062	-0.0093	0.0062
	Bank size growth*C	-0.0025	0.0500	-0.0050	0.0494	-0.1765	0.0142***	-0.1757	0.0142***
	Loan growth*C	-0.0961	0.0289***	-0.0947	0.0291***	0.1056	0.0101***	0.1050	0.0101***
	Claims on MFI*C	0.0416	0.0604	0.0377	0.0612	0.0300	0.0110***	0.0298	0.0109***
	Claims on non-MFI*C	0.1440	0.0889	0.1404	0.0883	0.0315	0.0089***	0.0323	0.0088***
	Board size*C	-0.0582	0.1741	-0.0742	0.1735	0.0438	0.0206**	0.0466	0.0207**
	Bank size*S	0.6247	1.8421	0.6643	1.8486	-0.1519	0.1496	-0.1649	0.1504
	Bank efficiency*S	0.0154	0.0324	0.0151	0.0323	-0.0296	0.0062***	-0.0299	0.0063***
	Bank size growth*S	-0.1468	0.0250***	-0.1462	0.0248***	-0.1353	0.0110***	-0.1352	0.0110***
	Loan growth*S	0.0676	0.0116***	0.0664	0.0114***	0.0958	0.0059***	0.0960	0.0059***
	Claims on MFI*S	0.0155	0.0302	0.0148	0.0301	-0.0220	0.0080***	-0.0217	0.0080***
	Claims on non-MFI*S	0.0105	0.0458	0.0099	0.0465	0.0176	0.0083**	0.0163	0.0084**
	Board size*S	0.0494	0.1056	0.0444	0.1061	0.0398	0.0120***	0.0406	0.0119***
Macroeconomic and structural environment	East/West	-5.6937	1.6715***	-5.6803	1.6868***	0.1436	0.2734	0.1427	0.2736
	GDP per capita	0.0378	0.0738	0.0420	0.0732	-0.0417	0.0087***	-0.0414	0.0087***
	Population	-0.7573	0.8120	-0.8379	0.8095	-0.1757	0.0622***	-0.1662	0.0621***
	constant	67.5626	62.3129	69.1274	62.5231	16.2852	3.7900***	15.0631	3.7116***
	Wald Chi^2	222.61	***	222.00	***	1031.42	***	1049.92	***
	R-sq	0.1129		0.1153		0.3078		0.3116	
	No of observations	2,278		2,278		2,259		2,259	

* indicates significance at the 10% level, ** at the 5% level, and *** at the 1% level, respectively.
Standard errors control for clustering at the bank level.

Appendix IV.6.23: Comparison coefficients with dependent variables z-score and NPL ratio, Top 200 banks, 5% outlier correction

Variable		z-score (RE) Financial expertise		z-score (RE) Out. Fin. expertise		NPL ratio (RE) Financial expertise		NPL ratio (RE) Out. fin. expertise	
		chi^2	P>chi^2	chi^2	P>chi^2	chi^2	P>chi^2	chi^2	P>chi^2
Financial expertise	Financial expertise: C vs. S	0.5700	0.4513			2.5600	0.1093		
	Out. financial expertise: C vs. S			1.7400	0.1868			7.9300	0.0049 ***
Bank level	Bank size: C vs. S	0.8400	0.3603	0.8600	0.3527	8.6700	0.0032 ***	6.8600	0.0088 ***
	Bank efficiency: C vs. S	6.2500	0.0124 **	5.9600	0.0146 **	5.4800	0.0192 **	5.5000	0.0190 **
	Bank size growth: C vs. S	6.8200	0.0090 ***	6.7000	0.0096 ***	5.2700	0.0217 **	5.0900	0.0241 **
	Board size: C vs. S	0.3000	0.5857	0.3600	0.5478	0.0300	0.8672	0.0700	0.7967
	Loan growth: C vs. S	28.0000	0.0000 ***	27.0400	0.0000 ***	0.7000	0.4023	0.6600	0.4402
	Claims on MFI: C vs. S	0.1500	0.6976	0.1100	0.7352	14.7400	0.0001 ***	14.5300	0.0001 ***
	Claims on non-MFI: C vs. S	2.0000	0.1574	1.9200	0.1655	1.2700	0.2596	1.6800	0.1944

* indicates significance at the 10% level, ** at the 5% level, and *** at the 1% level, respectively.

Appenix IV.6.24: Random-effect regressions with dependent variables RORWA and ROE, Top 200 banks, 5% outlier correction

Variable		RORWA (RE) Financial expertise Coeff.	SE (robust)	RORWA (RE) Out. fin. expertise Coeff.	SE (robust)	ROE (RE) Financial expertise Coeff.	SE (robust)	ROE (RE) Out. fin. expertise Coeff.	SE (robust)
Financial expertise	Financial expertise*C	-0.0006	0.0011			-0.0018	0.0115		
	Out. financial expertise*C			-0.0009	0.0011			-0.0055	0.0107
	Financial expertise*S	0.0023	0.0013 *			0.0381	0.0139 ***		
	Out. financial expertise*S			0.0023	0.0010 **			0.0333	0.0100 ***
Bank level	Savings	-2.1237	1.4824	-2.2516	1.4682	-6.8771	15.2530	-7.3802	15.0451
	Bank size*C	-0.2665	0.0575 ***	-0.2666	0.0559 ***	-1.6467	0.5878 ***	-1.6252	0.5713 ***
	Bank efficiency*C	-0.0232	0.0030 ***	-0.0232	0.0030 ***	-0.2482	0.0289 ***	-0.2472	0.0289 ***
	Bank size growth*C	-0.0392	0.0063 ***	-0.0393	0.0063 ***	-0.2771	0.0617 ***	-0.2784	0.0617 ***
	Loan growth*C	0.0407	0.0032 ***	0.0407	0.0032 ***	0.2493	0.0313 ***	0.2497	0.0313 ***
	Claims on MFI*C	-0.0074	0.0046	-0.0073	0.0046	-0.1048	0.0436 **	-0.1042	0.0437 **
	Claims on non-MFI*C	-0.0117	0.0025 ***	-0.0116	0.0025 ***	-0.0344	0.0255	-0.0335	0.0255
	Board size*C	0.0044	0.0062	0.0041	0.0062	0.0594	0.0629	0.0563	0.0632
	Bank size*S	-0.0536	0.0602	-0.0487	0.0604	-0.2821	0.5679	-0.2270	0.5677
	Bank efficiency*S	-0.0452	0.0037 ***	-0.0452	0.0037 ***	-0.4871	0.0394 ***	-0.4873	0.0394 ***
	Bank size growth*S	-0.0219	0.0052 ***	-0.0221	0.0052 ***	-0.0747	0.0562	-0.0782	0.0560
	Loan growth*S	0.0301	0.0030 ***	0.0303	0.0030 ***	0.1436	0.0280 ***	0.1471	0.0282 ***
	Claims on MFI*S	-0.0126	0.0043 ***	-0.0127	0.0043 ***	-0.1440	0.0427 ***	-0.1452	0.0428 ***
	Claims on non-MFI*S	-0.0212	0.0027 ***	-0.0209	0.0027 ***	-0.1161	0.0285 ***	-0.1131	0.0283 ***
	Board size*S	-0.0146	0.0053 ***	-0.0138	0.0053 ***	-0.0820	0.0533	-0.0696	0.0533
Macroeconomic and structural environment	East/West	-0.0556	0.0968	-0.0416	0.0968	0.5346	0.9569	0.7249	0.9620
	GDP per capita	-0.0069	0.0034 **	-0.0070	0.0034 **	-0.1412	0.0347 ***	-0.1424	0.0348 ***
	Population	0.0125	0.0228	0.0118	0.0229	-0.0019	0.1975	-0.0072	0.1987
	constant	9.1314	1.1325 ***	9.1466	1.1028 ***	69.1807	11.8283 ***	68.8446	11.5145 ***
	Wald Chi²	1036.85	***	1,034.31	***	727.27	***	722.93	***
	R-sq	0.3237		0.3249		0.2612		0.2623	
	No of observations	2,278		2,278		2,278		2,278	

* indicates significance at the 10% level, ** at the 5% level, and *** at the 1% level, respectively.
Standard errors control for clustering at the bank level.

Appendix IV.6.25: Comparison coefficients with dependent variables RORWA and ROE, Top 200 banks, 5% outlier correction

Variable		RORWA (RE) Financial expertise chi²	P>chi²	RORWA (RE) Out. fin. expertise chi²	P>chi²	ROE (RE) Financial expertise chi²	P>chi²	ROE (RE) Out. fin. expertise chi²	P>chi²
Financial expertise	Financial expertise: C vs. S	2.6500	0.1038			4.8700	0.0273 **		
	Out. financial expertise: C vs. S			4.7100	0.0300 **			7.0100	0.0081 ***
Bank level	Bank size: C vs. S	9.3700	0.0022 ***	10.1000	0.0015 **	3.8400	0.0499 **	4.2000	0.0405 **
	Bank efficiency: C vs. S	21.3700	0.0000 ***	21.4200	0.0000 ***	24.2500	0.0000 ***	24.4800	0.0000 ***
	Bank size growth: C vs. S	4.5200	0.0335 **	4.4400	0.0350 **	5.9200	0.0149 **	5.8100	0.0160 **
	Board size: C vs. S	5.4200	0.0199 **	4.7900	0.2860 **	2.9400	0.0866 *	2.3100	0.1283
	Loan growth: C vs. S	5.7600	0.0164 **	5.5400	0.1860 **	6.3200	0.0119 **	5.9200	0.0149 **
	Claims on MFI: C vs. S	0.7000	0.4016	0.7400	0.3883	0.4100	0.5198	0.4500	0.5025
	Claims on non-MFI: C vs. S	8.0300	0.0046 ***	7.5800	0.0059 ***	5.4400	0.0196 **	5.2300	0.0222 **

* indicates significance at the 10% level, ** at the 5% level, and *** at the 1% level, respectively.

Appendix IV.6.26: Random-effect regressions with dependent variables z-score and NPL ratio, Top 150 banks, 5% outlier correction

Variable		z-score (RE) Financial expertise		z-score (RE) Out. fin. expertise		NPL ratio (RE) Financial expertise		NPL ratio (RE) Out. fin. expertise	
		Coeff.	SE (robust)	Coeff.	SE (robust)	Coeff.	SE (robust)	Coeff.	SE (robust)
Financial expertise	Financial expertise*C	-0.0083	0.0140			0.0126	0.0044***		
	Out. financial expertise*C			-0.0146	0.0131			0.0128	0.0040***
	Financial expertise*S	0.0163	0.0099*			0.0044	0.0040		
	Out. financial expertise*S			0.0099	0.0083			0.0011	0.0031
Bank level	Savings	-48.8893	26.9543*	-49.3610	26.6148*	-14.3194	4.3610***	-12.7041	4.4035***
	Bank size*C	-3.4897	0.8135***	-3.4703	0.7943***	-0.6052	0.1561***	-0.5534	0.1551***
	Bank efficiency*C	-0.0315	0.0091***	-0.0310	0.0091***	-0.0085	0.0072	-0.0088	0.0072
	Bank size growth*C	-0.0790	0.0173***	-0.0799	0.0172***	-0.1745	0.0163***	-0.1738	0.0163***
	Loan growth*C	-0.0084	0.0115	-0.0078	0.0115	0.1050	0.0106***	0.1047	0.0106***
	Claims on MFI*C	-0.0426	0.0199**	-0.0439	0.0199**	0.0170	0.0122	0.0172	0.0122
	Claims on non-MFI*C	0.0340	0.0263	0.0332	0.0260	0.0369	0.0100***	0.0377	0.0100***
	Board size*C	0.0185	0.0841	0.0128	0.0832	0.0662	0.0284**	0.0684	0.0284**
	Bank size*S	-1.0985	1.1021	-1.0596	1.0913	0.1652	0.1591	0.1565	0.1601
	Bank efficiency*S	-0.0427	0.0130***	-0.0427	0.0129***	-0.0256	0.0070***	-0.0260	0.0070***
	Bank size growth*S	-0.1256	0.0187***	-0.1259	0.0186***	-0.1272	0.0124***	-0.1273	0.0125***
	Loan growth*S	0.0662	0.0081***	0.0668	0.0081***	0.0898	0.0069***	0.0900	0.0069***
	Claims on MFI*S	0.0229	0.0241	0.0232	0.0241	-0.0170	0.0089*	-0.0167	0.0089*
	Claims on non-MFI*S	0.0547	0.0327*	0.0548	0.0325*	0.0244	0.0091***	0.0232	0.0091***
	Board size*S	-0.0168	0.0447	-0.0059	0.0466	0.0329	0.0200*	0.0338	0.0198*
Macroeconomic and structural environment	East/West	-4.0013	1.4602***	-3.9041	1.4509***	0.4157	0.3305	0.4097	0.3322
	GDP per capita	0.1345	0.0312***	0.1365	0.0313***	-0.0376	0.0101***	-0.0377	0.0101***
	Population	0.5366	0.2132**	0.5203	0.2151**	-0.2550	0.0682***	-0.2456	0.0676***
	constant	85.4147	16.5889***	85.3585	16.2398***	13.5450	3.4162***	12.4214	3.4173***
	Wald Chi^2	317.48	***	314.55	***	809.16	***	819.36	***
	R-sq	0.0572		0.0600		0.3352		0.3379	
	No of observations	1,796		1,796		1,781		1,781	

* indicates significance at the 10% level, ** at the 5% level, and *** at the 1% level, respectively.
Standard errors control for clustering at the bank level.

Appendix IV.6.27: Comparison coefficients with dependent variables z-score and NPL ratio, Top 150 banks, 5% outlier correction

Variable		z-score (RE) Financial expertise		z-score (RE) Out. fin. expertise		NPL ratio (RE) Financial expertise		NPL ratio (RE) Out. fin. expertise	
		chi^2	P>chi^2	chi^2	P>chi^2	chi^2	P>chi^2	chi^2	P>chi^2
Financial expertise	Financial expertise: C vs. S	2.0800	0.1488			1.9300	0.1648		
	Out. financial expertise: C vs. S			2.5000	0.1135			5.4800	0.0192 **
Bank level	Bank size: C vs. S	3.7600	0.0524 **	3.9500	0.0470	16.5900	0.0000 ***	13.9300	0.0002 ***
	Bank efficiency: C vs. S	0.5100	0.4771	0.5500	0.4567	2.9100	0.0878 *	2.9200	0.0873 *
	Bank size growth: C vs. S	3.2400	0.0719 *	3.2000	0.0738 *	5.2700	0.0217 **	5.0900	0.0241 **
	Board size: C vs. S	0.1400	0.7108	0.0400	0.8444	0.9500	0.3305	1.0300	0.3111
	Loan growth: C vs. S	28.1800	0.0000 ***	28.1800	0.0000 ***	1.4600	0.2265	1.3600	0.2444
	Claims on MFI: C vs. S	4.4500	0.0348 **	4.6800	0.0305 **	5.0700	0.0243 **	5.0600	0.0245 **
	Claims on non-MFI: C vs. S	0.2400	0.6222	0.2700	0.6034	0.7900	0.3754	1.0700	0.3001

* indicates significance at the 10% level, ** at the 5% level, and *** at the 1% level, respectively.

Appendix IV.6.28: Random-effect regressions with dependent variables RORWA and ROE, Top 150 banks, 5% outlier correction

Variable		RORWA (RE) Financial expertise		RORWA (RE) Out. fin. expertise		ROE (RE) Financial expertise		ROE (RE) Out. fin. expertise	
		Coeff.	SE (robust)	Coeff.	SE (robust)	Coeff.	SE (robust)	Coeff.	SE (robust)
Financial expertise	Financial expertise*C	-0.0002	0.0013			-0.0057	0.0143		
	Out. financial expertise*C			-0.00070	0.0013			-0.0102	0.0136
	Financial expertise*S	0.0025	0.0015*			0.0320	0.0148**		
	Out. financial expertise*S			0.0024	0.0011**			0.0306	0.0110***
Bank level	Savings	-2.3228	1.5546	-2.4137	1.5246	-12.2695	17.0263	-13.6796	16.7380
	Bank size*C	-0.2747	0.0579***	-0.2735	0.0565***	-1.6353	0.6189***	-1.6337	0.6023***
	Bank efficiency*C	-0.0277	0.0035***	-0.0276	0.0035***	-0.3002	0.0347***	-0.2994	0.0347***
	Bank size growth*C	-0.0371	0.0072***	-0.0373	0.0073***	-0.2302	0.0710***	-0.2324	0.0713***
	Loan growth*C	0.0377	0.0038***	0.0378	0.0038***	0.2267	0.0351***	0.2273	0.0351***
	Claims on MFI*C	-0.0113	0.0049**	-0.0112	0.0049**	-0.1520	0.0496***	-0.1516	0.0497***
	Claims on non-MFI*C	-0.0124	0.0031***	-0.0125	0.0031***	-0.0319	0.0327	-0.0330	0.0328
	Board size*C	0.0082	0.0099	0.0077	0.0099	0.1352	0.0992	0.1297	0.1000
	Bank size*S	-0.0642	0.0567	-0.0598	0.0566	-0.2424	0.6472	-0.1870	0.6457
	Bank efficiency*S	-0.0449	0.0039***	-0.0449	0.0038***	-0.4721	0.0436***	-0.4722	0.0433***
	Bank size growth*S	-0.0220	0.0055***	-0.0220	0.0055***	-0.0906	0.0595	-0.0933	0.0594
	Loan growth*S	0.0272	0.0029***	0.0274	0.0029***	0.1178	0.0278***	0.1207	0.0280***
	Claims on MFI*S	-0.0080	0.0043*	-0.0081	0.0043*	-0.0779	0.0448*	-0.0788	0.0449*
	Claims on non-MFI*S	-0.0203	0.0032***	-0.0201	0.0031***	-0.0925	0.0320***	-0.0899	0.0313***
	Board size*S	-0.0191	0.0069***	-0.0179	0.0069***	-0.0938	0.0761	-0.0780	0.0760
Macroeconomic and structural environment	East/West	-0.0172	0.1268	-0.0046	0.1264	0.9329	1.2033	1.0943	1.1936
	GDP per capita	-0.0074	0.0041*	-0.0075	0.0041*	-0.1356	0.0431***	-0.1367	0.0433***
	Population	0.0702	0.0276**	0.0682	0.0279**	0.4186	0.2828	0.3947	0.2875
	constant	9.4332	1.0922***	9.4422	1.0718***	70.5962	11.9407***	70.9067	11.6758***
	Wald Chi^2	877.31	***	875.11	***	613.13	***	613.08	***
	R-sq	0.3226		0.3239		0.2506		0.2528	
	No of observations	1,796		1,796		1,796		1,796	

* indicates significance at the 10% level, ** at the 5% level, and *** at the 1% level, respectively.
Standard errors control for clustering at the bank level.

Appendix IV.6.29: Comparison coefficients with dependent variables RORWA and ROE, Top 150 banks, 5% outlier correction

Variable		RORWA (RE) Financial expertise		RORWA (RE) Out. fin. expertise		ROE (RE) Financial expertise		ROE (RE) Out. fin. expertise	
		chi^2	P>chi^2	chi^2	P>chi^2	chi^2	P>chi^2	chi^2	P>chi^2
Financial expertise	Financial expertise: C vs. S	1.9700	0.1601			3.3800	0.0659 *		
	Out. financial expertise: C vs. S			3.4400	0.0636 *			5.4800	0.0193 **
Bank level	Bank size: C vs. S	8.6300	0.0033 ***	9.3200	0.0023 ***	3.2900	0.0698 *	3.7100	0.0541 *
	Bank efficiency: C vs. S	10.8400	0.0010 ***	10.9900	0.0009 ***	9.7100	0.0018 ***	9.8900	0.0017 ***
	Bank size growth: C vs. S	2.8200	0.0933 *	2.7900	0.0948 *	2.2900	0.1302	2.2700	0.1322
	Board size: C vs. S	5.0900	0.0241 **	4.4700	0.0346 **	3.3400	0.0675 *	2.7200	0.0990 *
	Loan growth: C vs. S	4.8400	0.0279 **	4.6600	0.0310 **	5.9400	0.0148 **	5.6600	0.0170 **
	Claims on MFI: C vs. S	0.2500	0.6155	0.2400	0.6264	1.2100	0.2703	1.1700	0.2801
	Claims on non-MFI: C vs. S	3.7700	0.0523 *	3.5900	0.0581 *	2.0700	0.1498	1.8800	0.1704

* indicates significance at the 10% level, ** at the 5% level, and *** at the 1% level, respectively.

V Bank Performance and Risk: Contest of the Risk Advocate Hypothesis

Abstract

We analyze the impact of ownership concentration on the performance and risk of banks. The results are based on a panel analysis of 400 banks from 44 countries for the period 2004-2008. The results show that ownership concentration negatively affects return on risk-weighted assets. With regard to bank risk, results are not consistent between market-based and accounting-based risk indicators (beta vs. z-score). For lower levels of ownership concentration, large shareholders increase bank beta, whereas for higher levels, the effect inverts. With regard to the z-score, concentrated concentration consistently increases bank risk. Interaction with regulation shows that the impact of regulation on bank performance and risk depends on ownership concentration. Overall, the study shows that ownership concentration is more relevant for bank performance and less for bank risk.

V.1 Introduction

A too short funding horizon, high leverage, and riskiness in pre-crisis returns are among the many root causes of the 2008 banking crisis under discussion in related studies (e.g., Beltratti and Stulz, 2010). Initially, there was no difference in the impact of the crisis between bank business models or ownership types. Among the most severely hit institutions were private as well as public banks. For some banks, the final consequence was bankruptcy, whereas other banks were saved in bailouts through government intervention. Through direct capital injections some governments became major blockholders of banks. However, government investment in banks was not made on the basis of strategic investment considerations. The intention to stabilize the banking system was the rationale behind. First, the government can closely monitor bank management, as this is supposed to increase bank stability. Second, it will result in bank management having more predictability of owners' expectations

In addition to the quantifiable causes, which can be proved with accounting data, further in-depth discussions are also centered around the failure of the governance structures of banks (Kirkpatrick, 2009). Governance-related crisis analysis leads to the fundamental principal agent dilemma, which is the mismatch of interests between shareholders and managers (Jensen and Meckling, 1976). Consequently, the two parties may differ in their views on performance and risk-taking. Beyond the banking crisis, this gives rise to the question whether it is the shareholders or the managers who are responsible for the performance and risk of banks.

With the government being a major shareholder, the questions on banks' risk and performance profiles arise, whether banks with a concentrated ownership structure have a higher risk-adjusted performance, and whether a high degree of ownership concentration increases a bank's riskiness. It is of fundamental importance in economic development that banks take some risks in order to finance corporate and private investments (Kroszner, Laeven, and Klingebiel, 2007; Levine, 2006). Hence, due to banks being large creditors and their significant shareholdings in many countries, they are important in the corporate governance of industrial firms (Caprio, Laeven, and Levine, 2007).

Agency theory proposes that ownership structure has an effect on corporate risk-taking due to the diverging interests of shareholders and managers of firms (Jensen and Meckling, 1976; John, Litov, and Yeung, 2008). Bank management has to strike a balance between the interests of the more risk averse depositors and the more risk prone shareholders. It is for this reason that governance mechanisms that align only the interests of shareholders with those of managers are inappropriate for banks (Mullineux, 2006). Shareholders have an upside potential in risk-taking, whereas depositors only experience the downside potential when the bank cannot meet its obligations anymore. Furthermore, with regard to governance mechanisms, some are particular to banks (Levine, 2004). First, banks are more opaque in the sense that there is greater information asymmetry than at nonfinancial firms. Hence, changes in the risk profiles of banks are not immediately observable. Second, due the importance of banks in economic development, they are more regulated than other industries. Theoretical evidence on the impact of ownership structure on bank risk and performance leads to unequivocal predictions.

A major school of thought in theoretical considerations holds that it is the large shareholders who advocate risk (Esty, 1998; John, Litov, and Yeung, 2008). Shareholders may induce management toward more risk-taking after collecting funds from depositors, consequently shifting risks to them (Galai and Masulis, 1976). The limited liability of shareholders additionally supports the incentive to take risks (Grossman, 2001). At the same time, banks with large shareholders could have a weaker performance than those with dispersed ownership structures. Bank performance may be negatively affected by external ownership, as large shareholders may limit managerial incentives that could worsen bank performance. The reason for this is potential loss of control, as managers fear interference from large shareholders and therefore show less initiative in recommending new investment projects (Burkart, Gromb, and Panunzi, 1997). In effect, the "bargaining problem" between multiple controlling shareholders and minority shareholders could prevent efficient decisions (Gomes and Novaes, 1999).

A contradictory school of thought proposes that banks with dispersed ownership structures have more risk and that controlling shareholders therefore reduce bank risk. This view is based on the assumption that ownership concentration enhances management monitoring, which in turn can reduce bank risk (Berle and Means, 1933). Banks without large shareholders lack efficient and strong management oversight (Shleifer and Vishny, 1986). Hence, large shareholders can improve corporate control and simultaneously lower risk. The question whether performance is affected positively remains unanswered.

Beyond pure theory, the influence that large shareholders can actually exert depends on legal and regulatory restrictions (La Porta, Lopez-de-Silanes, Shleifer, and Vishny, 1998; Saunders, Strock, and Travlos, 1990). The heavy regulations in the banking industry, compared with other industries, is due to the relevance of banks in economic development and the potential to generate systemic risk (Levine, 2004). Intuitively, banks in less regulated countries provide a better playing field for shareholders' interference than do banks in heavily regulated countries, as regulation imposes restrictions on banks in various fields. Therefore, any evaluation of governance mechanisms for banks has to be viewed in the context of the regulatory framework in which the respective bank operates.

Although the main idea of bank regulation is to make banks more stable, various studies show that this goal is only partially achieved, if at all (Barth, Caprio, and Levine, 2004; González, 2005; Kahane, 1977). In the case of capital regulation, it can be argued that stricter capital requirements have, in fact, achieved the opposite (Koehn and Santomero, 1980). In order to fulfill capital requirements in the next period, a bank may be induced to increase risk today and simple capital ratios do not necessarily reduce the riskiness of a bank (Blum, 1999; Kim and Santomero, 1988). In addition, shareholders of well-capitalized banks have the least incentive to increase risk, as the bank then would risk its charter value (Keeley, 1990; Marcus, 1984). Consequently, shareholders of weakly capitalized banks have the greatest incentive to take high risks.

Deposit insurance schemes are a special mechanism to regulate the shareholder-depositor antagonism. As depositors are exposed to the downside risk of a bank, insurance schemes protect them from excessive risk shifting. Especially fixed rate deposit insurance schemes that do not vary with bank risk may add to moral hazard problems as they increase risk shifting incentives for equity holders (John, John, and Senbet, 1991; Kareken and Wallace, 1978). Studies based on the option price theory also indicate this aspect (Merton, 1977; Sharpe, 1977). The scheme is like a put option to equity holders, and increases in value with an increase in asset risk. Hence, value-maximizing investors have an interest in increasing the bank's risk. At the same time, deposit insurance schemes have an adverse effect on management monitoring by depositors, as they create a safety net for depositors. The protection of deposits reduces the incentive for depositors to monitor banks and to discipline bank management (Demirgüç-Kunt and Detragiache, 2002; Levine, 2004; O'Hara and Shaw, 1990). The crisis of American thrift institutions in the 1980s and 1990s was explained by moral hazard problems arising from deposit insurance (Barth, 1991).

Previous studies on these issues have often focused on accounting-based risk measures such as z-scores, non-performing loans ratio, and capital adequacy ratio. However, market-based risk measures have the advantage of timeliness and cleanness (Baele, De Jonghe, and Vander Vennet, 2007; Saunders, Strock, and Travlos, 1990). In addition, a market-based risk measure allows the application of a forward-looking risk metric that is not distorted by differences in accounting practices among countries. The impacts of ownership on market-based vs. accounting-based indicators have hardly been contrasted in previous studies. With regard to performance, asset-based profit ratios are widely used whereas risk-weighted assets are barely used. Instead, the standard deviation is calculated for risk-adjustment. However, performance measures that only consider total assets as the base do not incorporate the different risk profiles of banks.

Our study tries to close this research gap on the impact of ownership concentration on bank performance and risk. For this reason, we focus on two aspects: First, bank performance analysis focuses on banks' individual risk profiles, on the basis of risk-weighted capital, and examines the impact of ownership concentration on risk-adjusted bank performance. For this reason, the primary performance measure is return on risk-weighted assets (RORWA). Second, the impact of ownership concentration on market-based and accounting-based risk measures is comparatively analyzed. Annual beta is applied as a market-based risk measure and is contrasted with z-score, which is used as an accounting-based risk metric. In order to consider changes over time, the analysis uses panel data with a horizon of five years. To account for cross-country differences, regulatory banking sector variables and other country-specific variables are included.

The remainder of this study is structured in the following manner: Chapter V.2 presents relevant related literature. Predictions and findings on the impact of ownership concentration and its effects on bank performance and bank risk in relevant previous studies are compared. Chapter V.3 describes the data and methodology applied. First, the data, definitions, and sources are outlined. Second, the empirical model for the analysis is presented. Chapter V.4 contains the descriptive statistics and regression results. Chapter V.5 concludes the study and evaluates the results, which is also in comparison to other related studies.

V.2 Related Literature

As a result of unequivocal theoretical predictions, the economic importance of banks, and the prominent role of the principal agent theory in corporate governance issues, the relationships among ownership, performance, valuation, and risk have been analyzed from different viewpoints. However, there are still not many studies that focus on ownership, risk-adjusted performance, and bank risk while simultaneously taking regulation into account.

Related studies differ in terms of the following characteristics: ownership focus, risk metrics, and performance measurement. With regard to the first characteristic, some studies focus solely on the proportion of shares held by bank management. This is justified as one can argue that it is the managers who decide on the bank's portfolio and risk-taking, not the shareholders, for example, lending decisions (Gorton and Rosen, 1995). Saunders, Strock, and Travlos (1990) differentiate between management-controlled and shareholder-controlled banks and show that the former exhibit less risk than the latter. Conversely, other studies find that managerial holdings are positively related to risk (Anderson and Fraser, 2000; Sullivan and Spong, 2007). However, as Anderson and Fraser (2000) indicate, these results depend on the level of deregulation. More recently, Gropp and Köhler (2010) focus on the issue of manager- vs. owner-controlled banks in the context of the recent banking crisis and conclude that owner-controlled banks had higher profits before the crisis but also experienced higher losses during the crisis. A study with a more detailed differentiation between ownership types concludes that the type of ownership is significant only for private banks (Barry, Lepetit, and Tarazi, 2011). They report higher stakes by institutional investors and non-financial companies result in more risk-taking.

Other studies consider ownership from a different viewpoint and differentiate not only between stockholders and managers but also between different levels of shareholdings. Iannotta, Nocera, and Sironi (2007) show that higher ownership concentration in European banks is associated with less risk and better loan quality. Return volatility, loan losses, and z-score are used for risk measurement. Profitability does not significantly vary with different ownership concentration levels. Garcia-Marco and Robles-Fernández (2008) confirm these results on the Spanish market only partially. They report that a higher degree of ownership concentration is related to less risk. However, this only holds true for large banks. For small commercial banks, the result is the opposite. Again, the applied risk measure is the z-score. Ownership concentration is measured using Herfindahl's index.

At least three recent studies have a comparable focus to that of the present study, which is the impact of ownership concentration on the performance and risk of global banks taking national regulation into account. Magalhaes, Gutiérrez, and Tribó (2008) conclude that ownership concentration has an effect on bank performance in particular. With regard to risk-taking, they find that there is a relationship between ownership concentration and risk-taking only in small banks. Earnings volatility and z-score were used for risk measurement, and the ratio of return on assets (ROA) to the standard deviation of ROA was used for risk-adjusted performance. Ownership concentration was measured via the equity stake of the largest shareholder. Laeven and Levine (2009) find that banks with a concentrated ownership tend to be more risky than banks with dispersed ownership structures. They also show that the impact of regulation on bank risk-taking varies according to the ownership structure of the bank. In contrast to Magalhaes, Gutiérrez, and Tribó (2008), Laeven and Levine's (2009) results hold for all sizes of banks in their sample. Ownership structure is measured via ownership level thresholds of 10% and 20%. For risk measurement, z-scores calculated over a six-year window are used. For the robustness test, equity volatility was applied as a market-based risk measure. In order to control for different country regulations on banks, indices such as capital stringency, activity restrictions, and deposit insurance scheme are applied. Furthermore, they control for country influences such as economic development as well as for ownership restrictions and shareholder protection. Shehzad, de Haan, and Scholtens (2010) analyze the effect of ownership concentration on bank risk, which is measured via non-performing loans and the capital adequacy ratio. They conclude that tight ownership reduces the non-performing loans ratio (NPL ratio), conditional on supervisory control and shareholder protection rights. In addition, it improves a bank's capital adequacy ratio, conditional on shareholder protection rights. In contrast to Laeven and Levine (2009), the three thresholds of ownership by the largest owner are 10%, 25%, and 50%, and these thresholds allow for differentiating between different levels of holdings.

Summing up, the three studies show contradictory results. With regard to the two main theoretical strands, Laeven and Levine (2009) and Magalhaes, Gutiérrez, and Tribó (2008) find that tight ownership results in more risk-taking.

On the other hand, Shehzad, de Haan, and Scholtens (2010) observe an increase in ownership concentration which leads to lower bank risk. Two of these studies focus solely on the relationship between ownership and risk-taking, Magalhaes, Gutiérrez, and Tribó (2008) include the performance aspect as well. Moreover, all three studies mainly focus on accounting-based risk measures. Risk-weighted assets to proxy a bank's risk profile are left out in all three studies. With regard to methodology, only Magalhaes, Gutiérrez, and Tribó (2008) conduct a panel analysis to consider changes over time from 2000-2006.

V.3 Data and Methodology

V.3.1 Sample and Data

The present study is based on a balanced panel with 400 exchange-listed banks from 44 countries, encompassing the years 2004-2008. Crisis-related changes in banks' ownership structure mainly took place at the end of 2008 and in 2009. For this reason, the years 2007 and 2008 are included in the analysis although the crisis had already begun. The final sample includes 400 banks, resulting in 2,000 observations per variable. Due to data limitations for the risk-adjusted performance measure, only 802 observations were available, thereby resulting in an unbalanced panel. The selection of banks is begun by ranking banks by size. First, data on 867 banks from 52 countries are collected. Second, only banks for which ownership, Balance sheet, and Profit & Loss statement data are available through the years 2004-2008 are used. Third, banks in which the three largest shareholders own over 80% of the bank's shares are excluded from the analysis. If this is not done, the tradable volumes would distort the market-based risk measure that we use. Of the remaining banks, the largest 400 banks are selected. The average total assets are USD 99.8 billion. The smallest bank in the sample has average total assets of USD 1.1 billion, and the largest bank has average total assets of USD 1,993.3 billion.

Overall, four dependent variables are used. The primary performance measure is RORWA. Robustness is tested with ROA. On the risk side, annual beta is the primary risk measure. Z-score is used as accounting-based measure for the purpose of robustness.

Balance sheet and Profit & Loss statement data come from the Thomson Reuters Knowledge database. Data on historic annual beta is taken from the Bloomberg database. The data source for bank ownership structures is Thomson ONE Banker. Further data was collected manually from annual reports. Data for the sector level and country level control variables comes from various sources.

The regulation control variables are built on the basis of the 2003 and 2008 regulation surveys (Barth, Caprio, and Levine, 2004, 2008). National banking sector data comes from the Financial Structure Dataset (Beck and Demirgüç-Kunt, 2009). The governance indicators are from the Aggregate Governance Indicators (Kaufmann, Kraay, and Mastruzzi, 2009). The economic data are from the World Development Indicators (World Bank, 2010).

V.3.2   Ownership Concentration

Unlike most previous related studies, the proportion of shares held by the three largest shareholders (*CR3*) is examined. This allows to analyze ownership concentration as well, instead of only focusing on the largest shareholder. In addition, a group of the largest shareholders of a bank may collude and exert more power than a single shareholder. The use of the *CR3* as an ownership measure follows previous studies (e.g., La Porta, Lopez-de-Silanes, Shleifer, and Vishny, 1998). *CR3* is defined as:

$$CR3_{it} = \sum_{j=1}^{3} os_{jt} \qquad (V.1)$$

where os_{jt} is the ownership share of shareholder j of bank i at time t. For robustness reasons, we measure CR3 in two ways. For the first regression analyses, the ownership concentration threshold is defined at 20%. If the *CR3* of a bank exceeds 20%, a binary variable value of 1 is assigned. For the second regression, the ownership concentration threshold is defined at 50%. Again, if the *CR3* of a bank exceeds 50%, a binary variable value of 1 is assigned.

V.3.3   Risk-Adjusted Performance and Risk

For risk-adjusted performance, risk-weighted assets are used as the base. This allows the consideration of each bank's risk profile and changes to this profile over time. RORWA is defined as profit before tax divided by average risk-weighted assets. Risk-weighted assets include an adjustment for risk as they are weighted for credit and market risks. ROA is the second applied performance measure. It is defined as profit before tax divided by average total assets. Higher values for both measures indicate better performance.

The primary measure of risk is historic annual beta[19], as this is a relevant indicator from the diversified investor's perspective (Amihud and Lev, 1981). For the beta calculation, the respective national stock index was used. A higher beta indicates higher systematic risk from an investor's perspective. The second risk measure is the z-score, which is based on accounting data; this is a measure of bank stability and indicates a bank's default risk (Boyd and Runkle, 1993). The calculation of the probability of insolvency (z-score) follows that of Laeven and Levine (2009). Insolvency is defined as the state in which a bank's capital is not sufficient to absorb losses. The z-score indicates the distance to default (Roy, 1952). Accordingly, the probability of insolvency is defined as prob(-ROA<CAR). ROA is the return on assets and CAR is the capital assets ratio. Based on the assumption that profits are normally distributed, the probability of insolvency is (ROA+CAR)/σ(ROA), where σ(ROA) is the standard deviation of ROA. The standard deviation for z-scores is calculated over a five-year moving window. A higher z-value indicates a more stable bank. The z-score allows for consideration of the returns situation as well as the capital adequacy for absorbing losses.

V.3.4   Control Variables

The empirical model controls for bank-level, sector-level and country-level characteristics. To take into account for these different aspects, various data sources are used. On the bank-level, bank size, growth, efficiency, and capitalization are controlled. Data for all bank specific variables come from the Reuters Knowledge database. Previous studies have indicated that bank size has an ambiguous effect on stability, ranging from positive to negative effects (Boyd and Runkle, 1993; De Nicolo, 2000). With regard to efficiency, more efficient banks tend to be more stable and should therefore display less risk (Wheelock and Wilson, 2000). Higher efficiency is indicated by a lower cost-income ratio (CIR).

Due to differences in regulations and the structure of the financial sector among countries, there are seven sector-level control variables. More specifically, sector control variables comprise audit and disclosure requirements,

---

19   Beta is defined as $\beta_i = \dfrac{Cov(R_i, R_m)}{\sigma^2(R_m)}$, where $Cov(R_i, R_m)$ is the covariance between the

return on asset i and the return on the market and $\sigma^2(R_m)$ is the variance of the market

(Ross, Westefield, and Jaffe, 2003).

authorities' power, bank activities restrictions, capital regulation, deposit insurance requirements, ownership limitation, and concentration of the banking sector. The sector level variables on regulation come from the surveys retrieved from the World Bank Web site (Barth, Caprio, and Levine, 2004, 2008). The banking sector concentration data comes from the World Bank Financial Structure Dataset (Beck and Demirgüç-Kunt, 2009). The banking sector concentration ratio and the ownership limitation regulation are straightforward. The other variables are indices generated on the basis of the survey data. For details on the regulation indices, see Appendix V.6.1.

Since countries differ in their economic development stages and in their political and legal systems, political stability, legal certainty (rule of law), Gross Domestic Product (GDP) per capita, and stock market development are controlled at the country level. The first two are sourced from Aggregate Governance Indicators (Kaufmann, Kraay, and Mastruzzi, 2009). The latter two are taken from the World Bank database on World Development Indicators (World Bank, 2010).

Table V.1:   Definition of control variables and sources.

Bank level control variables	Description	Source
a. Bank size	Ln of total assets	Thomson Reuters Knowledge
b. Bank growth	Year-on-year change in total assets	Thomson Reuters Knowledge
c. Bank efficiency	Operating expenses divided by net interest and non-interest income (CIR)	Thomson Reuters Knowledge
d. Bank capitalization	Total Equity divided by total assets	Thomson Reuters Knowledge
Sector level control variables		
e. Audit and disclosure	Index based on World Bank regulation survey	Barth, Caprio, and Levine (2004), Barth, Caprio, and Levine (2008)
f. Authorities power	Index based on World Bank regulation survey	Barth, Caprio, and Levine (2004), Barth, Caprio, and Levine (2008)
g. Bank activities	Index based on World Bank regulation survey	Barth, Caprio, and Levine (2004), Barth, Caprio, and Levine (2008)
h. Capital	Index based on World Bank regulation survey	Barth, Caprio, and Levine (2004), Barth, Caprio, and Levine (2008)
i. Deposit insurance	Index based on World Bank regulation survey	Barth, Caprio, and Levine (2004), Barth, Caprio, and Levine (2008)
j. Ownership limitation	Binary variable based on World Bank regulation survey	Barth, Caprio, and Levine (2004), Barth, Caprio, and Levine (2008)
k. Sector CR3	Share in total assets of largest three banks (CR3)	Beck and Demirgüç-Kunt (2009)
Country level control variables		
l. Economic strength	GDP per capita in USD at current prices	World Bank (2010)
m. Political stability	Index	Kaufmann, Kraay, and Mastruzzi (2009)
n. Rule of law	Index	Kaufmann, Kraay, and Mastruzzi (2009)
o. Stock market development	Stock market capitalization divided by GDP	World Bank (2010)

V.3.5 Model

In order to capture as much information as possible, the methodology applied in our examination is based on panel data analysis. This allows the evaluation of differences among banks as well as of developments over time. First, a random-effect model is estimated. Since many control variables such as regulation indices are constant over time in many countries, a regulation fixed-effect model is also estimated in order to isolate effects in development over time at individual banks. A regression model of the following form is applied:

$$DV_{it} = \alpha + \beta OC_{it} + \gamma B_{it} + \delta S_{it} + \tau C_{it} + \varepsilon_{it} \qquad (V.2)$$

where DV is the dependent variable (beta, z-score, RORWA, ROA), OC is ownership concentration, B comprises bank-level control variables, S sector-level control variables, and C country-level control variables, respectively. ε is the error term. B comprises the following bank variables: (a) bank size, (b) bank growth, (c) bank efficiency, and (d) bank capitalization. Vector S comprises the following sector control variables: (e) audit and disclosure index, (f) authorities power index, (g) bank activities index, (h) capital regulation index, (i) deposit insurance index (j) ownership limitation, and (k) sector concentration ratio CR3. Vector C includes the following country control variables: (l) economic strength, (m) political stability index, (n) rule of law index, and (o) stock market development. For the fixed-effect regression, z_t for time effects is added to the above equation (Schröder, 2007).

V.4 Results

V.4.1 Summary Statistics

The banks in our sample show a wide variation in performance as well as in risk. To a certain extent, the huge gap in profitability between minimum and maximum value can be attributed to the banking crisis. The crisis led to huge performance gaps in 2008 that divided banks and pushed some banks to the lowest bounds. RORWA and ROA have coefficients of variation of 190% and 119%, respectively. RORWA ranges from -42.80% to 46.81% and ROA from -14.64% to 23.58%, respectively. Remarkably, the mean value for beta is below 1.0, which implies that the banks included in the sample were considered less risky on average than the stock market in their respective countries. The beta values range from -0.76 to 3.32. Through the standard deviation of 0.46, the beta coefficient of variation results in 53%. The second risk measure z-score shows a larger dispersion, with a coefficient of variation of 104%.

In terms of ownership concentration, the largest three owners hold, on average, less than 25%. Of the banks encompassed, 40% have a CR3 above 20% and 15% have a CR3 above 50%. Regulation indices reveal significant differences among countries. The values of the regulation indices range from absolute minimum to maximum values. Country statistics show large differences. Countries with risky banks in terms of beta are not the same as those that have the most risky banks in terms of z-score. The cross-country comparison also shows that countries with more risky banks are not the same as those with the highest performances. At first sight, this indicates that banks in these countries are not compensated for their risk-taking at least on a short horizon. For details on the cross-country comparison, see Appendix V.6.2.

Table V.2:   Summary statistics.

Dependent variables	Observations	Mean	Std. Dev.	Coeff. of Variation	Min	Max
RORWA (%)	802	3.66	6.95	189.73	-42.80	46.81
ROA (%)	2,000	1.25	1.49	119.31	-14.64	23.58
Beta	2,000	0.88	0.46	52.57	-0.76	3.32
z-score	2,000	40.89	42.72	104.47	-0.96	630.11
Bank level variables						
CR3 (20% Threshold)	2,000	0.40	0.49	123.79	0.00	1.00
CR3 (50% Threshold)	2,000	0.15	0.36	238.11	0.00	1.00
CR3 stake (%)	2,000	23.43	19.89	84.90	0.10	80.00
Bank size (ln '000 USD)	2,000	7.23	0.74	10.24	5.85	9.55
Bank growth (%)	2,000	13.86	18.96	136.79	-86.46	178.87
Bank efficiency (%)	2,000	63.58	25.65	40.34	19.20	752.64
Bank capitalization (%)	2,000	7.88	4.13	52.42	1.39	45.92
Sector level variables						
Activities index	2,000	10.24	1.99	19.40	4.00	16.00
Audit and disclosure index	2,000	8.82	0.78	8.88	7.00	11.00
Authorities index	2,000	5.48	1.44	26.35	1.00	7.00
Capital index	2,000	4.07	1.22	29.98	2.00	6.00
Deposit insurance index	2,000	4.06	1.77	43.68	0.00	6.00
Ownership limitation	2,000	0.15	0.36	234.89	0.00	1.00
Sector CR3 (%)	2,000	48.64	20.83	42.83	14.01	100.00
Country level variables						
Rule of law	2,000	1.23	0.63	51.11	-0.95	2.04
GDP per capita (USD)	2,000	33,723	15,911	47.18	644	94,759
Political stability index	2,000	0.47	0.62	132.75	-2.61	1.60
Stock market development (%)	2,000	114.16	66.92	58.62	14.28	561.44

Development over time shows a downward trend of RORWA. The mean value dropped from 4.46% in 2005 to 3.86% in 2007, before a sharper drop to 1.71% in 2008. The ROA numbers confirm this. Further, development over time shows that capital markets anticipated rising risk during the period 2004-2008. The average beta rose from 0.69 in 2004 to 0.95 in 2008. This finding is in line with previous studies, in which market-based risk measures are used because of more timeliness and less accounting distortion (Baele, De Jonghe, and Vander

Vennet, 2007). In contrast to bank beta, the accounting-based z-score did not indicate any change in bank risk before 2008. Taking into account that the financial crisis begun in 2007 and worsened in 2008, beta development reflected bank risk more accurately than did the z-score. Bank capitalization did not change significantly, either.

Following the constantly improving GDP per capita over time, total bank assets grew steadily until 2007. At the same time, bank efficiency remained stable before the crisis in 2008; however, CIR increased by almost 10 percentage points from 2007 to 2008. The ownership concentration rose slowly but steadily, from 21.19% in 2004 to 25.62% in 2008. Bank ownership structures tightened slightly from 2004 to 2008. On average, approximately 25% was held by the largest three owners in 2008. The same applies to sector concentration. Compared to 2004, in 2008, approximately eight more percentage points of total sector assets were held by the largest three banks. Since the 2003 regulation survey was used for the year 2004, and since the 2008 update was used for the following years, there is a change only between 2004 and 2005.

Table V.3:   Development over time from 2004-2008 (mean values).

Dependent Variables	2008	2007	2006	2005	2004	Trend[1]
RORWA (%)	1.71	3.86	4.21	4.46	4.19	↓
ROA (%)	0.65	1.34	1.43	1.45	1.40	↓
Beta	0.95	0.97	0.92	0.85	0.69	↑
z-score	32.15	43.07	44.78	43.12	41.33	↓
Bank level						
CR3 (20% Threshold)	0.43	0.44	0.39	0.37	0.34	↑
CR3 (50% Threshold)	0.17	0.16	0.14	0.15	0.14	↑
CR3 stake (%)	25.62	25.14	22.93	22.27	21.19	↑
Bank size (ln '000 USD)	7.33	7.28	7.22	7.18	7.13	→
Bank growth (%)	11.52	16.05	13.64	10.35	17.73	↓
Bank efficiency (%)	71.19	61.91	60.78	60.81	63.22	↑
Bank capitalization (%)	7.93	8.00	7.83	7.78	7.87	→
Sector level						
Activities index	10.27	10.27	10.27	10.27	10.13	n/a[2]
Auditing and disclosure index	8.78	8.78	8.78	8.78	8.99	n/a[2]
Authorities index	5.47	5.47	5.47	5.47	5.49	n/a[2]
Capital index	4.32	4.32	4.32	4.32	3.08	n/a[2]
Deposit insurance index	4.06	4.06	4.06	4.06	4.07	n/a[2]
Ownership limitation	0.16	0.16	0.16	0.16	0.15	n/a[2]
Sector CR3 (%)	54.06	50.00	46.46	46.41	46.29	↑
Country level						
Rule of law	1.28	1.23	1.23	1.21	1.20	↑
GDP per capita (USD)	37,585	35,346	33,214	31,914	30,559	↑
Political stability index	0.54	0.47	0.52	0.39	0.41	↑
Stock market development (%)	72.52	139.70	132.22	116.00	110.36	↓

1) A compounded annual upward or downward change by more than 1% is indicated by ↑ or ↓, respectively. A change of less than 1% is indicated by →.
2) Regulation surveys only changed between 2004 and 2005.

To analyze financial institutions by size, banks are divided into four clusters, with 100 banks in each cluster. Hence, Cluster 1 contains the largest 100 banks of the sample and Cluster 4 the smallest 100, respectively. In terms of profitability, the largest banks show the smallest average RORWA. However, this is not clearly confirmed by ROA, as the largest banks here display less profitability than the smallest banks; however, the clusters in between show an even weaker performance. Further, larger banks are not only less profitable but also more risky than smaller banks. This finding is supported by both risk measures. Comparably weak capitalization further underlines this finding. Obviously, bank size does not affect ownership concentration. There is no remarkable difference between large and small banks. For significance levels of the size cluster comparison see Appendix V.6.4.

Table V.4:   Banks clustered by size.

Dependent variables	Cluster 1	Cluster 2	Cluster 3	Cluster 4	Delta Cluster 1-4
RORWA (%)	2.14	2.36	3.92	11.00	-8.86
ROA (%)	1.19	1.01	1.13	1.67	-0.48
Beta	0.98	0.86	0.78	0.89	0.09
z-score	31.22	38.10	42.19	52.06	-20.84
Bank level variables					
CR3 (20% Threshold)	0.37	0.44	0.35	0.42	-0.05
CR3 (50% Threshold)	0.14	0.24	0.16	0.06	0.08
CR3 stake (%)	22.38	28.07	22.84	20.44	1.94
Bank size (ln '000 USD)	8.24	7.36	6.93	6.38	1.86
Bank growth (%)	18.26	12.12	12.12	12.93	5.33
Bank efficiency (%)	62.64	63.93	65.65	62.11	0.53
Bank capitalization (%)	6.09	6.71	8.83	9.90	-3.81

Since previous studies have emphasized the importance of regulation (Laeven and Levine, 2009; Saunders, Strock, and Travlos, 1990), the banks analyzed in our study are also clustered by regulation. The five regulation indices and the binary variable on ownership restriction are added up to a total regulation index. Following this, the range between minimum and maximum total regulation is divided into four clusters. This results in unbalanced clusters, with 176 banks in Cluster 1, 118 banks in Cluster 2, 63 banks in Cluster 3, and 43 banks in Cluster 4.

As performance measures show, heavily regulated banks do not suffer inferior returns. The average RORWA is higher for strongly regulated banks than for less regulated banks. This finding is confirmed by the ROA comparison between Clusters 1 and 4. Cluster 1, which includes banks with the strongest regulation, has the highest average beta. This implies that capital markets view banks, which operate in a strongly regulated environment, as more risky than banks in less restricted countries. However, from an accounting viewpoint, banks with stricter regulation have a lower risk of insolvency. In addition, heavily regulated banks fulfill capital requirements, as they have a clearly higher equity-to-total-assets ratio (capitalization). From an accounting viewpoint, regulation achieves its goals but capital markets obviously do not follow this judgment. The differentiation along the level of regulation shows that less regulated banks have a much higher ownership concentration than do strongly regulated banks. This is of relevance, as regulation determines the extent to which shareholders can interfere (Saunders, Strock, and Travlos, 1990). For significance levels of the regulation cluster comparison see Appendix V.6.5.

Table V.5:   Banks clustered by regulation.

Dependent variables	Cluster 1	Cluster 2	Cluster 3	Cluster 4	Delta Cluster 1-4
RORWA (%)	6.04	2.34	1.92	2.14	3.90
ROA (%)	1.32	0.99	1.54	1.25	0.07
Beta	0.96	0.91	0.60	0.86	0.10
z-score	49.89	29.26	41.42	35.19	14.70
Bank level variables					
CR3 (20% Threshold)	0.42	0.26	0.47	0.55	-0.13
CR3 (50% Threshold)	0.06	0.15	0.23	0.37	-0.31
CR3 stake (%)	21.23	20.47	27.17	35.07	-13.84
Bank size (ln '000 USD)	6.87	7.31	7.69	7.76	-0.89
Bank growth (%)	11.46	13.62	17.14	19.52	-8.06
Bank efficiency (%)	62.68	66.84	62.29	60.23	2.45
Bank capitalization (%)	9.61	6.16	7.00	6.86	2.75

Summary statistics show that in the years before the financial crisis, there was weakening profitability and increasing risk, as indicated by RORWA and beta. However, the bank default risk (z-score) did not indicate such trends or any worsening of the situation of banks. The differentiation by size shows that larger banks have higher risk and lower profitability. Regulation does not lead to clear results. In strongly regulated countries, banks' profitability is higher and default risk is lower. However, capital markets arrive at different conclusions. Beta is higher for banks in heavily regulated countries than for banks in less regulated countries.

V.4.2   Regression Results

The regression results show that risk-adjusted performance is negatively related to ownership concentration (see Table V.6). This holds for both levels of ownership concentration. Although the negative impact of ownership concentration decreases for higher levels, the relationship remains negative. This finding is consistent with the theory of Burkart, Gromb, and Panunzi (1997), who suggest that shareholder interference might negatively affect bank performance. In addition, the bargaining problem between multiple large shareholders, which is outlined by Gomes and Novaes (1999), can adversely affect bank performance. However, beyond certain thresholds, the problems between multiple shareholders are obviously resolved, since the impact is less for higher levels of ownership concentration. This general result on performance is confirmed by the ROA regressions (see Table V.7). Again, the negative effect of ownership concentration diminishes with higher threshold levels. These findings are contrary to those of Iannotta, Nocera, and Sironi (2007), who find no significant relationship between ownership structure and bank performance. However, the results are similar to those of Magalhaes, Gutiérrez, and Tribó (2008), who find the same for intermediate ownership levels.

With regard to risk, the results differ according to market-based and accounting-based risk measures. For the lower cutoff point, ownership concentration increases beta, whereas, for higher ownership levels, the sign changes and ownership concentration reduces risk (see Table V.8). Shehzad, de Haan, and Scholtens (2010) find a similar pattern with non-performing loans as a risk measure. In contrast, increasing ownership concentration consistently increases accounting-based bank risk when measured with z-score (see Table V.9). For higher levels of ownership concentration, the effect becomes even more pronounced. The results of the z-score regressions confirm the findings of Laeven and Levine (2009), who find that a concentrated ownership structure increases bank risk.

All regression models are significant at the 1% level, as indicated by the Wald chi-square value for random-effect regressions and by the F-test for fixed-effect regressions. The overall result shows that ownership concentration is negatively related to risk-adjusted performance; this is confirmed by the regression with the CR3 20% cutoff point for ownership concentration as well as by the regression with the CR3 50% cutoff point (see Table V.6). However, the effect on RORWA is less at the 50% cutoff point than at the CR3 20% cutoff point. All ownership coefficients of the random-effect model are significant at the 1% level. The regression with a fixed-effect model confirms the results. Again, the coefficients with the CR3 20% threshold and the CR3 50% threshold are significant at the 1% and 5% levels, respectively.

Table V.6: *Random-effect and fixed-effect regressions with dependent variable RORWA.*

Variable		RORWA (RE) CR3 20% Coeff.	SE (robust)	RORWA (RE) CR3 50% Coeff.	SE (robust)	RORWA (FE) CR3 20% Coeff.	SE (robust)	RORWA (FE) CR3 50% Coeff.	SE (robust)
Ownership	CR3 Threshold 20	-2.1964	0.7565 ***			-2.2909	0.8569 ***		
	CR3 Threshold 50			-0.9050	0.3337 ***			-0.8047	0.3182 **
Bank level	Bank size	-2.4580	0.4810 ***	-2.3011	0.4674 ***	-3.5535	1.9144 *	-4.1629	2.0506 **
	Bank size growth	0.0073	0.0050	0.0084	0.0050 *	0.0095	0.0049 *	0.0098	0.0047 **
	Bank efficiency	-0.0255	0.0100 **	-0.0261	0.0104 **	-0.0270	0.0103 ***	-0.0281	0.0110 **
	Bank capitalization	-0.2606	0.1106 **	-0.2498	0.1138 **	-0.4890	0.1799 ***	-0.5128	0.1925 ***
Sector level	Activities	-0.2272	0.0975 **	-0.1861	0.0919 **	-0.0978	0.1333	-0.0485	0.1221
	Capital	-0.2027	0.1272	-0.2618	0.1278 **	-0.1623	0.1318	-0.2311	0.1235 *
	Audit and disclosure	-0.0102	0.1627	0.0090	0.1563	0.0617	0.1858	0.0513	0.1876
	Authorities	-0.1827	0.1351	-0.1673	0.1348	-0.1446	0.1432	-0.1080	0.1317
	Deposit	0.5395	0.1527 ***	0.5477	0.1509 ***	0.1430	0.1336	0.1485	0.0892 *
	Ownership	-1.1454	0.6996	-1.2640	0.6609 *	1.7556	0.8399 **	0.8831	0.6755
	Sector CR3	-0.0369	0.0120 ***	-0.0437	0.0118 ***	0.0019	0.0204	0.0012	0.0207
Country level	Stock market development	0.0166	0.0042 ***	0.0158	0.0040 ***	0.0124	0.0033 ***	0.0117	0.0030 ***
	Economic strength	0.0000	0.0000 ***	0.0000	0.0000 ***	0.0000	0.0000	0.0000	0.0000
	Political stability	-3.9043	0.8416 ***	-3.8388	0.8415 ***	-3.8283	1.3072 ***	-3.8034	1.3451 ***
	Rule of law	1.3432	0.8036 *	1.4945	0.8032 *	-6.1633	2.1890 ***	-6.3409	2.2744 ***
	constant	28.3838	5.0602 ***	26.1746	4.6761 ***	44.8714	14.0911 ***	48.8350	15.0694 ***
	Wald chi²	77.02	***	78.40	***	--		--	
	F-Test	--		--		3.55	***	3.33	***
	R-sq	0.2704		0.2679		0.0191		0.0230	
	No of observations	802		802		802		802	

* indicates significance at the 10% level, ** at the 5% level, and *** at the 1% level, respectively.
Standard errors control for clustering at the bank level.

The signs of the coefficients of the ROA regression confirm the findings of the RORWA regression (see Table V.7). However, in contrast to the RORWA regressions, the coefficients are not significant at the 10% level or higher. For higher ownership concentration levels, the effect also decreases, as shown with RORWA. In the case of the fixed-effect model, even the sign for the higher threshold changes.

Table V.7: *Random-effect and fixed-effect regressions with dependent variable ROA.*

Variable		ROA (RE) CR3 20%		ROA (RE) CR3 50%		ROA (FE) CR3 20%		ROA (FE) CR3 50%	
		Coeff.	SE (robust)	Coeff.	SE (robust)	Coeff.	SE (robust)	Coeff.	SE (robust)
Ownership	CR3 Threshold 20	-0.1335	0.0915			-0.0655	0.0996		
	CR3 Threshold 50			-0.1033	0.0963			0.0657	0.0730
Bank level	Bank size	-0.1792	0.0770 **	-0.1761	0.0759 **	-1.7549	0.4657 ***	-1.8004	0.4898 ***
	Bank size growth	0.0018	0.0021	0.0018	0.0022	0.0011	0.0022	0.0011	0.0022
	Bank efficiency	-0.0199	0.0086 **	-0.0199	0.0087 **	-0.0196	0.0086 **	-0.0197	0.0086 **
	Bank capitalization	0.1013	0.0468 **	0.1021	0.0473 **	0.0649	0.0219 ***	0.0648	0.0220 ***
Sector level	Activities	-0.0502	0.0197 **	-0.0502	0.0194 ***	-0.0372	0.0338	-0.0374	0.0334
	Capital	-0.0827	0.0229 ***	-0.0863	0.0237 ***	-0.0197	0.0254	-0.0233	0.0259
	Audit and disclosure	-0.0397	0.0376	-0.0412	0.0380	-0.0373	0.0460	-0.0433	0.0462
	Authorities	-0.0654	0.0332 **	-0.0641	0.0331 *	0.0569	0.0509	0.0568	0.0507
	Deposit	-0.0390	0.0411	-0.0438	0.0432	0.0690	0.0301 **	0.0670	0.0293 **
	Ownership	-0.2488	0.1246 **	-0.2522	0.1251 **	0.2504	0.2985	0.2454	0.3001
	Sector CR3	0.0014	0.0033	0.0010	0.0033	0.0011	0.0046	0.0009	0.0046
Country level	Stock market development	0.0043	0.0010 ***	0.0042	0.0010 ***	0.0039	0.0010 ***	0.0039	0.0010 ***
	Economic strength	0.0000	0.0000	0.0000	0.0000	0.0000	0.0000 *	0.0000	0.0000 *
	Political stability	-0.5800	0.1207 ***	-0.5701	0.1208 ***	-0.8733	0.1681 ***	-0.8630	0.1671 ***
	Rule of law	-0.2010	0.1635	-0.2051	0.1640	-0.8674	0.4706 *	-0.8532	0.4726 *
	constant	4.7287	1.0639 ***	4.7311	1.0627 ***	15.1471	2.9994 ***	15.4905	3.1628 ***
	Wald chi^2	444.79	***	443.93	***	--		--	
	F-Test	--		--		21.25	***	20.73	***
	R-sq	0.4311		0.4313		0.1744		0.1710	
	No of observations	2,000		2,000		2,000		2,000	

* indicates significance at the 10% level, ** at the 5% level, and *** at the 1% level, respectively.
Standard errors control for clustering at the bank level.

Regressions on beta show mixed results (see Table V.8). Initially, the relationship is positive. However, this relation becomes negative with an increase in ownership concentration. At lower levels of ownership concentration (CR3 20% threshold), beta is positively associated with ownership. However, at the CR3 50% threshold level, ownership concentration is negatively associated with bank risk. This implies that the impact of ownership structure on bank risk depends on the ownership level. At higher levels of concentration, ownership reduces bank risk. The ownership coefficients fail to show significance at the 10% level or over. Shehzad, de Haan, and Scholtens (2010) also find changing signs with regard to risk measured with non-performing loans.

Table V.8: Random-effect and fixed-effect regressions with dependent variable beta.

Variable		beta (RE) CR3 20%		beta (RE) CR3 50%		beta (FE) CR3 20%		beta (FE) CR3 50%	
		Coeff.	SE (robust)	Coeff.	SE (robust)	Coeff.	SE (robust)	Coeff.	SE (robust)
Ownership	CR3 Threshold 20	0.0185	0.0258			0.0052	0.0318		
	CR3 Threshold 50			-0.0530	0.0415			-0.0422	0.0555
Bank level	Bank size	0.1858	0.0261 ***	0.1848	0.0261 ***	0.2958	0.0970 ***	0.3082	0.0984 ***
	Bank size growth	-0.0011	0.0004 **	-0.0011	0.0004 ***	-0.0012	0.0004 ***	-0.0012	0.0004 ***
	Bank efficiency	0.0003	0.0002	0.0003	0.0002	0.0003	0.0002	0.0003	0.0002
	Bank capitalization	0.0033	0.0037	0.0032	0.0037	-0.0038	0.0091	-0.0038	0.0092
Sector level	Activities	0.0160	0.0075 **	0.0164	0.0075 **	0.0110	0.0174	0.0116	0.0175
	Capital	0.0711	0.0099 ***	0.0726	0.0100 ***	0.0508	0.0140 ***	0.0518	0.0140 ***
	Audit and disclosure	-0.0797	0.0179 ***	-0.0777	0.0179 ***	-0.0617	0.0288 **	-0.0594	0.0286 **
	Authorities	0.0721	0.0109 ***	0.0705	0.0112 ***	0.0899	0.0278 ***	0.0896	0.0277 ***
	Deposit	-0.0194	0.0118	-0.0200	0.0117 *	-0.0988	0.0212 ***	-0.0984	0.0212 ***
	Ownership	-0.0262	0.0382	-0.0379	0.0398	-0.0125	0.1052	-0.0158	0.1050
	Sector CR3	-0.0023	0.0008 ***	-0.0020	0.0008 **	-0.0017	0.0015	-0.0017	0.0015
Country level	Stock market development	-0.0007	0.0002 ***	-0.0007	0.0002 ***	0.0003	0.0002	0.0003	0.0002
	Economic strength	0.0000	0.0000	0.0000	0.0000	0.0000	0.0000 **	0.0000	0.0000 *
	Political stability	-0.0509	0.0301 *	-0.0545	0.0304 *	0.0349	0.0640	0.0311	0.0637
	Rule of law	-0.0309	0.0465	-0.0298	0.0464	0.8463	0.1853 ***	0.8401	0.1855 ***
	constant	-0.2890	0.3180	-0.2905	0.3191	-2.2971	0.7279 ***	-2.3958	0.7339 ***
	Wald chi^2	285.57	***	285.26	***	--		--	
	F-Test	--		--		14.14	***	14.14	***
	R-sq	0.1565		0.1566		0.0001		0.0000	
	No of observations	2,000		2,000		2,000		2,000	

* indicates significance at the 10% level, ** at the 5% level, and *** at the 1% level, respectively.
Standard errors control for clustering at the bank level.

The regression with the accounting-based risk measure z-score shows a negative relationship between ownership concentration and bank risk (see Table V.9). The effect remains the same regardless of the cutoff point for the CR3 threshold. The regression with the fixed-effect model confirms the results of the random-effect model. However, in the case of the fixed-effect model, the ownership coefficients are significant at the 10% level for the CR3 20% threshold and at the 5% level for the CR3 50% threshold.

Table V.9: *Random-effect and fixed-effect regressions with dependent variable z-score.*

Variable		z-score (RE) CR3 20%		z-score (RE) CR3 50%		z-score (FE) CR3 20%		z-score (FE) CR3 50%	
		Coeff.	SE (robust)	Coeff.	SE (robust)	Coeff.	SE (robust)	Coeff.	SE (robust)
Ownership	CR3 Threshold 20	-3.5136	2.4048			-4.9156	2.8123*		
	CR3 Threshold 50			-4.1715	3.6492			-12.2038	5.3189**
Bank level	Bank size	-4.6789	1.9255**	-4.5808	1.9420**	-4.1589	10.2187	-3.5208	10.3986
	Bank size growth	-0.0255	0.0316	-0.0246	0.0315	-0.0111	0.0329	-0.0100	0.0325
	Bank efficiency	-0.1000	0.0378***	-0.1004	0.0382***	-0.0705	0.0355**	-0.0724	0.0363**
	Bank capitalization	1.2253	0.5387**	1.2466	0.5427**	3.0791	1.0051***	3.0990	1.0026***
Sector level	Activities	0.4450	0.7269	0.4167	0.7276	0.8516	1.1245	1.1324	1.1048
	Capital	-0.2388	0.9704	-0.3097	0.9707	3.6878	2.2737	3.7680	2.2792*
	Audit and disclosure	-1.0558	1.0758	-1.0389	1.0917	4.2941	2.2050*	4.6741	2.2900**
	Authorities	0.1809	1.1089	0.2124	1.1272	4.2792	3.5386	4.1345	3.5287
	Deposit	1.1174	1.0519	0.9594	1.0481	2.0585	1.7987	2.0386	1.7917
	Ownership	-5.5605	3.0904*	-5.7595	3.0599*	17.5344	5.6892***	15.4495	5.6785***
	Sector CR3	0.1245	0.0602**	0.1182	0.0592**	0.4989	0.1583***	0.5092	0.1593***
Country level	Stock market development	0.1113	0.0251***	0.1108	0.0254***	0.0964	0.0314***	0.0941	0.0316***
	Economic strength	-0.0002	0.0002	-0.0002	0.0002	-0.0008	0.0005*	-0.0008	0.0005*
	Political stability	-13.0577	2.8878***	-12.8183	2.8852***	-27.6147	5.7358***	-28.2681	5.7532***
	Rule of law	21.3345	5.0791***	21.1267	5.1005***	-19.8009	19.9672	-21.0859	20.0002
	constant	40.8294	22.2818*	40.7146	22.3959*	-13.7223	71.0506	-20.9655	73.0615
	Wald chi^2	180.20	***	166.56	***	--		--	
	F-Test	--		--		7.48	***	7.54	***
	R-sq	0.1282		0.1271		0.0050		0.0058	
	No of observations	2,000		2,000		2,000		2,000	

* indicates significance at the 10% level, ** at the 5% level, and *** at the 1% level, respectively.
Standard errors control for clustering at the bank level.

V.4.3 Regulation, Bank Size, and Ownership

As initially outlined, regulation is responsible for the extent to which shareholders can exert influence on bank performance and risk-taking (Saunders, Strock, and Travlos, 1990). As indicated in previous studies, regulation does not necessarily achieve its objectives. For example, restrictions on bank activities can make banking systems more risky. Countries with restrictions on the securities activities of commercial banks are more likely to suffer a major banking crisis (Barth, Caprio, and Levine, 2000). For this reason, we analyze the effect of bank ownership structure on risk-adjusted performance and bank risk, conditional on regulation. In order to analyze the effect of ownership concentration on risk-adjusted performance and risk the one hand and the interaction of regulation and ownership concentration on the other hand, regressions are conducted including interaction terms between regulation indices and ownership variables (for details see Appendices V.6.5 and V.6.7). With regard to shareholder incentives that advocate bank risk, restrictions on bank activities, capital regulation, and deposit insurance schemes are of special interest as they are supposed to increase moral hazard problems. For this reason, the focus of the interaction analysis is on these three regulations.

Restrictions on bank activities directly reduce RORWA and ROA. The interaction term between activities restrictions and ownership shows that shareholders can offset the effect with regard to ROA performance. However, risk-adjusted performance is not positively influenced by shareholders. Capital regulation directly reduces performance. In contrast to restrictions on bank activities, the original negative effect of capital regulation on risk-adjusted performance can be clearly offset by large shareholders. Performance measured with ROA confirms this where the offsetting effect is clearer in higher ownership concentration levels. Deposit insurance leads to unequivocal results. RORWA is being increased, whereas ROA is being reduced. A higher ownership concentration changes the signs in both cases, thereby indicating that it reduces risk-adjusted performance but increases ROA performance.

Capital markets view some essential regulations on banks as directly risk increasing. In these cases, a tight ownership structure reduces bank risk. Bank activities restrictions and capital regulation increase bank beta. In both cases, large shareholders reduce bank risk. Only deposit insurance directly reduces beta, whereas ownership concentration offsets this effect. The z-score shows different results. Activities restrictions and deposit insurance directly increase bank stability. Large shareholders only evade activities restrictions as the interaction term enters the regression negatively. Capital regulation displays mixed results. At higher ownership concentration levels, it reduces banks stability, but ownership concentration offsets this. For lower concentration levels, the effect is the opposite. Overall, the results show that the effects of regulations are to a vast extent dependent on the ownership structure of the bank.

Beyond the interaction between ownership structure and regulation, the regressions for size and regulation clusters show whether large shareholders exert their influence differently in large vs. small banks and strongly regulated banks vs. weakly regulated banks (for details, see Appendices V.6.8–15). Overall, there are no major deviations from the general regression results. The only size-related deviation appears for ROA where, for lower ownership levels, ROA increases in large banks. Further, in large banks and lower ownership levels, beta is reduced but the overall impact is beta-increasing. In addition, random-effect regression shows that for larger banks, z-score increases. This holds true for both ownership thresholds.

The analysis of regulation clusters shows almost no deviation from the general results. Only with regard to beta, higher ownership concentration levels increase beta at weaker regulated banks. This contradicts the general results on higher ownership concentration levels.

V.5 Conclusion

This study analyzes the effect of bank ownership structures on risk-adjusted performance and risk for the period 2004-2008. Special attention is paid to bank regulatory frameworks. As the base of this study, 802 observations for risk-adjusted performance and 2,000 observations for risk metrics of global banks have been used.

The results show that ownership concentration is negatively associated with risk-adjusted bank performance. This finding holds for two ownership concentration thresholds and for random- as well as fixed-effect regressions. It is in line with theoretical considerations that large owners tend to reduce bank performance (Burkart, Gromb, and Panunzi, 1997; Gomes and Novaes, 1999). The finding confirms the empirical evidence of Magalhaes, Gutiérrez, and Tribó (2008) for intermediate levels of ownership. At the same time, it contradicts the findings of Iannotta, Nocera, and Sironi (2007), who report performance numbers which do not vary significantly with ownership structure.

The impact of ownership concentration on bank risk depends on the applied measures. Ownership concentration tends to result in higher bank betas. However, this finding only holds for lower levels of ownership concentration. The effect inverts at higher levels of ownership concentration. This observation is in line with the results by Shehzad, de Haan, and Scholtens (2010), who also find that the effect of ownership on bank risk is not equal for all levels of ownership. According to Shleifer and Vishny (1986), the results document that higher ownership concentration improves management oversight, which can reduce risk. In contrast, the z-score results indicate that higher ownership concentration is associated with higher bank risk at all ownership levels. From an accounting viewpoint, ownership concentration is generally associated with more risk. This is in line with theoretical models, e.g. Galai and Masulis (1976), predicting that large shareholders advocate for more risk, and confirms the empirical findings of Laeven and Levine (2009).

Some theoretical models highlight the possibility that regulation may even result in greater bank risk (Koehn and Santomero, 1980). For example, activities restriction and capital regulation increase bank beta and decrease risk-adjusted performance. As our results show, ownership structure may offset these effects. It is for this reason that regulation cannot be evaluated without taking ownership structure into account and vice versa.

Overall, the present study shows the dependence of the results on the risk metrics applied. Furthermore, it shows that capital markets evaluate regulation at least in parts as different from accounting-based risk measures. Whereas, in some cases, accounting-based measures show a reduction in bank risk, capital markets provide evidence for the opposite. Large shareholders who try to increase their return potential are likely to cause countermeasures to regulations aimed at reducing bank profits.

V.6 Appendix

Appendix V.6.1:   Regulation Indices

Activities index	Auditing and disclosure index	Authorities index
Securities activities	External audit required	Suspension of dividends by supervisor possible
Insurance activities	Licensed or certified Auditors compulsory	Suspension of bonuses by supervisor possible
Real estate activities	Supervisors informed of the auditor's report	Suspension of management fees by supervisor possible
Ownership of voting shares	Right to meet with external auditors for supervisory agency	Replacement of management by supervisor possible
	Potential legal actions of supervisors against external auditors for negligence	Replacement of directors by supervisor possible
	Consolidated accounts covering all bank and any non-bank financial subsidiaries necessary	Existence of more than one supervisory body
	Disclosure of off-balance sheet items to supervisors	Replacement of head of supervisory body possible
	Disclosure of off-balance sheet items to public	Liability of supervisory body for damages to a bank by its actions
	Disclose of risk management procedures to public	
	Liability of bank directors for erroneous information	
	Credit ratings required for commercial banks	

Capital index	Deposit insurance index
Minimum capital requirement	Explicit deposit insurance protection system
Accordance with 1988 Basel Accord	Ex-ante collection of premia
Minimum ratio as function of credit risk	Fees based on some risk assessment
Minimum ratio as function of market risk	Insurance limit per person
Subordinated debt allowed as part of regulatory capital	Coverage of interbank deposits
Revaluation gains allowed as part of capital	Participation compulsory for all banks
Formal definition of a non-performing loan	

Source: Barth, Caprio, and Levine (2004, 2008)

Appendix V.6.2: Country Summary Statistics (Mean values)

Country	No of Banks	CR3 ownership	CR3 (20%)	CR3 (50%)	beta	z-score	RORWA	ROA
Argentina	3	21.08	0.33	0.07	0.90	10.38	-	2.30
Australia	7	9.05	0.09	0.00	0.92	38.08	2.09	1.56
Austria	3	61.58	1.00	0.73	0.40	110.64	1.70	0.77
Belgium	3	48.32	1.00	0.47	0.87	25.54	2.25	0.55
Brasil	2	10.72	0.10	0.00	0.93	16.16	1.76	3.54
Canada	8	12.59	0.00	0.00	0.54	33.48	1.98	0.99
Chile	3	67.28	1.00	1.00	0.63	50.77	0.01	1.82
China	4	20.03	0.50	0.00	0.96	26.93	0.22	0.99
Czech Republic	1	68.81	1.00	1.00	1.16	22.67	0.24	2.45
Denmark	5	18.34	0.40	0.00	0.49	29.38	0.38	1.52
Egypt	1	1.87	0.00	0.00	0.51	13.39	-	2.19
Finland	1	38.92	1.00	0.00	0.62	21.82	2.00	0.76
France	9	17.13	0.18	0.16	0.40	65.53	4.02	1.26
Germany	3	10.17	0.07	0.00	0.78	16.91	1.40	0.54
Greece	7	14.42	0.29	0.06	1.08	21.25	4.38	1.00
HongKong	7	56.01	0.86	0.71	0.74	61.32	0.54	1.47
India	10	25.55	0.34	0.24	1.14	21.32	10.06	1.67
Indonesia	3	37.00	0.53	0.53	0.79	24.46	0.00	2.12
Ireland	2	11.06	0.00	0.00	0.94	27.15	2.41	1.27
Israel	6	54.66	1.00	0.70	1.14	23.89	2.53	0.80
Italy	9	29.79	0.49	0.33	0.83	28.86	2.16	1.18
Japan	64	14.21	0.09	0.05	0.90	32.01	0.01	0.41
Malaysia	5	29.66	0.56	0.20	1.16	42.68	1.40	1.31
Mexico	1	13.46	0.40	0.00	1.15	13.59	-	3.20
Morocco	2	7.12	0.10	0.10	0.81	25.70	-	1.77
Netherlands	2	44.63	0.80	0.30	0.36	19.29	2.10	0.59
Norway	4	16.82	0.25	0.15	0.40	17.48	0.68	1.39
Pakistan	1	6.15	0.00	0.00	1.25	10.76	0.13	4.51
Peru	1	40.73	1.00	0.00	0.41	22.71	-	2.63
Philippines	6	8.72	0.13	0.03	0.78	35.68	0.06	1.55
Poland	5	57.35	0.76	0.76	0.98	15.46	1.18	2.05
Portugal	3	40.79	0.80	0.53	0.89	29.39	1.71	0.89
Russia	1	39.18	0.60	0.60	0.95	9.35	-	2.90
Saudi-Arabia	1	20.32	0.60	0.00	0.56	19.67	1.33	3.35
Singapore	4	32.22	0.90	0.25	0.90	55.32	1.56	1.50
South Africa	3	32.23	0.73	0.27	0.69	12.45	-	7.79
South Korea	4	41.50	0.85	0.30	1.00	17.19	0.01	1.40
Spain	8	25.23	0.60	0.10	0.73	35.17	2.55	1.17
Sweden	4	31.71	1.00	0.05	0.85	38.62	0.86	0.92
Switzerland	15	41.89	0.63	0.61	0.42	59.81	1.98	0.90
Taiwan	13	18.43	0.32	0.05	0.96	13.29	-0.01	-0.32
Turkey	5	42.09	0.60	0.60	1.19	12.64	7.88	2.96
UK	6	19.39	0.37	0.07	1.08	27.90	3.37	1.29
USA	145	20.17	0.40	0.04	0.95	55.04	9.40	1.44

Country	Bank size	MarketCap/ GDP (in %)	GDP per capita (in USD)	Activities	Auditing and disclosure	Authorities	Capital	Deposit insurance
Argentina	6.62	30.02	5,815	11.0	10.0	4.8	5.6	4.0
Australia	8.04	124.98	36,830	10.2	9.8	6.8	4.8	0.0
Austria	7.47	41.85	41,102	7.0	8.0	5.2	2.6	2.0
Belgium	8.49	73.90	39,687	7.4	9.0	5.8	3.6	4.0
Brasil	8.00	61.81	5,871	8.8	8.2	4.8	4.0	3.0
Canada	8.06	120.42	38,731	7.8	8.4	3.2	4.0	5.0
Chile	7.17	112.95	8,407	13.8	10.0	3.0	3.0	2.0
China	7.85	81.60	2,213	15.0	9.0	4.0	3.0	0.0
Czech Republic	7.42	31.57	14,861	12.0	8.0	3.8	4.0	3.0
Denmark	7.35	68.68	52,428	9.2	9.8	2.8	2.4	3.2
Egypt	6.63	76.87	1,438	10.0	11.0	5.4	3.0	0.0
Finland	7.46	107.60	42,194	8.8	9.2	2.8	3.0	4.0
France	7.62	84.77	37,657	8.4	9.0	2.0	4.8	4.0
Germany	8.38	47.48	37,441	7.0	8.8	3.2	2.0	3.2
Greece	7.55	60.28	25,312	8.4	9.8	3.2	2.8	3.0
HongKong	7.41	408.30	27,801	5.2	9.0	6.0	3.4	3.2
India	7.19	84.67	855	11.2	8.6	5.8	3.0	3.0
Indonesia	6.78	32.69	1,660	16.0	9.0	6.0	2.0	3.0
Ireland	8.26	53.08	53,298	7.0	9.0	6.8	4.2	3.0
Israel	7.44	98.33	21,917	12.2	9.0	5.8	5.0	0.0
Italy	7.94	43.81	33,150	11.6	8.0	1.0	3.0	3.0
Japan	7.31	91.90	35,713	11.0	9.0	7.0	3.0	3.2
Malaysia	7.32	138.59	6,314	11.0	9.8	5.8	4.8	3.2
Mexico	7.35	29.57	8,942	6.0	10.8	4.2	3.4	3.0
Morocco	7.13	67.85	2,205	11.6	9.0	5.2	3.0	3.0
Netherlands	7.18	92.81	43,672	6.0	9.8	2.8	2.8	2.8
Norway	7.31	64.25	74,228	10.2	9.8	3.2	4.2	4.0
Pakistan	6.73	34.11	804	12.8	10.8	6.0	4.6	0.0
Peru	7.10	56.09	3,383	11.0	9.2	4.0	4.0	4.0
Philippines	6.61	47.00	1,402	7.0	9.6	5.8	5.0	4.8
Poland	7.14	33.70	9,709	7.8	8.0	3.0	4.0	3.0
Portugal	7.84	43.25	19,404	11.6	9.8	5.2	4.8	4.0
Russia	8.05	83.69	7,471	8.0	7.2	3.0	3.8	2.0
Saudi-Arabia	7.30	121.08	14,949	11.8	10.0	6.6	2.8	0.0
Singapore	7.68	204.73	32,055	10.0	10.0	7.0	6.0	3.2
South Africa	7.15	238.53	5,377	9.6	10.0	3.2	4.6	0.0
South Korea	7.29	78.49	18,611	9.6	10.2	5.2	3.0	3.0
Spain	7.89	93.31	29,138	6.8	9.4	3.8	5.2	3.0
Sweden	8.43	109.90	45,017	9.6	8.0	5.0	4.0	3.2
Switzerland	7.30	253.22	54,373	7.8	9.2	6.0	5.6	1.8
Taiwan	7.14	81.60	2,213	13.0	10.0	5.2	5.4	4.2
Turkey	7.22	29.86	7,713	8.0	10.0	5.0	6.0	4.0
UK	8.63	124.98	40,851	4.2	8.8	4.6	4.0	2.0
USA	6.80	130.83	43,489	11.0	8.2	6.0	4.4	6.0

158

Appendix V.6.3: Correlation Matrix

	RORWA	ROA	Beta	Zscore	CR3 (20%)	CR3 (50%)
RORWA	1.0000					
ROA	0.3076*	1.0000				
Beta	0.0242	-0.0214	1.0000			
Zscore	0.2337*	0.1006*	-0.1051*	1.0000		
CR3 (20%)	-0.0981*	0.0387	-0.0218	0.0142	1.0000	
CR3 (50%)	-0.1092*	0.0277	-0.0742*	-0.0162	0.5199*	1.0000
CR3 stake	-0.0897*	0.0317	-0.0370	0.0016	0.7747*	0.8638*
Bank size	-0.2873*	-0.1437*	0.1290*	-0.1747*	-0.0457*	0.0577*
Bank size growth	0.0361	0.1911*	-0.0206	-0.0563*	0.0052	0.0217
Efficiency	-0.1585*	-0.4739*	0.0519*	-0.1100*	-0.0811*	-0.0467*
Capitalization	0.1731*	0.4523*	-0.0037	0.1534*	0.0121	-0.0103
Activities	0.0054	-0.0630*	0.1530*	-0.0220	-0.0722*	-0.1430*
Audit and disclosure	-0.2398*	0.0148	-0.1275*	-0.1765*	0.0028	0.1086*
Authorities	0.1697*	-0.1288*	0.1566*	0.0953*	-0.1130*	-0.1387*
Capital	0.0460	0.0298	0.1206*	0.0762*	0.1289*	0.0445*
Deposit	0.3490*	-0.0127	0.0709*	0.1900*	-0.0607*	-0.2718*
Ownership	-0.1812*	-0.0575*	0.0125	-0.1453*	-0.0802*	-0.0701*
MarketCap/GDP	0.1322*	0.1317*	-0.1010*	0.2301*	0.1438*	0.1397*
GDP per capita	0.1270*	-0.1345*	-0.0995*	0.2141*	-0.0413	-0.1389*
Political stability	-0.1825*	-0.2821*	-0.1456*	0.0512*	-0.0712*	-0.0253
Rule of law	0.0806*	-0.1996*	-0.1007*	0.2280*	-0.0176	-0.1063*
Sector CR3	-0.2846*	0.0322	-0.1747*	-0.0835*	0.2082*	0.2938*

* indicates significance at the 5% level

	CR3 stake	Bank size	Bank size growth	Efficiency	Capitalization
RORWA					
ROA					
Beta					
Zscore					
CR3 (20%)					
CR3 (50%)					
CR3 stake	1.0000				
Bank size	0.0239	1.0000			
Bank size growth	0.0141	0.1078*	1.0000		
Efficiency	-0.0560*	0.0443*	-0.1486*	1.0000	
Capitalization	-0.0045	-0.3693*	0.0531*	-0.1191*	1.0000
Activities	-0.1269*	-0.2751*	-0.1085*	0.0432	0.0784*
Audit and disclosure	0.0389	0.1493*	0.0605*	-0.0300	-0.0941*
Authorities	-0.1342*	-0.2471*	-0.1744*	0.0926*	-0.0201
Capital	0.0792*	-0.0756*	-0.0374	0.0026	0.2521*
Deposit	-0.1741*	-0.3892*	-0.1193*	0.0056	0.2754*
Ownership	-0.0917*	0.0983*	0.1098*	-0.0085	-0.0620*
MarketCap/GDP	0.1670*	-0.0800*	-0.0339	-0.0949*	0.0929*
GDP per capita	-0.0919*	-0.0310	-0.1569*	0.0666*	-0.0779*
Political stability	-0.0309	0.1984*	-0.1517*	0.1241*	-0.2408*
Rule of law	-0.0493*	0.0081	-0.1705*	0.0645*	-0.1154*
Sector CR3	0.2609*	0.3686*	0.1144*	-0.0492*	-0.1937*

* indicates significance at the 5% level

	Activities	Audit and disclosure	Authorities	Capital	Deposit	Ownership
RORWA						
ROA						
Beta						
Zscore						
CR3 (20%)						
CR3 (50%)						
CR3 stake						
Bank size						
Bank size growth						
Efficiency						
Capitalization						
Activities	1.0000					
Audit and disclosure	-0.1220*	1.0000				
Authorities	0.2582*	-0.0562*	1.0000			
Capital	-0.0626*	-0.1584*	0.0192	1.0000		
Deposit	0.1788*	-0.5076*	0.1688*	0.1588*	1.0000	
Ownership	0.0918*	0.3153*	-0.1118*	0.0754*	-0.1977*	1.0000
MarketCap/GDP	-0.2389*	-0.0712*	0.2361*	0.1765*	0.0359	-0.1425*
GDP per capita	-0.1523*	-0.4068*	0.1510*	0.0811*	0.3710*	-0.4591*
Political stability	-0.2043*	0.0103	0.0980*	-0.0577*	-0.0535*	-0.1845*
Rule of law	-0.1828*	-0.2883*	0.2304*	0.0897*	0.3106*	-0.3218*
Sector CR3	-0.4842*	0.4031*	-0.3106*	0.0705*	-0.6123*	0.0161

* indicates significance at the 5% level

	Market Cap/GDP	GDP per capita	Political stability	Rule of law	Sector CR3
RORWA					
ROA					
Beta					
Zscore					
CR3 (20%)					
CR3 (50%)					
CR3 stake					
Bank size					
Bank size growth					
Efficiency					
Capitalization					
Activities					
Audit and disclosure					
Authorities					
Capital					
Deposit					
Ownership					
MarketCap/GDP	1.0000				
GDP per capita	0.2547*	1.0000			
Political stability	0.2374*	0.5457*	1.0000		
Rule of law	0.3761*	0.8614*	0.6929*	1.0000	
Sector CR3	0.0838*	-0.0091	0.2017*	0.0029	1.0000

* indicates significance at the 5% level

Appendix V.6.4:   Mean comparison, bank size clusters

Dependent variables	Cluster 1 vs. 2	Cluster 1 vs. 3	Cluster 1 vs. 4	Cluster 2 vs. 3	Cluster 2 vs. 4	Cluster 3 vs. 4
	t	t	t	t	t	t
	(p-value)	(p-value)	(p-value)	(p-value)	(p-value)	(p-value)
Beta	5.0689 ***	7.3135 ***	3.0155 ***	2.5992 ***	-1.0671	-3.2205 ***
	0.0000	0.0000	0.0026	0.0095	0.2862	0.0013
Z-score	-2.8556 ***	-4.7686 ***	-8.4886 ***	-1.4341	-4.6870 ***	-3.4129 ***
	0.0044	0.0000	0.0000	0.1519	0.0000	0.0007
RORWA	-0.5750	-3.3115 ***	-12.3623 ***	-2.1263 **	-8.9053 ***	-6.1168 ***
	0.5656	0.0010	0.0000	0.0342	0.0000	0.0000
ROA	2.9615 ***	0.7635	-4.4003 ***	-1.6899 *	-6.0439 ***	-4.6023 ***
	0.0031	0.4453	0.0000	0.0914	0.0000	0.0000
Bank level variables						
CR3 (20% Threshold)	-2.3879 **	0.4605	-1.5549	2.8513 ***	0.8301	-2.0167 **
	0.0171	0.6453	0.1203	0.0044	0.4067	0.0440
CR3 (50% Threshold)	-4.2987 ***	-1.0623	4.4190 ***	3.2370 ***	8.6205 ***	5.4521 ***
	0.0000	0.2884	0.0000	0.0012	0.0000	0.0000
CR3 stake	-4.2178 ***	-0.3644	1.9049 *	3.6342 ***	6.2291 ***	2.1179 **
	0.0000	0.7156	0.0571	0.0003	0.0000	0.0344
Bank size	38.4563 ***	56.9446 ***	79.0500 ***	43.2757 ***	88.4160 ***	49.5837 ***
	0.0000	0.0000	0.0000	0.0000	0.0000	0.0000
Bank size growth	43.8177 ***	4.9441 ***	4.3766 ***	-0.0062	-0.7170	-0.7356
	0.0000	0.0000	0.0000	0.9951	0.4735	0.4621
Bank efficiency	-0.7207	-1.5022	0.2794	-1.3185	1.6405	2.4941 **
	0.4713	0.1333	0.7800	0.1876	0.1012	0.0128
Bank capitalization	-3.8027 ***	-11.0323 ***	-15.6565 ***	-8.7858 ***	-13.4954 ***	-3.5344 ***
	0.0002	0.0000	0.0000	0.0000	0.0000	0.0004

* indicates significance at the 10% level, ** at the 5% level, and *** at the 1% level, respectively.

Appendix V.6.5: Mean comparison, bank regulation clusters

Dependent variables	Cluster 1 vs. 2	Cluster 1 vs. 3	Cluster 1 vs. 4	Cluster 2 vs. 3	Cluster 2 vs. 4	Cluster 3 vs. 4
	t	t	t	t	t	t
	(p-value)	(p-value)	(p-value)	(p-value)	(p-value)	(p-value)
Beta	1.7514 *	11.8399 ***	2.9567 ***	10.0384 ***	1.7085 *	-6.4760 ***
	0.0801	0.0000	0.0032	0.0000	0.0879	0.0000
Z-score	9.7515 ***	2.8526 ***	4.0118 ***	-5.3687 ***	-2.0597 **	1.4985
	0.0000	0.0044	0.0001	0.0000	0.0398	0.1346
RORWA	4.8234 ***	5.9430 ***	4.2847 ***	0.9530	0.3913	-0.8681
	0.0000	0.0000	0.0000	0.3412	0.6959	0.3861
ROA	5.2936 ***	-1.8325 *	0.7563	-4.4680 ***	-3.3995 ***	1.5059
	0.0000	0.0671	0.4496	0.0000	0.0007	0.1327
Bank level variables						
CR3 (20% Threshold)	6.2932 ***	-1.5534	-3.5656 ***	-6.4853 ***	-8.0521 ***	-1.8940 *
	0.0000	0.1206	0.0004	0.0000	0.0000	0.0588
CR3 (50% Threshold)	-5.6429 ***	-8.6285 ***	-13.2293 ***	-3.0773 ***	-6.9437 ***	-3.4470 ***
	0.0000	0.0000	0.0000	0.0022	0.0000	0.0006
CR3 stake	0.8657	-5.4819 ***	-10.3784 ***	-4.4935 ***	-7.9803 ***	-3.4940 ***
	0.3868	0.0000	0.0000	0.0000	0.0000	0.0005
Bank size	-13.9755 ***	-17.6738 ***	-17.4266 ***	-8.4222 ***	-9.7207 ***	-1.0220
	0.0000	0.0000	0.0000	0.0000	0.0000	0.3073
Bank size growth	2.3847 **	-4.9363 ***	-5.8162 ***	-2.5968 ***	-3.6166 ***	-1.1767
	0.0172	0.0000	0.0000	0.0096	0.0003	0.2398
Bank efficiency	-3.8062 ***	0.1955	1.4037	2.2969 **	5.3878 ***	0.6459
	0.0001	0.8450	0.1607	0.0219	0.0000	0.5186
Bank capitalization	17.7515 ***	9.0086 ***	9.0164 ***	-3.3283 ***	-3.2084 ***	0.3542
	0.0000	0.0000	0.0000	0.0009	0.0014	0.7233

* indicates significance at the 10% level, ** at the 5% level, and *** at the 1% level, respectively.

Appendix V.6.6: Random-effect regressions with interaction terms

Variable		beta (RE) CR3 20%		beta (RE) CR3 50%	
		Coeff.	SE (robust)	Coeff.	SE (robust)
Ownership	CR3 Threshold 20	0.1733	0.3306		
	CR3 Threshold 50			-0.0419	0.3766
Bank level	Bank size	0.1868	0.0260 ***	0.1785	0.0265 ***
	Bank size growth	-0.0010	0.0004 **	-0.0011	0.0004 ***
	Bank efficiency	0.0003	0.0002	0.0003	0.0002
	Bank capitalization	0.0030	0.0038	0.0032	0.0037
Sector level	Activities	0.0275	0.0094 ***	0.0171	0.0085 **
	Capital	0.0798	0.0136 ***	0.0769	0.0109 ***
	Audit and disclosure	-0.0749	0.0216 ***	-0.0786	0.0183 ***
	Authorities	0.0693	0.0144 ***	0.0758	0.0134 ***
	Deposit	-0.0426	0.0147 ***	-0.0274	0.0132 **
	Ownership	-0.0580	0.0464	-0.0459	0.0440
	Interaction activities	-0.0204	0.0105 *	-0.0051	0.0132
	Interaction capital	-0.0137	0.0164	-0.0264	0.0207
	Interaction audit and disclosure	-0.0060	0.0296	0.0266	0.0452
	Interaction authorities	-0.0076	0.0207	-0.0356	0.0262
	Interaction deposit	0.0465	0.0154 ***	0.0220	0.0231
	Interaction ownership	0.0662	0.0570	0.0824	0.0721
	Sector CR3	-0.0023	0.0008 ***	-0.0019	0.0008 ***
Country level	Stock market development	-0.0007	0.0002 ***	-0.0006	0.0002 ***
	Economic strength	0.0000	0.0000	0.0000	0.0000
	Political stability	-0.0731	0.0319 **	-0.0637	0.0332 *
	Rule of law	-0.0069	0.0475	-0.0246	0.0501
	constant	-0.3868	0.3443	-0.2782	0.3295
	Wald chi^2	306.67	***	298.36	***
	R-sq	0.1582		0.1583	
	No of observations	2,000		2,000	

* indicates significance at the 10% level, ** at the 5% level, and *** at the 1% level, respectively.
Standard errors control for clustering at the bank level.

Appendix V.6.6: Random-effect regressions with interaction terms (*continued*)

Variable		z-score (RE) CR3 20%		z-score (RE) CR3 50%	
		Coeff.	SE (robust)	Coeff.	SE (robust)
Ownership	CR3 Threshold 20	-14.4753	18.2165		
	CR3 Threshold 50			12.9705	31.3947
Bank level	Bank size	-4.8546	1.9195 **	-4.5385	1.9986 **
	Bank size growth	-0.0235	0.0323	-0.0249	0.0316
	Bank efficiency	-0.1006	0.0379 ***	-0.0981	0.0382 ***
	Bank capitalization	1.2218	0.5362 **	1.2428	0.5396 **
Sector level	Activities	0.8468	0.6577	0.6242	0.6450
	Capital	0.0995	0.9163	-0.5092	0.8040
	Audit and disclosure	-1.8541	1.2003	-0.8343	1.1373
	Authorities	0.0774	1.1412	0.0331	1.0663
	Deposit	0.6736	1.0911	0.9832	1.0443
	Ownership	-7.0039	3.6114 *	-7.0191	3.5722 **
	Interaction activities	-0.8745	0.8870	-0.4156	1.3940
	Interaction capital	-0.6146	1.7685	2.0850	4.2935
	Interaction audit and disclosure	2.1780	1.9639	-2.7146	4.7352
	Interaction authorities	-0.0206	1.6979	0.1788	3.1954
	Interaction deposit	0.6604	1.4899	0.1812	2.0555
	Interaction ownership	3.8239	3.7910	8.8188	5.5579
	Sector CR3	0.1165	0.0638 *	0.1239	0.0645 *
Country level	Stock market development	0.1093	0.0258 ***	0.1100	0.0274 ***
	Economic strength	-0.0002	0.0002	-0.0002	0.0002
	Political stability	-13.4757	2.7806 ***	-12.8536	2.8200 ***
	Rule of law	22.0069	4.9967 ***	21.6827	5.5799 ***
	constant	46.4877	24.2115 *	38.3072	23.0054 *
	Wald chi^2	188.96	***	180.57	***
	R-sq	0.1289		0.1270	
	No of observations	2,000		2,000	

* indicates significance at the 10% level, ** at the 5% level, and *** at the 1% level, respectively.
Standard errors control for clustering at the bank level.

Appendix V.6.6: Random-effect regressions with interaction terms (*continued*)

Variable		RORWA (RE) CR3 20%		RORWA (RE) CR3 50%	
		Coeff.	SE (robust)	Coeff.	SE (robust)
Ownership	CR3 Threshold 20	-6.7193	3.6206 *		
	CR3 Threshold 50			-5.6225	3.4067
Bank level	Bank size	-2.5537	0.5082 ***	-2.3068	0.4715
	Bank size growth	0.0061	0.0048	0.0081	0.0050
	Bank efficiency	-0.0258	0.0098 ***	-0.0260	0.0104
	Bank capitalization	-0.2657	0.1152 **	-0.2491	0.1153
Sector level	Activities	-0.2629	0.1198 **	-0.1900	0.0902
	Capital	-0.2716	0.1962	-0.3192	0.1314
	Audit and disclosure	-0.3552	0.2620	-0.0845	0.1686
	Authorities	0.0984	0.1867	-0.1609	0.1457
	Deposit	0.8667	0.2405 ***	0.5183	0.1579
	Ownership	-1.2987	1.1992	-1.1976	0.7471
	Interaction activities	0.0070	0.1044	-0.0600	0.0870
	Interaction capital	0.2965	0.2474	0.4474	0.1886
	Interaction audit and disclosure	0.9068	0.4298 **	0.4681	0.3284
	Interaction authorities	-0.5415	0.2283 **	-0.1344	0.1468
	Interaction deposit	-0.6513	0.2879 **	-0.0325	0.2609
	Interaction ownership	0.4612	1.1768	-0.2286	0.7666
	Sector CR3	-0.0338	0.0128 ***	-0.0463	0.0127
Country level	Stock market development	0.0156	0.0037 ***	0.0158	0.0040
	Economic strength	0.0000	0.0000 ***	0.0000	0.0000
	Political stability	-3.5377	0.7774 ***	-3.7973	0.8430
	Rule of law	0.9345	0.8719	1.4354	0.7998
	constant	30.3461	5.7715 ***	27.5442	4.9001
	Wald chi^2	96.63	***	96.15	
	R-sq	0.2690		0.2763	
	No of observations	802		802	

* indicates significance at the 10% level, ** at the 5% level, and *** at the 1% level, respectively.
Standard errors control for clustering at the bank level.

Appendix V.6.6: Random-effect regressions with interaction terms (*continued*)

Variable		ROA (RE) CR3 20%		ROA (RE) CR3 50%	
		Coeff.	SE (robust)	Coeff.	SE (robust)
Ownership	CR3 Threshold 20	-0.2937	0.7453		
	CR3 Threshold 50			-0.7367	0.6986
Bank level	Bank size	-0.1781	0.0797 **	-0.1820	0.0816 **
	Bank size growth	0.0019	0.0020	0.0018	0.0022
	Bank efficiency	-0.0199	0.0087 **	-0.0199	0.0087 **
	Bank capitalization	0.1026	0.0464 **	0.1038	0.0477 **
Sector level	Activities	-0.0585	0.0240 **	-0.0683	0.0216 ***
	Capital	-0.0828	0.0272 ***	-0.0952	0.0244 ***
	Audit and disclosure	-0.0402	0.0492	-0.0514	0.0403
	Authorities	-0.0481	0.0455	-0.0368	0.0343
	Deposit	-0.0629	0.0702	-0.0563	0.0526
	Ownership	-0.2708	0.1840	-0.2058	0.1314
	Interaction activities	0.0181	0.0257	0.0516	0.0329
	Interaction capital	0.0005	0.0365	0.0717	0.0449
	Interaction audit and disclosure	0.0026	0.0732	0.0368	0.0619
	Interaction authorities	-0.0532	0.0370	-0.1357	0.0358 ***
	Interaction deposit	0.0523	0.0665	0.0704	0.0520
	Interaction ownership	0.0568	0.2364	-0.1360	0.1508
	Sector CR3	0.0017	0.0033	0.0012	0.0032
Country level	Stock market development	0.0043	0.0010 ***	0.0043	0.0010 ***
	Economic strength	0.0000	0.0000	0.0000	0.0000
	Political stability	-0.5938	0.1138 ***	-0.5749	0.1153 ***
	Rule of law	-0.1918	0.1502	-0.2048	0.1586
	constant	4.7778	1.0894 ***	4.9103	1.0651 ***
	Wald chi^2	477.85	***	477.13	***
	R-sq	0.4383		0.4396	
	No of observations	2,000		2,000	

* indicates significance at the 10% level, ** at the 5% level, and *** at the 1% level, respectively.
Standard errors control for clustering at the bank level.

Appendix V.6.7: Fixed-effect regressions interaction terms

Variable		Beta (FE) CR3 20%		Beta (FE) CR3 50%	
		Coeff.	SE (robust)	Coeff.	SE (robust)
Ownership	CR3 Threshold 20	-0.2894	0.3992		
	CR3 Threshold 50			-0.0327	0.5138
Bank level	Bank size	0.3391	0.1022***	0.3104	0.1009***
	Bank size growth	-0.0010	0.0004**	-0.0012	0.0004***
	Bank efficiency	0.0003	0.0002	0.0003	0.0002
	Bank capitalization	-0.0040	0.0094	-0.0034	0.0092
Sector level	Activities	0.0191	0.0187	0.0098	0.0186
	Capital	0.0525	0.0171***	0.0525	0.0149***
	Audit and disclosure	-0.0681	0.0304**	-0.0601	0.0286**
	Authorities	0.1033	0.0290***	0.0968	0.0287***
	Deposit	-0.1420	0.0245***	-0.1148	0.0241***
	Ownership	-0.0112	0.1160	-0.0194	0.1131
	Interaction activities	-0.0148	0.0125	0.0015	0.0183
	Interaction capital	0.0003	0.0184	0.0036	0.0259
	Interaction audit and disclosure	0.0253	0.0341	0.0097	0.0590
	Interaction authorities	-0.0160	0.0285	-0.0532	0.0474
	Interaction deposit	0.0726	0.0197***	0.0481	0.0279*
	Interaction ownership	0.0329	0.0782	-0.0266	0.0911
	Sector CR3	-0.0023	0.0015	-0.0018	0.0015
Country level	Stock market development	0.0002	0.0003	0.0002	0.0003
	Economic strength	0.0000	0.0000*	0.0000	0.0000*
	Political stability	0.0392	0.0650	0.0374	0.0635
	Rule of law	0.7996	0.1868***	0.8103	0.1885***
	constant	-2.4279	0.7651***	-2.3237	0.7462***
	F-Test	10.77	***	10.45	***
	R-sq	0.0001		0.0000	
	No of observations	2,000		2,000	

* indicates significance at the 10% level, ** at the 5% level, and *** at the 1% level, respectively.
Standard errors control for clustering at the bank level.

Appendix V.6.7: Fixed-effect regressions interaction terms (*continued*)

Variable		z-score (FE) CR3 20%		z-score (FE) CR3 50%	
		Coeff.	SE (robust)	Coeff.	SE (robust)
Ownership	CR3 Threshold 20	-60.5951	40.5739		
	CR3 Threshold 50			-120.8583	123.5642
Bank level	Bank size	-2.2342	10.5344	-1.6765	11.2106
	Bank size growth	-0.0111	0.0333	-0.0143	0.0326
	Bank efficiency	-0.0689	0.0359*	-0.0699	0.0373*
	Bank capitalization	3.1611	1.0652***	3.2054	1.0655***
Sector level	Activities	0.7265	1.2647	0.9365	1.2770
	Capital	3.3487	1.5701**	3.2502	1.4887**
	Audit and disclosure	2.6522	1.9198	4.2425	1.9829**
	Authorities	4.0932	3.0173	3.4067	2.6701
	Deposit	2.1724	1.8630	1.3631	1.8641
	Ownership	24.5095	7.9438***	17.7387	7.5019**
	Interaction activities	-0.6925	0.8319	-0.6673	2.6979
	Interaction capital	1.3975	2.8172	5.0859	8.6996
	Interaction audit and disclosure	6.1049	3.0413**	5.7995	7.6315
	Interaction authorities	1.2152	2.1485	6.6797	9.4452
	Interaction deposit	-0.1818	1.4897	2.7332	2.9956
	Interaction ownership	-9.9181	5.7242*	1.3818	8.7974
	Sector CR3	0.4944	0.1567***	0.4831	0.1479***
Country level	Stock market development	0.1033	0.0288***	0.0943	0.0290***
	Economic strength	-0.0009	0.0005*	-0.0009	0.0005*
	Political stability	-27.9875	5.9110***	-27.4591	5.7068***
	Rule of law	-17.0489	18.0181	-20.2867	17.4687
	constant	-14.4386	71.1502	-20.6292	76.2954
	F-Test	6.28	***	6.25	***
	R-sq	0.0049		0.0062	
	No of observations	2,000		2,000	

* indicates significance at the 10% level, ** at the 5% level, and *** at the 1% level, respectively.
Standard errors control for clustering at the bank level.

Appendix V.6.7: Fixed-effect regressions interaction terms (*continued*)

Variable		RORWA (FE) CR3 20%		RORWA (FE) CR3 50%	
		Coeff.	SE (robust)	Coeff.	SE (robust)
Ownership	CR3 Threshold 20	-4.3232	4.1409		
	CR3 Threshold 50			-4.6460	2.9767
Bank level	Bank size	-3.5087	1.7204**	-4.1884	2.0906**
	Bank size growth	0.0081	0.0046*	0.0098	0.0047**
	Bank efficiency	-0.0272	0.0101***	-0.0281	0.0110**
	Bank capitalization	-0.4872	0.1808***	-0.5147	0.1962***
Sector level	Activities	-0.1347	0.1424	-0.0165	0.1166
	Capital	-0.1699	0.2022	-0.2361	0.1314*
	Audit and disclosure	-0.2136	0.2616	0.0296	0.2005
	Authorities	0.1185	0.1729	-0.1363	0.1376
	Deposit	0.6196	0.2614**	0.1570	0.1032
	Ownership	0.7678	1.3200	1.0472	0.6747
	Interaction activities	-0.0460	0.1348	-0.1223	0.0984
	Interaction capital	0.1785	0.2671	0.1424	0.1425
	Interaction audit and disclosure	0.8220	0.4610*	0.3178	0.2635
	Interaction authorities	-0.6032	0.2555**	0.3910	0.2045*
	Interaction deposit	-0.7396	0.3231**	-0.1584	0.1725
	Interaction ownership	0.4075	1.2703	0.3878	0.6158
	Sector CR3	0.0043	0.0205	-0.0004	0.0210
Country level	Stock market development	0.0120	0.0031***	0.0117	0.0030***
	Economic strength	0.0000	0.0000	0.0000	0.0000
	Political stability	-3.3933	1.1899***	-3.8323	1.3569***
	Rule of law	-6.0585	2.0395***	-6.3491	2.3212***
	constant	43.8449	13.4282***	49.1136	15.3003***
	F-Test	2.93	***	2.52	***
	R-sq	0.0311		0.0241	
	No of observations	802		802	

* indicates significance at the 10% level, ** at the 5% level, and *** at the 1% level, respectively.
Standard errors control for clustering at the bank level.

Appendix V.6.7: Fixed-effect regressions interaction terms (*continued*)

Variable		ROA (FE) CR3 20%		ROA (FE) CR3 50%	
		Coeff.	SE (robust)	Coeff.	SE (robust)
Ownership	CR3 Threshold 20	1.1206	1.0205		
	CR3 Threshold 50			1.2953	0.8497
Bank level	Bank size	-1.8512	0.5218***	-1.7955	0.4998***
	Bank size growth	0.0010	0.0021	0.0011	0.0022
	Bank efficiency	-0.0197	0.0086**	-0.0197	0.0087**
	Bank capitalization	0.0626	0.0209***	0.0630	0.0217***
Sector level	Activities	-0.0159	0.0325	-0.0426	0.0312
	Capital	-0.0020	0.0339	-0.0258	0.0280
	Audit and disclosure	-0.0073	0.0610	-0.0437	0.0475
	Authorities	0.0318	0.0591	0.0672	0.0515
	Deposit	0.0843	0.0396**	0.0906	0.0312***
	Ownership	0.1285	0.3608	0.2041	0.2943
	Interaction activities	-0.0306	0.0336	0.0081	0.0403
	Interaction capital	-0.0430	0.0502	-0.0020	0.0450
	Interaction audit and disclosure	-0.0922	0.1033	-0.0581	0.0746
	Interaction authorities	0.0417	0.0623	-0.1062	0.0437**
	Interaction deposit	-0.0319	0.0629	-0.0725	0.0397*
	Interaction ownership	0.1768	0.3132	-0.0408	0.1373
	Sector CR3	0.0008	0.0044	0.0012	0.0045
Country level	Stock market development	0.0039	0.0009***	0.0040	0.0010***
	Economic strength	0.0000	0.0000*	0.0000	0.0000*
	Political stability	-0.8647	0.1685***	-0.8766	0.1670***
	Rule of law	-0.8509	0.4682*	-0.8277	0.4832*
	constant	15.3667	3.2932***	15.3311	3.2193***
	F-Test	15.88	***	16.71	***
	R-sq	0.1648		0.1689	
	No of observations	2,000		2,000	

* indicates significance at the 10% level, ** at the 5% level, and *** at the 1% level, respectively.
Standard errors control for clustering at the bank level.

Appendix V.6.8:   Random-effect regressions for large banks

Risk

Variable		beta (RE) CR3 20% Coeff.	SE (robust)	beta (RE) CR3 50% Coeff.	SE (robust)	z-score (RE) CR3 20% Coeff.	SE (robust)	z-score (RE) CR3 50% Coeff.	SE (robust)
Ownership	CR3 Threshold 20	-0.0148	0.0316			0.3693	2.7314		
	CR3 Threshold 50			-0.0758	0.0483			2.2436	4.0747
Bank Level	Bank size	0.2793	0.0362***	0.2751	0.0361***	-8.3541	3.1778***	-8.1944	3.1640***
	Bank size growth	-0.0011	0.0005**	-0.0011	0.0005**	0.0304	0.0424	0.0313	0.0425
	Bank efficiency	0.0008	0.0002***	0.0008	0.0002***	-0.0642	0.0361*	-0.0649	0.0362*
	Bank capitalization	0.0084	0.0071	0.0084	0.0070	2.9688	0.8991***	2.9718	0.8915***
Sector Level	Activities	0.0095	0.0085	0.0091	0.0085	0.5817	1.0107	0.5997	0.9749
	Capital	0.0008	0.0133	0.0023	0.0135	0.1565	1.8269	0.0997	1.8095
	Audit and disclosure	0.0022	0.0211	0.0047	0.0209	-2.0008	1.5542	-2.0793	1.5840
	Authorities	0.0634	0.0097***	0.0616	0.0100***	-0.4705	1.0076	-0.4136	1.0355
	Deposit	-0.0317	0.0130**	-0.0326	0.0130**	-0.9471	1.4268	-0.9260	1.3624
	Ownership	-0.0965	0.0555*	-0.1060	0.0557*	-0.9655	3.6049	-0.6614	3.5486
	Sector CR3	-0.0012	0.0008	-0.0011	0.0008	0.0459	0.0722	0.0431	0.0667
Country Level	Stock market development	-0.0007	0.0002***	-0.0007	0.0002***	0.0571	0.0347*	0.0566	0.0344*
	Economic strength	0.0000	0.0000**	0.0000	0.0000**	-0.0002	0.0002	-0.0001	0.0002
	Political stability	-0.0264	0.0384	-0.0297	0.0387	-8.1212	3.5216**	-7.9779	3.5632**
	Rule of law	-0.0290	0.0552	-0.0323	0.0545	24.3137	6.3272***	24.3705	6.3654***
	constant	-1.3152	0.3865***	-1.2798	0.3900***	73.4170	36.8323***	72.1170	35.8717**
	Wald chi²	172.46	***	172.66	***	101.28	***	99.51	***
	R-sq	0.2233		0.2273		0.1321		0.1338	
	No of observations	1,000		1,000		1,000		1,000	

Performance

Variable		RORWA (RE) CR3 20% Coeff.	SE (robust)	RORWA (RE) CR3 50% Coeff.	SE (robust)	ROA (RE) CR3 20% Coeff.	SE (robust)	ROA (RE) CR3 50% Coeff.	SE (robust)
Ownership	CR3 Threshold 20	-0.7327	0.5288			0.0089	0.0612		
	CR3 Threshold 50			-0.3920	0.2842			-0.0254	0.0730
Bank level	Bank size	-1.2625	0.8316	-1.1936	0.8125	0.0961	0.0631	0.0935	0.0628
	Bank size growth	0.0061	0.0037*	0.0064	0.0037*	0.0034	0.0013**	0.0034	0.0013**
	Bank efficiency	-0.0225	0.0073***	-0.0225	0.0073***	-0.0085	0.0046*	-0.0085	0.0046*
	Bank capitalization	-0.2336	0.1300*	-0.2294	0.1279*	0.1508	0.0223***	0.1508	0.0222***
Sector level	Activities	-0.1716	0.0907*	-0.1503	0.0889*	-0.0466	0.0217**	-0.0467	0.0218**
	Capital	-0.2015	0.1722	-0.2137	0.1708	-0.0991	0.0282***	-0.0979	0.0286***
	Audit and disclosure	0.0061	0.1148	0.0076	0.1171	0.0642	0.0361*	0.0658	0.0367*
	Authorities	0.0070	0.0991	0.0082	0.1022	-0.0354	0.0220	-0.0365	0.0223
	Deposit	0.2056	0.1304	0.2013	0.1272	0.0002	0.0226	0.0003	0.0227
	Ownership	-0.0686	0.8262	-0.2250	0.7409	-0.0259	0.0976	-0.0300	0.0984
	Sector CR3	-0.0332	0.0090***	-0.0357	0.0089***	-0.0006	0.0021	-0.0005	0.0020
Country level	Stock market development	0.0078	0.0025***	0.0072	0.0024***	0.0031	0.0007***	0.0031	0.0007***
	Economic strength	0.0000	0.0000	0.0000	0.0000	0.0000	0.0000	0.0000	0.0000
	Political stability	-1.9352	0.7862**	-1.8324	0.7545**	-0.3206	0.0888***	-0.3231	0.0878***
	Rule of law	-0.2109	0.8722	-0.1317	0.8567	-0.2069	0.1486	-0.2088	0.1488
	constant	19.3935	7.8825**	18.5721	7.5416**	0.5611	0.8837	0.5745	0.8794
	Wald chi²	60.36	***	63.89	***	339.71	***	347.75	***
	R-sq	0.0921		0.0861		0.4686		0.4689	
	No of observations	1,000		1,000		1,000		1,000	

* indicates significance at the 10% level, ** at the 5% level, and *** at the 1% level, respectively.
Standard errors control for clustering at the bank level.

Risk

Variable		beta (FE) CR3 20%		beta (FE) CR3 50%		z-score (FE) CR3 20%		z-score (FE) CR3 50%	
		Coeff.	SE (robust)	Coeff.	SE (robust)	Coeff.	SE (robust)	Coeff.	SE (robust)
Ownership	CR3 Threshold 20	-0.06	0.0389			-5.69	2.8154 **		
	CR3 Threshold 50			-0.11	0.0790			-8.96	4.5661 *
Bank level	Bank size	0.49	0.1287 ***	0.49	0.1358 ***	-4.76	17.1380	-5.02	16.9780
	Bank size growth	0.00	0.0005 **	0.00	0.0005 **	0.04	0.0411	0.04	0.0409
	Bank efficiency	0.00	0.0002 ***	0.00	0.0002 ***	-0.04	0.0332	-0.04	0.0330
	Bank capitalization	0.02	0.0145	0.02	0.0142	4.32	2.4766 *	4.34	2.4845 *
Sector level	Activities	0.03	0.0200	0.03	0.0199	-0.75	1.4472	-0.47	1.3878
	Capital	0.00	0.0170	0.00	0.0169	6.72	4.8782	6.74	4.8750
	Audit and disclosure	0.03	0.0319	0.03	0.0320	4.44	2.6040 *	4.79	2.7000 *
	Authorities	0.06	0.0246 **	0.06	0.0246 **	5.18	5.0047	4.90	4.9196
	Deposit	-0.08	0.0202 ***	-0.08	0.0208 ***	0.65	1.5441	0.54	1.5544
	Ownership	0.08	0.1416	0.07	0.1303	23.93	8.8414 ***	22.86	8.8604 **
	Sector CR3	0.00	0.0016	0.00	0.0016	0.47	0.1800 ***	0.48	0.1839 ***
Country level	Stock market development	0.00	0.0003	0.00	0.0003	0.06	0.0389	0.05	0.0398
	Economic strength	0.00	0.0000	0.00	0.0000	0.00	0.0008	0.00	0.0008
	Political stability	0.09	0.0845	0.09	0.0840	-40.56	11.0846 ***	-39.98	11.0038 ***
	Rule of law	0.72	0.2141 ***	0.70	0.2130 ***	-5.51	24.3698	-6.96	24.6653
	constant	-4.34	1.0737 ***	-4.36	1.1125 ***	-9.30	130.0078	-9.81	130.0556
	F-Test	4.81	***	4.73	***	5.80	***	5.28	***
	R-sq	0.0007		0.0013		0.001		0.0020	
	No of observations	1,000		1,000		1,000		1,000	

Performance

Variable		RORWA (FE) CR3 20%		RORWA (FE) CR3 50%		ROA (FE) CR3 20%		ROA (FE) CR3 50%	
		Coeff.	SE (robust)	Coeff.	SE (robust)	Coeff.	SE (robust)	Coeff.	SE (robust)
Ownership	CR3 Threshold 20	-0.63	0.4696			0.17	0.0972 *		
	CR3 Threshold 50			-0.36	0.2943			0.06	0.0799
Bank level	Bank size	-3.38	2.4149	-3.48	2.5947	-1.33	0.4540 ***	-1.24	0.4364 ***
	Bank size growth	0.01	0.0036	0.01	0.0036 *	0.00	0.0013 *	0.00	0.0013 *
	Bank efficiency	-0.02	0.0073 ***	-0.02	0.0073 ***	-0.01	0.0044 *	-0.01	0.0044 *
	Bank capitalization	-0.40	0.2005 **	-0.40	0.1994 **	0.12	0.0365 ***	0.12	0.0371 ***
Sector level	Activities	0.09	0.1051	0.12	0.1109	-0.02	0.0317	-0.02	0.0331
	Capital	-0.28	0.1711	-0.29	0.1667 *	-0.08	0.0257 ***	-0.08	0.0261 ***
	Audit and disclosure	-0.01	0.1878	0.00	0.1900	-0.02	0.0367	-0.02	0.0369
	Authorities	-0.04	0.1069	-0.05	0.1077	-0.01	0.0421	-0.01	0.0421
	Deposit	0.13	0.0832	0.13	0.0809	0.05	0.0253 **	0.06	0.0264 **
	Ownership	1.39	0.7741 *	1.16	0.6150 *	0.17	0.2195	0.21	0.2447
	Sector CR3	-0.03	0.0162 *	-0.03	0.0166	0.00	0.0052	0.00	0.0053
Country level	Stock market development	0.01	0.0024 ***	0.01	0.0022 ***	0.00	0.0007 ***	0.00	0.0008 ***
	Economic strength	0.00	0.0000	0.00	0.0000	0.00	0.0000	0.00	0.0000
	Political stability	-1.01	1.0981	-0.89	1.1462	-1.07	0.2410 ***	-1.11	0.2434 ***
	Rule of law	-2.07	1.4091	-2.09	1.4256	-1.61	0.4576 ***	-1.61	0.4584 ***
	constant	36.00	16.8908 **	36.41	17.7776 **	13.46	3.5049 ***	12.85	3.4113 ***
	F-Test	4.70	***	4.27	***	13.10	***	12.61	***
	R-sq	0.0128		0.0099		0.2127		0.2196	
	No of observations	528		528		1,000		1,000	

* indicates significance at the 10% level, ** at the 5% level, and *** at the 1% level, respectively.
Standard errors control for clustering at the bank level.

Appendix V.6.10:   Random-effect regressions for small banks

Risk

Variable		beta (RE) CR3 20% Coeff.	SE (robust)	beta (RE) CR3 50% Coeff.	SE (robust)	z-score (RE) CR3 20% Coeff.	SE (robust)	z-score (RE) CR3 50% Coeff.	SE (robust)
Ownership	CR3 Threshold 20	0.0340	0.0371			-5.4919	3.7568		
	CR3 Threshold 50			-0.0091	0.0711			-14.8226	7.6732*
Bank level	Bank size	0.2274	0.0753***	0.2260	0.0757***	1.6603	6.3850	2.6052	6.3724
	Bank size growth	-0.0010	0.0008	-0.0010	0.0008	-0.1019	0.0528*	-0.0971	0.0515*
	Bank efficiency	-0.0002	0.0005	-0.0002	0.0005	-0.1554	0.0415***	-0.1639	0.0416***
	Bank capitalization	0.0066	0.0046	0.0065	0.0046	0.9841	0.5446*	1.0106	0.5614*
Sector level	Activities	0.0283	0.0149*	0.0283	0.0152*	-0.1679	1.1935	-0.0827	1.2136
	Capital	0.0860	0.0138***	0.0872	0.0137***	-0.3730	1.0032	-0.4694	1.0218
	Audit and disclosure	-0.1612	0.0296***	-0.1606	0.0297***	0.8049	2.0756	0.9231	2.1501
	Authorities	0.0906	0.0263***	0.0911	0.0264***	0.6065	2.3843	0.9233	2.4067
	Deposit	-0.0164	0.0255	-0.0161	0.0255	4.5278	2.0435**	4.0830	2.1371*
	Ownership	0.1091	0.0592*	0.1029	0.0605*	-9.8558	4.7006**	-11.5371	5.1342**
	Sector CR3	-0.0031	0.0020	-0.0029	0.0021	0.2251	0.1401	0.2817	0.1463*
Country level	Stock market development	-0.0005	0.0003*	-0.0005	0.0003	0.1724	0.0431***	0.1792	0.0433***
	Economic strength	0.0000	0.0000	0.0000	0.0000	-0.0002	0.0002	-0.0002	0.0002
	Political stability	-0.0616	0.0547	-0.0648	0.0553	-14.1861	5.4568***	-14.3704	5.4579***
	Rule of law	-0.0309	0.0829	-0.0241	0.0829	17.9372	8.0136**	18.9292	8.1933**
	constant	-0.2233	0.6852	-0.2286	0.6918	-28.3463	53.6110	-38.1301	54.6324
	Wald chi^2	246.75	***	245.64	***	135.87	***	123.96	***
	R-sq	0.2230		0.2231		0.1295		0.1313	
	No of observations	1,000		1,000		1,000		1,000	

Performance

Variable		RORWA (RE) CR3 20% Coeff.	SE (robust)	RORWA (RE) CR3 50% Coeff.	SE (robust)	ROA (RE) CR3 20% Coeff.	SE (robust)	ROA (RE) CR3 50% Coeff.	SE (robust)
Ownership	CR3 Threshold 20	-3.6970	1.2091***			-0.1282	0.1181		
	CR3 Threshold 50			-2.5524	0.9823***			-0.2093	0.1602
Bank level	Bank size	-2.0388	2.0848	-2.2185	2.1411	-1.2461	0.5191**	-1.2140	0.5104**
	Bank size growth	0.0031	0.0181	0.0019	0.0175	-0.0005	0.0042	-0.0004	0.0042
	Bank efficiency	-0.0369	0.0321	-0.0450	0.0339	-0.0398	0.0053***	-0.0400	0.0053***
	Bank capitalization	-0.1857	0.1230	-0.1597	0.1267	0.0790	0.0462*	0.0810	0.0474*
Sector level	Activities	-0.3059	0.1707*	-0.1949	0.1801	-0.0118	0.0345	-0.0088	0.0334
	Capital	-0.0542	0.1973	-0.1297	0.1596	-0.0276	0.0328	-0.0319	0.0324
	Audit and disclosure	0.4079	0.5082	0.6683	0.4613	-0.0269	0.0732	-0.0282	0.0715
	Authorities	-0.6308	0.5290	-0.5946	0.5830	-0.0841	0.0572	-0.0842	0.0559
	Deposit	1.3146	0.4727***	1.3096	0.4718***	-0.0651	0.0643	-0.0767	0.0689
	Ownership	-3.3519	1.2801***	-3.1812	1.2904**	-0.3718	0.2376	-0.4097	0.2228*
	Sector CR3	-0.0591	0.0377	-0.0573	0.0394	0.0087	0.0067	0.0089	0.0068
Country level	Stock market development	0.0357	0.0117***	0.0384	0.0126***	0.0047	0.0017***	0.0047	0.0017***
	Economic strength	0.0000	0.0000	0.0000	0.0000	0.0000	0.0000	0.0000	0.0000
	Political stability	-5.0967	1.2040***	-5.2615	1.2686***	-0.3648	0.1716**	-0.3685	0.1702**
	Rule of law	4.1555	1.5800***	4.1954	1.6210***	-0.2921	0.3137	-0.2899	0.3082
	constant	19.0961	15.2204	15.5197	14.6998	12.5401	3.2454***	12.3520	3.1926***
	Wald chi^2	72.87	***	79.27	***	388.00	***	369.72	***
	R-sq	0.4389		0.4191		0.5494		0.5571	
	No of observations	274		274		1,000		1,000	

* indicates significance at the 10% level, ** at the 5% level, and *** at the 1% level, respectively.
Standard errors control for clustering at the bank level.

173

Appendix V.6.11: Fixed-effect regressions for small banks

Risk

Variable		Beta (FE) CR3 20%		Beta (FE) CR3 50%		z-score (FE) CR3 20%		z-score (FE) CR3 50%	
		Coeff.	SE (robust)	Coeff.	SE (robust)	Coeff.	SE (robust)	Coeff.	SE (robust)
Ownership	CR3 Threshold 20	0.0575	0.0439			-4.4501	4.3477		
	CR3 Threshold 50			0.0173	0.0642			-17.9652	11.9132
Bank level	Bank size	0.2506	0.1632	0.2621	0.1662	5.7781	13.4485	6.5085	13.6424
	Bank size growth	-0.0010	0.0008	-0.0010	0.0009	-0.0932	0.0568	-0.0897	0.0552
	Bank efficiency	0.0000	0.0005	0.0001	0.0005	-0.1381	0.0490***	-0.1435	0.0492***
	Bank capitalization	-0.0095	0.0107	-0.0096	0.0106	2.8708	1.0307***	2.8799	1.0248***
Sector level	Activities	0.0010	0.0317	0.0013	0.0318	2.2590	2.5099	2.7974	2.3996
	Capital	0.0138	0.0219	0.0161	0.0217	2.1198	1.7555	2.1245	1.7732
	Audit and disclosure	-0.2329	0.0558***	-0.2291	0.0553***	3.9235	3.1495	4.0564	3.2862
	Authorities	0.1543	0.0907*	0.1545	0.0905*	4.2520	4.7700	5.0554	4.9321
	Deposit	-0.1578	0.0414***	-0.1572	0.0413***	6.2429	4.6347	6.1646	4.6038
	Ownership	-0.0769	0.1766	-0.0687	0.1769	6.4395	9.9266	-0.2241	9.5850
	Sector CR3	-0.0015	0.0028	-0.0013	0.0028	0.3837	0.2386	0.3993	0.2364*
Country level	Stock market development	0.0011	0.0004***	0.0011	0.0004***	0.1328	0.0547**	0.1326	0.0545**
	Economic strength	0.0000	0.0000***	0.0000	0.0000***	-0.0005	0.0005	-0.0005	0.0005
	Political stability	-0.1094	0.1010	-0.1071	0.1001	-15.0995	8.0517*	-16.9175	8.1268**
	Rule of law	1.3093	0.3159***	1.2979	0.3156***	-47.5348	31.0823	-47.9204	30.9850
	constant	-1.1698	1.0958	-1.2679	1.1206	-76.2881	90.0807	-89.9902	93.5557
	F-Test	14.55	***	14.42	***	3.80	***	3.97	***
	R-sq	0.0001		0.0001		0.0153		0.0128	
	No of observations	1,000		1,000		1,000		1,000	

Performance

Variable		RORWA (FE) CR3 20%		RORWA (FE) CR3 50%		ROA (FE) CR3 20%		ROA (FE) CR3 50%	
		Coeff.	SE (robust)	Coeff.	SE (robust)	Coeff.	SE (robust)	Coeff.	SE (robust)
Ownership	CR3 Threshold 20	-3.7909	1.3367***			-0.1128	0.1250		
	CR3 Threshold 50			-3.0106	1.6953*			-0.0080	0.1256
Bank level	Bank size	-1.8358	3.7645	-3.6818	3.7964	-2.1027	0.8287**	-2.1279	0.8538**
	Bank size growth	0.0171	0.0165	0.0126	0.0158	-0.0011	0.0044	-0.0010	0.0044
	Bank efficiency	-0.0446	0.0352	-0.0532	0.0372	-0.0395	0.0055***	-0.0397	0.0055***
	Bank capitalization	-0.4049	0.2789	-0.4367	0.3246	0.0320	0.0217	0.0322	0.0223
Sector level	Activities	-0.3295	0.4824	-0.1725	0.4907	-0.0289	0.0619	-0.0304	0.0629
	Capital	0.0234	0.3250	-0.1432	0.2965	-0.0080	0.0507	-0.0128	0.0522
	Audit and disclosure	0.3367	1.0055	0.0279	0.8861	-0.0058	0.1011	-0.0139	0.1011
	Authorities	-1.0309	0.9002	-0.1594	0.8540	0.0171	0.1242	0.0154	0.1219
	Deposit	-0.0035	1.0799	-0.4647	1.0502	0.0670	0.0667	0.0660	0.0663
	Ownership	-0.1183	2.4909	-1.6707	3.5434	0.0648	0.7506	0.0582	0.7541
	Sector CR3	0.0665	0.0496	0.0591	0.0533	0.0087	0.0065	0.0083	0.0063
Country level	Stock market development	0.0158	0.0092*	0.0195	0.0095**	0.0050	0.0019**	0.0050	0.0019**
	Economic strength	0.0000	0.0001	0.0000	0.0001	0.0000	0.0000	0.0000	0.0000
	Political stability	-5.1482	1.5945***	-5.7651	1.6625***	-0.5280	0.1408***	-0.5301	0.1427***
	Rule of law	-14.8604	7.1193**	-15.1970	7.6264**	0.4990	0.8488	0.5233	0.8674
	constant	49.1775	28.2496*	60.4380	26.4867**	15.8946	4.2768***	16.1204	4.4846***
	F-Test	5.33	***	4.23	***	23.19	***	22.72	***
	R-sq	0.0307		0.0141		0.3030		0.2950	
	No of observations	274		274		1,000		1,000	

* indicates significance at the 10% level, ** at the 5% level, and *** at the 1% level, respectively.
Standard errors control for clustering at the bank level.

Appendix V.6.12: Random-effect regressions for strongly regulated banks

Risk

Variable		beta (RE) CR3 20% Coeff.	SE (robust)	beta (RE) CR3 50% Coeff.	SE (robust)	z-score (RE) CR3 20% Coeff.	SE (robust)	z-score (RE) CR3 50% Coeff.	SE (robust)
Ownership	CR3 Threshold 20	0.0207	0.0287			-4.6626	2.8536		
	CR3 Threshold 50			-0.0111	0.0529			-5.5276	3.6305
Bank level	Bank size	0.0991	0.0338***	0.0995	0.0342***	-4.6995	2.5067*	-4.4263	2.5355*
	Bank size growth	-0.0016	0.0007**	-0.0016	0.0006**	-0.0321	0.0476	-0.0272	0.0475
	Bank efficiency	0.0000	0.0005	0.0000	0.0005	-0.1746	0.0407***	-0.1778	0.0400***
	Bank capitalization	0.0041	0.0043	0.0039	0.0043	1.2651	0.4940***	1.2831	0.4964***
Sector level	Activities	0.0086	0.0152	0.0091	0.0154	1.7223	0.7795**	1.6200	0.7651**
	Capital	0.0810	0.0116***	0.0822	0.0116***	-1.6652	0.7673**	-1.7843	0.7722**
	Audit and disclosure	-0.1333	0.0234***	-0.1309	0.0237***	-2.3774	1.4741	-2.3614	1.4559
	Authorities	0.0597	0.0255**	0.0575	0.0260**	4.9546	2.0101**	4.8986	1.9995**
	Deposit	-0.0469	0.0155***	-0.0461	0.0154***	3.3560	0.9875***	3.1067	0.9928***
	Ownership	0.0276	0.0506	0.0227	0.0518	2.0020	3.7815	0.9850	3.8685
	Sector CR3	-0.0009	0.0013	-0.0008	0.0013	0.4166	0.0995***	0.4046	0.1002***
Country level	Stock market development	-0.0006	0.0003*	-0.0006	0.0003*	0.1781	0.0291***	0.1737	0.0294***
	Economic strength	0.0000	0.0000*	0.0000	0.0000*	0.0000	0.0001	0.0000	0.0001
	Political stability	-0.0314	0.0379	-0.0361	0.0380	-12.3626	3.1917***	-12.2391	3.2540***
	Rule of law	0.0835	0.0626	0.0881	0.0623	13.0312	4.4689***	13.2561	4.5345***
	constant	0.9261	0.4818*	0.9050	0.4858*	-7.7163	30.9800	-6.1969	31.1757
	Wald chi^2	243.87	***	242.90	***	166.88	***	158.53	***
	R-sq	0.1099		0.1094		0.1524		0.1524	
	No of observations	1,470		1,470		1,470		1,470	

Performance

Variable		RORWA (RE) CR3 20% Coeff.	SE (robust)	RORWA (RE) CR3 50% Coeff.	SE (robust)	ROA (RE) CR3 20% Coeff.	SE (robust)	ROA (RE) CR3 50% Coeff.	SE (robust)
Ownership	CR3 Threshold 20	-2.6224	0.9071***			-0.0610	0.0566		
	CR3 Threshold 50			-1.0554	0.5401*			-0.0537	0.0792
Bank level	Bank size	-2.9756	0.6986***	-3.0605	0.6702***	-0.1177	0.0486**	-0.1148	0.0488**
	Bank size growth	0.0078	0.0094	0.0077	0.0094	0.0035	0.0015**	0.0036	0.0015**
	Bank efficiency	-0.0461	0.0304	-0.0498	0.0311	-0.0389	0.0043***	-0.0390	0.0043***
	Bank capitalization	-0.3370	0.1489**	-0.3256	0.1551**	0.0359	0.0121***	0.0362	0.0122***
Sector level	Activities	-0.6483	0.2395***	-0.5453	0.2289**	-0.1094	0.0302***	-0.1108	0.0301***
	Capital	-0.2072	0.1501	-0.2651	0.1337**	-0.0886	0.0288***	-0.0906	0.0291***
	Audit and disclosure	0.3351	0.3512	0.3892	0.3148	-0.0423	0.0608	-0.0433	0.0626
	Authorities	-0.8490	0.3980**	-0.6633	0.3692**	-0.0952	0.0498**	-0.0948	0.0505**
	Deposit	0.5202	0.1947***	0.5184	0.1865***	0.0255	0.0319	0.0223	0.0321
	Ownership	-1.5995	1.1474	-1.7166	1.1105	-0.3602	0.1390***	-0.3690	0.1403***
	Sector CR3	-0.0390	0.0215*	-0.0452	0.0213**	0.0050	0.0034	0.0048	0.0034
Country level	Stock market development	0.0239	0.0069***	0.0227	0.0067***	0.0049	0.0009***	0.0048	0.0009***
	Economic strength	0.0001	0.0000***	0.0000	0.0000**	0.0000	0.0000	0.0000	0.0000
	Political stability	-3.8420	0.9057***	-3.7904	0.9025***	-0.3575	0.0849***	-0.3538	0.0857***
	Rule of law	1.2489	1.1811	1.7361	1.1666	-0.2058	0.1595	-0.2058	0.1586
	constant	39.0538	7.6032***	36.5812	6.9295***	6.3353	0.8990***	6.3639	0.9111***
	Wald chi^2	62.71	***	60.31	***	690.84	***	669.87	***
	R-sq	0.2845		0.2811		0.6774		0.6766	
	No of observations	506		506		1,470		1,470	

* indicates significance at the 10% level, ** at the 5% level, and *** at the 1% level, respectively.
Standard errors control for clustering at the bank level.

Appendix V.6.13:   Fixed-effect regressions for strongly regulated banks

Risk

Variable		Beta (FE) CR3 20%		Beta (FE) CR3 50%		z-score (FE) CR3 20%		z-score (FE) CR3 50%	
		Coeff.	SE (robust)	Coeff.	SE (robust)	Coeff.	SE (robust)	Coeff.	SE (robust)
Ownership	CR3 Threshold 20	0.0162	0.0364			-5.2454	3.3738		
	CR3 Threshold 50			-0.0568	0.0620			-5.0107	4.0112
Bank level	Bank size	0.2424	0.1417*	0.2690	0.1463*	-15.4569	12.0331	-16.8681	11.8023
	Bank size growth	-0.0013	0.0007*	-0.0013	0.0007*	-0.0464	0.0524	-0.0415	0.0523
	Bank efficiency	0.0002	0.0005	0.0002	0.0005	-0.1584	0.0496***	-0.1638	0.0492***
	Bank capitalization	-0.0145	0.0104	-0.0144	0.0104	2.3721	0.9311**	2.3742	0.9352**
Sector level	Activities	0.0968	0.0256***	0.0969	0.0257***	-0.6067	0.9976	-0.4276	0.9359
	Capital	0.0322	0.0199	0.0342	0.0199*	0.5361	1.0726	0.5026	1.0795
	Audit and disclosure	-0.1498	0.0499***	-0.1451	0.0503***	-0.3344	2.0114	-0.3718	2.0378
	Authorities	0.1779	0.0574***	0.1788	0.0575***	7.5536	2.2840***	7.4839	2.2732***
	Deposit	-0.1365	0.0302***	-0.1373	0.0302***	1.9918	1.3033	1.8520	1.3155
	Ownership	0.2008	0.1275	0.1974	0.1295	8.1924	6.4379	6.1236	6.1262
	Sector CR3	-0.0001	0.0019	0.0000	0.0019	0.6536	0.1896***	0.6424	0.1893***
Country level	Stock market development	0.0008	0.0004*	0.0008	0.0004*	0.1288	0.0396***	0.1251	0.0398***
	Economic strength	0.0000	0.0000	0.0000	0.0000	0.0005	0.0002**	0.0005	0.0003*
	Political stability	0.0412	0.0754	0.0392	0.0755	-32.8726	6.4913***	-32.8568	6.5257***
	Rule of law	1.2319	0.2345***	1.2076	0.2364***	-18.2527	17.5409	-17.9288	17.3659
	constant	-2.6843	0.9406***	-2.8697	0.9760***	71.9860	74.7580	82.2735	73.6059
	F-Test	15.79	***	15.87	***	6.80	***	6.88	***
	R-sq	0.0024		0.0028		0.0139		0.0154	
	No of observations	1,470		1,470		1,470		1,470	

Performance

Variable		RORWA (FE) CR3 20%		RORWA (FE) CR3 50%		ROA (FE) CR3 20%		ROA (FE) CR3 50%	
		Coeff.	SE (robust)	Coeff.	SE (robust)	Coeff.	SE (robust)	Coeff.	SE (robust)
Ownership	CR3 Threshold 20	-2.8005	0.9813***			0.0200	0.0722		
	CR3 Threshold 50			-1.0799	0.5698*			-0.0788	0.0707
Bank level	Bank size	-3.0379	2.5427	-4.7120	2.8179*	-1.5336	0.2899***	-1.4981	0.2907***
	Bank size growth	0.0100	0.0086	0.0088	0.0085	0.0022	0.0013*	0.0023	0.0013*
	Bank efficiency	-0.0475	0.0309	-0.0524	0.0320	-0.0392	0.0047***	-0.0391	0.0047***
	Bank capitalization	-0.6295	0.2558**	-0.6665	0.2865**	0.0199	0.0156	0.0199	0.0157
Sector level	Activities	-0.2380	0.3135	-0.1312	0.3084	0.0543	0.0803	0.0544	0.0801
	Capital	-0.1052	0.1865	-0.1136	0.1674	-0.0178	0.0399	-0.0151	0.0404
	Audit and disclosure	0.1376	0.5410	0.2167	0.4910	-0.0822	0.0897	-0.0758	0.0909
	Authorities	-0.1928	0.5641	0.0723	0.5097	0.2534	0.1342*	0.2546	0.1346*
	Deposit	0.0452	0.1790	0.0729	0.1108	0.0956	0.0384**	0.0944	0.0386**
	Ownership	1.8675	1.6072	1.3987	1.4222	0.9899	0.4490**	0.9846	0.4477**
	Sector CR3	0.0288	0.0368	0.0256	0.0380	0.0118	0.0044***	0.0120	0.0044***
Country level	Stock market development	0.0128	0.0053**	0.0122	0.0051**	0.0043	0.0009***	0.0043	0.0009***
	Economic strength	0.0000	0.0000	0.0000	0.0001	0.0000	0.0000	0.0000	0.0000
	Political stability	-3.7642	1.2836***	-3.7732	1.3033***	-0.5378	0.1121***	-0.5406	0.1124***
	Rule of law	-10.8757	3.6242***	-10.1702	3.5958***	-0.8471	0.5121*	-0.8798	0.5124*
	constant	47.6116	18.6456**	55.4863	19.7272***	12.7472	2.3132***	12.4998	2.3347***
	F-Test	2.25	***	2.07	**	32.95	***	32.68	***
	R-sq	0.0019		0.0000		0.3337		0.3325	
	No of observations	506		506		1,470		1,470	

* indicates significance at the 10% level, ** at the 5% level, and *** at the 1% level, respectively.
Standard errors control for clustering at the bank level.

Appendix V.6.14: Random-effect regressions for weakly regulated banks

Risk

Variable		beta (RE) CR3 20% Coeff.	SE (robust)	beta (RE) CR3 50% Coeff.	SE (robust)	z-score (RE) CR3 20% Coeff.	SE (robust)	z-score (RE) CR3 50% Coeff.	SE (robust)
Ownership	CR3 Threshold 20	0.0457	0.0499			-0.9321	3.8441		
	CR3 Threshold 50			0.0256	0.0716			-3.5253	6.6578
Bank level	Bank size	0.3459	0.0362***	0.3440	0.0363***	-7.0801	3.4537**	-7.3669	3.6371**
	Bank size growth	-0.0002	0.0005	-0.0002	0.0005	-0.0177	0.0372	-0.0211	0.0389
	Bank efficiency	0.0005	0.0002***	0.0005	0.0002***	-0.0288	0.0175*	-0.0282	0.0169*
	Bank capitalization	0.0125	0.0077	0.0120	0.0077	1.2264	1.2718	1.2193	1.2995
Sector level	Activities	0.0046	0.0156	0.0055	0.0156	2.4390	1.2316**	2.3909	1.2262*
	Capital	-0.0253	0.0183	-0.0252	0.0182	6.0666	4.1431	6.1796	4.0605
	Audit and disclosure	0.0149	0.0254	0.0140	0.0256	0.8092	1.8633	0.7465	1.7916
	Authorities	0.0638	0.0166***	0.0648	0.0167***	3.1509	2.9719	3.2147	2.9467
	Deposit	0.0124	0.0170	0.0130	0.0171	3.2305	3.0857	3.2057	3.1009
	Ownership	-0.0714	0.0875	-0.0886	0.0879	-23.5310	10.7379**	-23.7530	10.4593**
	Sector CR3	-0.0005	0.0014	-0.0004	0.0013	-0.4166	0.1652**	-0.4184	0.1601***
Country level	Stock market development	-0.0003	0.0002	-0.0003	0.0002	0.0354	0.0550	0.0369	0.0560
	Economic strength	0.0000	0.0000	0.0000	0.0000	-0.0008	0.0004*	-0.0008	0.0004*
	Political stability	0.0215	0.0777	0.0161	0.0833	-6.6306	7.8646	-5.8172	8.2668
	Rule of law	-0.2337	0.0771***	-0.2275	0.0774***	37.7733	13.2696***	36.8405	13.9037***
	constant	-2.0820	0.4844***	-2.0557	0.4987***	24.9200	47.8810	28.2123	51.0348
	Wald chi^2	193.95	***	189.63	***	109.24	***	120.15	***
	R-sq	0.4084		0.4040		0.1598		0.1578	
	No of observations	530		530		530		530	

Performance

Variable		RORWA (RE) CR3 20% Coeff.	SE (robust)	RORWA (RE) CR3 50% Coeff.	SE (robust)	ROA (RE) CR3 20% Coeff.	SE (robust)	ROA (RE) CR3 50% Coeff.	SE (robust)
Ownership	CR3 Threshold 20	-0.5533	0.3161*			-0.1835	0.1994		
	CR3 Threshold 50			-0.6823	0.3430**			-0.2303	0.1668
Bank level	Bank size	0.2196	0.2931	0.2288	0.2883	0.2284	0.0985**	0.2210	0.1028**
	Bank size growth	0.0086	0.0045*	0.0086	0.0044**	-0.0002	0.0039	-0.0004	0.0040
	Bank efficiency	-0.0188	0.0048***	-0.0188	0.0048***	-0.0051	0.0027*	-0.0051	0.0027*
	Bank capitalization	0.1953	0.1371	0.1951	0.1390	0.3165	0.0922***	0.3178	0.0942***
Sector level	Activities	0.0105	0.0902	0.0134	0.0884	-0.0008	0.0348	-0.0035	0.0330
	Capital	0.1516	0.1027	0.1728	0.1032*	-0.0407	0.0447	-0.0369	0.0458
	Audit and disclosure	0.0415	0.1158	0.0595	0.1193	0.0215	0.0372	0.0214	0.0377
	Authorities	-0.0568	0.0928	-0.0656	0.0950	-0.0214	0.0587	-0.0211	0.0599
	Deposit	0.0285	0.2893	-0.0724	0.2625	-0.0939	0.0714	-0.0960	0.0724
	Ownership	-1.3320	1.0740	-0.9390	0.9128	0.2702	0.2882	0.3155	0.3128
	Sector CR3	-0.0391	0.0105***	-0.0393	0.0113***	-0.0016	0.0073	-0.0019	0.0070
Country level	Stock market development	0.0048	0.0029	0.0050	0.0029*	0.0032	0.0015**	0.0033	0.0015**
	Economic strength	0.0000	0.0000	0.0000	0.0000	0.0000	0.0000***	0.0000	0.0000***
	Political stability	-1.1309	0.5928*	-1.0389	0.5875*	-0.2698	0.2354	-0.2379	0.2291
	Rule of law	1.7780	0.8574**	1.5615	0.8100*	-0.0573	0.2434	-0.1074	0.2442
	constant	1.2724	3.1683	1.2602	3.2172	-1.3177	1.4778	-1.2751	1.5357
	Wald chi^2	110.69	***	98.16	***	192.77	***	203.54	***
	R-sq	0.2777		0.2876		0.6289		0.6353	
	No of observations	296		296		530		530	

* indicates significance at the 10% level, ** at the 5% level, and *** at the 1% level, respectively.
Standard errors control for clustering at the bank level.

Appendix V.6.15: Fixed-effect regressions for weakly regulated banks

Risk

Variable		Beta (FE) CR3 20% Coeff.	SE (robust)	Beta (FE) CR3 50% Coeff.	SE (robust)	Z-Score (FE) CR3 20% Coeff.	SE (robust)	Z-Score (FE) CR3 50% Coeff.	SE (robust)
Ownership	CR3 Threshold 20	-0.0007	0.0602			-4.8256	5.5748		
	CR3 Threshold 50			0.0280	0.0991			-20.7867	11.3441 *
Bank level	Bank size	0.4633	0.1693 ***	0.4597	0.1721 ***	70.0074	40.1215 *	71.2591	39.5495 *
	Bank size growth	-0.0004	0.0005	-0.0003	0.0005	0.0069	0.0362	-0.0065	0.0368
	Bank efficiency	0.0003	0.0002	0.0003	0.0002	0.0150	0.0248	0.0158	0.0237
	Bank cap.	0.0197	0.0161	0.0195	0.0163	6.2714	3.3850 *	6.4333	3.3606 *
Sector level	Activities	-0.0002	0.0236	-0.0006	0.0239	-2.4993	4.8829	-2.2193	4.7990
	Capital	0.0085	0.0235	0.0072	0.0230	10.5410	11.4416	11.2323	11.3286
	Audit and discl.	-0.0113	0.0371	-0.0125	0.0364	3.3633	3.2771	4.1773	3.3902
	Authorities	0.0751	0.0327 **	0.0756	0.0328 **	5.3284	8.0450	4.8843	7.9461
	Deposit	0.0116	0.0173	0.0109	0.0178	3.1193	4.4326	3.4490	4.3382
	Ownership	0.0312	0.0878	0.0311	0.0876	37.4197	10.8679 ***	38.7803	10.9379 ***
	Sector CR3	-0.0057	0.0026 **	-0.0057	0.0025 **	-0.0940	0.2195	-0.0514	0.2237
Country level	Stock market developm.	-0.0004	0.0003	-0.0004	0.0003	0.0587	0.0395	0.0613	0.0389
	Economic strength	0.0000	0.0000	0.0000	0.0000	-0.0026	0.0011 **	-0.0026	0.0011 **
	Political stability	-0.1585	0.1272	-0.1547	0.1215	-25.8960	15.3839 *	-27.5732	14.9929 *
	Rule of law	0.2355	0.2740	0.2341	0.2734	16.2786	17.8415	15.6534	17.7860
	constant	-3.1602	1.3627 **	-3.1178	1.3802 **	-540.4107	319.0222 *	-560.9642	317.3379 *
	F-Test	4.78	***	4.86	***	13.14	***	16.89	***
	R-sq	0.1334		0.1321		0.0265		0.0304	
	No of obs.	530		530		530		530	

Performance

Variable		RORWA (FE) CR3 20%		RORWA (FE) CR3 50%		ROA (FE) CR3 20%		ROA (FE) CR3 50%	
		Coeff.	SE (robust)	Coeff.	SE (robust)	Coeff.	SE (robust)	Coeff.	SE (robust)
Ownership	CR3 Threshold 20	-0.2575	0.2914			-0.1555	0.2725		
	CR3 Threshold 50			-0.3118	0.4091			0.1377	0.0944
Bank level	Bank size	0.7854	1.4304	0.8725	1.4122	-2.2932	1.5030	-2.3526	1.5601
	Bank size growth	0.0089	0.0049 *	0.0090	0.0049 *	-0.0018	0.0043	-0.0017	0.0044
	Bank efficiency	-0.0181	0.0048 ***	-0.0181	0.0048 ***	-0.0055	0.0027 **	-0.0055	0.0027 **
	Bank cap.	0.1015	0.0994	0.1001	0.0979	0.1624	0.0378 ***	0.1621	0.0372 ***
Sector level	Activities	0.1070	0.1088	0.1115	0.1080	-0.0444	0.0334	-0.0462	0.0318
	Capital	-0.0471	0.1107	-0.0367	0.1108	0.0041	0.0441	-0.0106	0.0472
	Audit and discl.	-0.0524	0.1240	-0.0444	0.1258	0.0311	0.0738	0.0222	0.0705
	Authorities	0.0808	0.0564	0.0732	0.0561	-0.0074	0.0432	-0.0050	0.0433
	Deposit	-0.0241	0.2098	-0.0704	0.1983	-0.0301	0.0498	-0.0380	0.0507
	Ownership		(dropped)		(dropped)	-1.1472	0.6632 *	-1.1106	0.5996 *
	Sector CR3	-0.0317	0.0151 **	-0.0312	0.0156 **	-0.0046	0.0105	-0.0048	0.0108
Country level	Stock market developm.	0.0065	0.0030 **	0.0064	0.0030 **	0.0053	0.0020 **	0.0052	0.0021 **
	Economic strength	0.0000	0.0000	0.0000	0.0000	0.0000	0.0000	0.0000	0.0000
	Political stability	-0.3121	0.6939	-0.3216	0.7073	0.1266	0.3943	0.1790	0.4163
	Rule of law	1.7044	1.1111	1.5835	1.0817	0.0716	0.5886	0.0181	0.5754
	constant	-3.1187	10.6709	-3.6506	10.5549	16.8105	9.6793 *	17.3310	10.0384 *
	F-Test	9.50	***	9.43	***	9.38	***	9.24	***
	R-sq	0.1664		0.1703		0.1359		0.1300	
	No of obs.	296		296		530		530	

* indicates significance at the 10% level, ** at the 5% level, and *** at the 1% level, respectively.
Standard errors control for clustering at the bank level.

VI Main Conclusion

The four studies illuminate two specific governance issues: financial expertise of supervisory board members and ownership structure. The first part – comprising the studies 1 to 3 – focuses on financial expertise of supervisory board members, its impact on banks' risk-return profile, and its impact on bank stability, and also across legal ownership structures. The recent 2008 banking crisis and the resulting urgent calls for more expertise in bank governance have further emphasized the relevance of this analysis (Ard and Berg, 2010; Walker, 2009). The second part – comprising the fourth study – analyses the impact of ownership concentration on bank performance and risk at the international level.

The first study reveals that cooperative and savings banks have relatively high levels of financial expertise. A comparison of both banking groups shows that savings banks have, on average, significantly more financial expertise than cooperative banks (65% vs. 48%). However, savings banks benefit not only from employee representation but also have more "freely eligible" members with financial expertise on the board. Controlling for insiders still leaves savings banks with significantly more financial experts than cooperative banks (53% vs. 45%). Despite a different methodology, the study of Hau and Thum (2008) provides benchmarks for private and large public banks. The values for private banks are between 31% and 40% and between 10% and 30% for large public banks, including Landesbanken.

Although cooperative and savings banks have relatively high levels of financial expertise, they still have 35% and 52% of the supervisory board members who cannot be assumed to be financial experts. Against the background of the recent banking crisis and the frequently discussed shortcomings in internal bank governance mechanisms, this inadequacy should make regulators react and force banks to increase their financial expertise levels on the supervisory boards. Furthermore, since the legal requirements do not state exceptions, regulators need to clarify their procedure for individuals who cannot be assumed to be financially literate.

Financial experts on supervisory boards can impact the risk-return profile of a bank, but they cannot suspend the risk-return trade-off as revealed by the second study. With regard to performance, it pays off to have a high level of financial expertise on the supervisory board. However, the positive impact on performance comes at the price of a reduction of stability and an increase in risk. Apparently, financial experts on savings banks' supervisory boards, mainly bank employees and local and regional politicians, advocate profitable business even if it increases risk. For authorities and bodies involved in decisions on bank regulations, this should be a warning sign. Financial experts on savings banks' supervisory boards are a double-edged sword. They boost performance significantly, but also reduce stability and increase risk.

For the banks and the regulatory bodies, the results lead to contrarian implications. The owners should strive for more financial experts on the supervisory boards. Although the positive performance impact comes at the price of higher loan portfolio risk and less stability, overall, the banks seem to benefit from expertise. Financial experts advocate more profitable business, even if that entails higher risk and less stability. For this reason, contrary to the owners' interest in better performance, regulatory bodies should be concerned about the impact on stability and risk.

The third study confirms the detrimental impact of financial expertise on stability and risk. This finding is robust across ownership types. This finding is deemed to be useful for politics and regulatory bodies in particular. Articles, consultation papers, and recommendations by international authorities and bodies urgently call for more expertise in internal bank governance. Although this seems perfectly logical at first sight, the present study refutes this view.

Behavioural finance theory provides an explanation for the unintended adverse effect of financial expertise. Individuals generally tend to be overconfident, especially if their expertise is enhanced (e.g., Fischhoff, Slovic, and Lichtenstein, 1977; Odean, 1998). In the context of investment decisions, individuals tend to underestimate risks and chose riskier securities (Chuang and Lee, 2006; Fellner, Güth, and Maciejovsky, 2004). Transferring these findings to bank supervisory boards suggests that self-perceived experts, in particular, tend to underestimate risks. For this reason, requiring supervisory boards to possess only 100% financial expertise, without other further requirements, is not necessarily beneficial to bank stability and risk. Instead of seeking universal financial experts on the boards, it might be more appropriate to make sure that the supervisory boards' core roles and responsibilities are defined and met. Regulators might think of introducing rules for the overall composition of the supervisory board, for example, to make sure that all core responsibilities are covered by the supervisory board members.

Building on these three studies, there are opportunities for further research at the national and international levels. The present studies are based on the professional background of the board members to gauge their financial expertise. Although the majority of similar studies also have used the professional background parameter, criteria such as education, previous industry experiences, and management experience also represent potential indicators to gauge financial expertise. Subsequently, the analysis could be extended to banks with other ownership types and to other countries if the effects of financial expertise in internal governance can unequivocally be analysed. Since the present results are based on banks with a two-tier board structure, the transfer to institutions with a one-tier structure also remains open. In addition, potential core responsibilities of supervisory boards provide a further research area. First, such core areas could be defined. Second, analyzing whether experts in all or some specific areas are beneficial to performance, risk, and stability could shed light on the recommendation that calls for experts for specific areas on supervisory boards.

The fourth study reveals that a concentrated ownership structure is disadvantageous in various ways. First, it has a negative impact on the (risk-adjusted) performance of banks. Second, it has a detrimental effect on risk. However, the latter finding depends on the use of accounting-based measures. From a capital markets perspective, the impact is mixed, as it is negative only at lower ownership levels. Furthermore, the development of both measures in the pre-crisis years also shows contradicting results. Contrary to z-score, beta indicates rising risk in the years before the 2008 banking crisis.

The results of the study are deemed useful for bank management as well as regulatory bodies. Bank managers would prefer a less concentrated ownership structure as this is beneficial to performance. Moreover, large shareholders are more likely to intervene and limit management's freedom (e.g., Burkart, Gromb, and Panunzi, 1997). From an accounting-based perspective, large shareholders increase bank risk. For regulatory bodies, three aspects are of particular interest. First, large shareholders decrease stability of banks which is not desirable from a regulatory point of view. Second, the study points out the relevance of accounting-based measures vs. market-based measures. For this reason, regulators might think of using more market-based measures instead of accounting-based measures. Third, the interaction of ownership and regulation variables shows that the impact of large shareholders and regulation are interrelated. Therefore, regulation should always be traded off against potential countermeasures by large shareholders.

References

Acharya, V. (2009). A theory of systemic risk and design of prudential bank regulation. *Journal of Financial Stability, 5 (3)*, 224-255.

Acharya, V., Richardson, M., van Nieuwerburgh, S., and White, L. J. (2011). *Guaranteed To Fail: Fannie Mae, Freddie Mac and the Debacle of Mortgage Finance*. Princeton: Princeton University Press.

Acharya, V. and Yorulmazer, T. (2007). Too many to fail - An analysis of time-inconsistency in bank closure policies. *Journal of Financial Intermediation, 16 (1)*, 1-31.

Adams, R. B. and Mehran, H. (2008). Corporate performance, board structure, and their determinants in the banking industry, *Staff Reports, no. 330*. New York: Federal Reserve Bank of New York.

Altunbas, Y., Evans, L., and Molyneux, P. (2001). Bank Ownership and Efficiency. *Journal of Money, Credit and Banking, 33 (4)*, 926-954.

Amihud, Y. and Lev, B. (1981). Risk Reduction as a Managerial Motive for Conglomerate Mergers. *The Bell Journal of Economics, 12 (2)*, 605-617.

Anderson, R. C. and Fraser, D. R. (2000). Corporate control, bank risk taking, and the health of the banking industry. *Journal of Banking & Finance, 24 (8)*, 1383-1398.

Andres, P. d. and Vallelado, E. (2008). Corporate governance in banking: The role of the board of directors. *Journal of Banking & Finance, 32 (12)*, 2570-2580.

Ard, L. and Berg, A. (2010). Bank Governance - Lessons from the Financial Crisis, *World Bank, Policy Briefs, Note no. 13*. Washington D.C.: The World Bank.

Ayadi, R., Llewellyn, D. T., Schmidt, R. H., Arbak, E., and Groen, W. P. D. (2010). *Investigating Diversity in the Banking Sector in Europe - Key Developments, Performance and Role of Cooperative Banks*. Brussels: Center for European Policy Studies.

Baele, L., De Jonghe, O., and Vander Vennet, R. (2007). Does the stock market value bank diversification? *Journal of Banking & Finance, 31 (7)*, 1999-2023.

BaFin and Deutsche Bundesbank. (2010). Merkblatt zur Kontrolle von Mitgliedern von Verwaltungs- und Aufsichtsorganen gemäß KWG und VAG. Retrieved from http://www.bafin.de/cln_152/nn_721290/SharedDocs/Veroeffentlichungen/DE/Servic e/Merkblaetter/mb__100222__Verwaltungs__und__Aufsichtsorgane.html?__nnn=true

Barry, T. A., Lepetit, L., and Tarazi, A. (2011). Ownership structure and risk in publicly held and privately owned banks. *Journal of Banking & Finance, 35 (5)*, 1327-1340.

Barth, J. R. (1991). *The great savings and loan debacle*. Washington, D.C.: AEI Press.

Barth, J. R., Caprio, G. J., and Levine, R. (2000). *Banking systems around the globe: Do regulation and ownership affect the performance and stability?* Washington D.C.: The World Bank.

Barth, J. R., Caprio, G. J., and Levine, R. (2004). Bank regulation and supervision: what works best? *Journal of Financial Intermediation, 13 (2)*, 205-248.

Barth, J. R., Caprio, G. J., and Levine, R. (2008). Bank Regulations Are Changing: For Better or Worse?, *World Bank Policy Research, Working Paper Series, no. 4646*. Washington D.C.: The World Bank.

Basel Committee on Banking Supervision. (1999). *Enhancing Corporate Governance for Banking Organisations*. Basel: Bank of International Settlements.

Basel Committee on Banking Supervision. (2006). *Enhancing Corporate Governance for Banking Organisations*. Basel: Bank of International Settlements.

Beck, T. and Demirgüç-Kunt, A. (2009). Financial Institutions and Markets Across Countries and over Time: Data and Analysis, *World Bank Policy Research, Working Paper Series, no. 4943*. Washington D.C.: The World Bank.

Beck, T., Hesse, H., Kick, T., and Westernhagen, N. v. (2009). *Bank Ownership and Stability: Evidence from Germany*. Paper presented at the FDIC - Center for Financial Research. Retrieved from http://www.fdic.gov/bank/analytical/cfr/2009/june/CFR_SS_2009 _beck.pdf

Becker, H. P. and Peppmeier, A. (2006). *Bankbetriebslehre* (Vol. 8). Ludwigshafen: Kiehl.

Beltratti, A. and Stulz, R. M. (2010). The credit crisis around the globe: Why did some banks perform better?, *Working Paper, Charles A. Dice Center for Research in Financial Economics, no. 2010-5*. Columbus: Ohio State University.

Berle, A. A. and Means, G. C. (1933). *The modern corporation and private property*. New York: MacMillan.

Bermig, A. and Frick, B. (2010). Board Size, Board Composition, and Firm Performance: Empirical Evidence from Germany, *Working Paper*. Paderborn: University of Paderborn.

Bhagat, S. and Black, B. (2000). Board Independence and Long-Term Firm Performance, *Working Paper*. Boulder: University of Colorado.

Bhattacharya, S., Boot, A. W. A., and Thakor, A. V. (1998). The economics of bank regulation. *Journal of Money, Credit, and Banking, 30 (4)*, 745-770.

Blum, J. (1999). Do capital adequacy requirements reduce risks in banking? *Journal of Banking & Finance, 23 (5)*, 755-771.

Böhm-Dries, A., Eggers, H., and Hortmann, S. (2010). Zukunft der Corporate Governance von Sparkassen. *Betriebswirtschaftliche Blätter, 01/2011*, 27-31.

Böhm, C., Froneberg, D., and Schiereck, D. (2012a). Financial Expertise of Supervisory Board Members, Overconfidence, and Bank Risk Taking, *Working Paper*. Darmstadt: University of Technology Darmstadt.

Böhm, C., Froneberg, D., and Schiereck, D. (2012b). Zum offensichtlich erkennbaren bankwirtschaftlichen Sachverstand in den Kontrollorganen deutscher Genossenschaftsbanken und Sparkassen, *Working Paper*. Darmstadt: University of Technology Darmstadt.

Börner, C. J. and Büschgen, H. E. (2003). *Bankbetriebslehre* (Vol. 4). Stuttgart: UTB.

Boyd, J. H. and Runkle, D. E. (1993). Size and performance of banking firms: Testing the predictions of theory. *Journal of Monetary Economics, 31 (1)*, 47-67.

Brämer, P., Gischer, H., Pfingsten, A., and Richter, T. (2010). Der öffentliche Auftrag der deutschen Sparkassen aus der Perspektive des Stakeholder-Managements. *Zeitschrift für öffentliche und gemeinwirtschaftliche Unternehmen, 33 (4)*, 311-332.

Breuer, W. and Mark, K. (2005). *Perspektiven der Verbundkooperation am Beispiel der Sparkassen-Finanzgruppe*. Berlin: Duncker & Humblot Verlag.

Brown, C. O. and Dinç, I. S. (2011). Too Many to Fail? Evidence of Regulatory Forbearance When the Banking Sector Is Weak. *Review of Financial Studies, 24 (4)*, 1378-1405.

Büschgen, H. E. (1998). *Bankbetriebslehre* (Vol. 5). Wiesbaden: Gabler.

Burkart, M., Gromb, D., and Panunzi, F. (1997). Large Shareholders, Monitoring, and the Value of the Firm. *Quarterly Journal of Economics, 112 (3)*, 693-728.

Caprio, G., Laeven, L., and Levine, R. (2007). Governance and bank valuation. *Journal of Financial Intermediation, 16 (4)*, 584-617.

Carcello, J. V., Hollingsworth, C. W., Klein, A., and Neal, T. L. (2008). *Audit Committee Financial Expertise, Competing Corporate Governance Mechanisms, and Earnings Management in a Post-SOX World*. Paper presented at the University of Illinois 18th

Symposium on Audit Research. Retrieved from http://www.business.illinois.edu/accountancy/events/symposium/audit/proceedings/proceedings_2008/Papers/Carcello. pdf

Choundhry, M. (2011). Effective bank corporate governance: observations from the market crash and recommendations for policy. *Journal of Applied Finance & Banking, 1 (1)*, 179-211.

Chuang, W.-I. and Lee, B.-S. (2006). An empirical evaluation of the overconfidence hypothesis. *Journal of Banking & Finance, 30 (9)*, 2489-2515.

Cihák, M. and Hesse, H. (2007). Cooperative Banks and Financial Stability, *Working Paper Series, WP/07/2*. Washington D.C.: International Monetary Fund.

Claessens, S. and Laeven, L. (2003). What drives bank competition? some international evidence, *World Bank Policy Research, Working Paper Series, no. 3113*. Washington D.C.: The World Bank.

Claussen, C. P. (2003). *Bank- und Börsenrecht* (Vol. 3). München: C.H. Beck.

Coles, J. L., Daniel, N. D., and Naveen, L. (2008). Boards: Does one size fit all. *Journal of Financial Economics, 87 (2)*, 329-356.

Cooper, A. C., Woo, C. Y., and Dunkelberg, W. C. (1988). Entrepreneurs' perceived chances for success. *Journal of Business Venturing, 3 (2)*, 97-108.

Davidson, W. N., Xie, B., and Xu, W. (2004). Market reaction to voluntary announcements of audit committee appointments: The effect of financial expertise. *Journal of Accounting and Public Policy, 23 (4)*, 279-293.

De Nicolo, G. (2000). Size, charter value and risk in banking: an international perspective, *International Finance Discussion Papers No. 689*. Washington: Board of Governors of the Federal Reserve System (U.S.).

De Vries, C. G. (2005). The simple economics of bank fragility. *Journal of Banking & Finance, 29 (4)*, 803-825.

DeFond, M. L., Hann, R. N., and Hu, X. (2005). Does the Market Value Financial Expertise on Audit Committees of Boards of Directors? *Journal of Accounting Research, 43 (2)*, 153-193.

Demirgüç-Kunt, A. and Detragiache, E. (2002). Does deposit insurance increase banking system stability? An empirical investigation. *Journal of Monetary Economics, 49 (7)*, 1373-1406.

Demirgüç-Kunt, A. and Huizinga, H. (2010). Bank activity and funding strategies: The impact on risk and returns. *Journal of Financial Economics, 98 (3)*, 626-650.

Dermine, J. (2003). Banking in Europe: Past, present and future. In V. Gaspar, Hartmann, P., Sleijpen, O. (Ed.), *Proceedings of the 2nd ECB Central Banking Conference on the Transformation of the European Financial System*. Frankfurt am Main: ECB.

Deutsche Bundesbank. (2011). Statistik: Zeitreihen. Retrieved 15.02.2011: http://www.bundesbank.de/statistik/statistik_zeitreihen.php.

DeYoung, R., Hunter, W. C., and Udell, G. F. (2004). The Past, Present, and Probable Future for Community Banks. *Journal of Financial Services Research, 25 (2/3)*, 85.

Dhaliwal, D. S., Naiker, V., and Navissi, F. (2006). Audit Committee Financial Expertise, Corporate Governance and Accruals Quality: An Empirical Analysis, *Working Paper*. Tucson: University of Arizona.

Diamond, D. W. (1991). Monitoring and Reputation: The Choice between Bank Loans and Directly Placed Debt. *Journal of Political Economy, 99 (4)*, 689-721.

Diamond, D. W. and Rajan, R. G. (2001). Liquidity Risk, Liquidity Creation, and Financial Fragility: A Theory of Banking. *Journal of Political Economy, 109 (2)*, 287-327.

Drees, F., Keisers, M., and Schiereck, D. (2006). Zum Erfolg von Sparkassenfusionen – Aktuelle kasuistische Evidenz. *Zeitschrift für öffentliche und gemeinwirtschaftliche Unternehmen, 29*, 24-49.

Eisenberg, T., Sundgren, S., and Wells, M. T. (1998). Larger board size and decreasing firm value in small firms. *Journal of Financial Economics, 48 (1)*, 35-54.

Engerer, H. and Schrooten, M. (2004). *Untersuchung der Grundlagen und Entwicklungsperspektiven des Bankensektors in Deutschland (Dreisäulensystem)*. Berlin: DIW.

Erkens, D., Hung, M., and Matos, P. (2009). *Corporate Governance in the 2007-2008 Financial Crisis: Evidence from Financial Institutions Worldwide*. Paper presented at the 9th Bank Research Conference. Retrieved from www.fdic.gov/bank/analytical/CFR/bank_research_conference/annual_9th/Matos_P.pdf

Esty, B. C. (1998). The impact of contingent liability on commercial bank risk taking. *Journal of Financial Economics, 47 (2)*, 189-218.

Fama, E. F. and Jensen, M. C. (1983). Separation of Ownership and Control. *Journal of Law and Economics, 26 (2)*, 301-325.

Fellner, G., Güth, W., and Maciejovsky, B. (2004). Illusion of expertise in portfolio decisions: an experimental approach. *Journal of Economic Behavior & Organization, 55 (3)*, 355-376.

Fernandes, N. and Fich, E. M. (2009). Does Financial Experience Help Banks during Credit Crises?, *Mimeo*. Lausanne: IMD.

Fischer, K.-H. and Pfeil, C. (2004). Regulation and Competition in German Banking: An Assessment. In J. P. Krahnen and R. H. Schmidt (Eds.), *The German Financial System* (pp. 291-350). Oxford: Oxford University Press.

Fischhoff, B., Slovic, P., and Lichtenstein, S. (1977). Knowing with certainty: The appropriateness of extreme confidence. *Journal of Experimental Psychology: Human Perception and Performance, 3 (4)*, 552-564.

Gabriel, O. W. and Holtmann, E. (2005). *Handbuch Politisches System der Bundesrepublik Deutschland* (Vol. 3). München: Oldenbourg.

Galai, D. and Masulis, R. W. (1976). The option pricing model and the risk factor of stock. *Journal of Financial Economics, 3 (1-2)*, 53-81.

Garcia-Marco, T. and Robles-Fernández, M. D. (2008). Risk-taking behaviour and ownership in the banking industry: The Spanish evidence. *Journal of Economics and Business, 60 (4)*, 332-354.

Geiger, H. (1992). *Die deutsche Sparkassenorganisation* (Vol. 2). Frankfurt am Main: Fritz Knapp Verlag.

Goddard, J., Molyneux, P., and Wilson, J. O. S. (2004). The Profitability of European Banks: A cross-sectional and dynamic Panel Analysis. *The Manchester School, 72 (3)*, 363–381.

Goddard, J., Molyneux, P., Wilson, J. O. S., and Tavakoli, M. (2007). European banking: An overview. *Journal of Banking & Finance, 31 (7)*, 1911-1935.

Gomes, A. and Novaes, W. (1999). Multiple Large Shareholders in Corporate Governance, *Working Paper 005-99 Wharton School Rodney L. White Center for Financial Research*. Philadelphia: Univeristy of Pennsylvania.

González, F. (2005). Bank regulation and risk-taking incentives: An international comparison of bank risk. *Journal of Banking & Finance, 29 (5)*, 1153-1184.

Gorton, G. and Rosen, R. (1995). Corporate Control, Portfolio Choice, and the Decline of Banking. *The Journal of Finance, 50 (5)*, 1377-1420.

Gropp, R. and Köhler, M. (2010). Bank Owners or Bank Managers: Who is Keen on Risk? Evidence from the Financial Crisis, *Discussion Paper No. 10-013*. Mannheim: ZEW.

Grossman, R. S. (2001). Double Liability and Bank Risk Taking. *Journal of Money, Credit and Banking, 33 (2)*, 143-159.

Güner, A. B., Malmendier, U., and Tate, G. (2008). Financial expertise of directors. *Journal of Financial Economics, 88 (2)*, 323-354.

Hackethal, A. (2004). German Banks and Banking Structure. In J. P. Krahnen and R. H. Schmidt (Eds.), *The German Financial System* (pp. 71-105). Oxford: Oxford University Press.

Hackethal, A. and Schmidt, R. H. (2005). Structural Change in the German Banking System?, *Working Paper Series, Finance & Accounting No. 147*. Frankfurt am Main: Johann-Wolfgang Goethe University.

Hakenes, H., Schmidt, R. H., and Xie, R. (2009). Regional Banks and Economic Development: Evidence from German Savings Banks, *Working Paper*. Frankfurt am Main: Johann-Wolfgang Goethe University.

Hartmann-Wendels, T., Pfingsten, A., and Weber, M. (2007). *Bankbetriebslehre* (Vol. 4). Berlin, Heidelberg: Springer.

Hau, H. and Thum, M. (2008). Wie (in-)kompetent sind die Aufsichtsräte deutscher Banken? *Ifo Schnelldienst, 61 (19)*, 27-29.

Hau, H. and Thum, M. (2009). Subprime crisis and board (in-)competence: private versus public banks in Germany. *Economic Policy, 24 (60)*, 701-752.

Hempell, H. S. (2002). Testing for Competition Among German Banks, *Discussion Paper 04/02 Economic Research Centre of the Deutsche Bundesbank*. Frankfurt am Main: Deutsche Bundesbank.

Hermalin, B. E. and Weisbach, M. S. (1991). The Effects of Board Composition and Direct Incentives on Firm Performance. *Financial Management, 20 (4)*, 101-112.

Hermalin, B. E. and Weisbach, M. S. (2003). Boards of directors as an endogenously determined institution: a survey of the economic literature. *Economic Policy Review (Apr)*, 7-26.

Hoggarth, G., Reidhill, J., and Sinclair, P. (2004). On the resolution of banking crises: theory and evidence, *Working Paper no. 229*. London: Bank of England.

Hopt, K. J. and Leyens, P. C. (2004). Board Models in Europe - Recent Developments of Internal Corporate Governance Structures in Germany, the United Kingdom, France, and Italy, *ECGI Working Paper Series in Law, No. 18/2004*. Brussels: European Corporate Governance Institute.

Iannotta, G., Nocera, G., and Sironi, A. (2007). Ownership structure, risk and performance in the European banking industry. *Journal of Banking & Finance, 31 (7)*, 2127-2149.

Illueca, M., Norden, L., and Udell, G., F. . (2009). Liberalization, Corporate Governance, and Savings Banks, *Money and Finance Research group (Mo.Fi.R.), Dept. Economics, Working Paper no. 17*. Ancona: Università Politecnica delle Marche.

International Monetary Fund. (2010). Global financial stability report, April 2010, *World economic and financial surveys*. Washington: International Monetary Fund.

Jensen, M. C. (1993). The Modern Industrial Revolution, Exit, and the Failure of Internal Control Systems. *The Journal of Finance, 48 (3)*, 831-880.

Jensen, M. C. and Meckling, W. H. (1976). Theory of the firm: Managerial behavior, agency costs and ownership structure. *Journal of Financial Economics, 3 (4)*, 305-360.

Jensen, M. C. and Ruback, R. S. (1983). The market for corporate control: The scientific evidence. *Journal of Financial Economics, 11 (1-4)*, 5-50.

John, K., John, T. A., and Senbet, L. W. (1991). Risk-shifting incentives of depository institutions: A new perspective on federal deposit insurance reform. *Journal of Banking & Finance, 15 (4-5)*, 895-915.

John, K., Litov, L., and Yeung, B. (2008). Corporate Governance and Risk-Taking. *Journal of Finance, 63 (4)*, 1679-1728.

John, K. and Senbet, L. W. (1998). Corporate governance and board effectiveness. *Journal of Banking & Finance, 22 (4)*, 371-403.

Jungmann, C. (2006). The Effectiveness of Corporate Governance in One-Tier and Two-Tier Board Systems –Evidence from the UK and Germany–. *European Company and Financial Law Review, 3 (4)*, 426-474.

Kahane, Y. (1977). Capital adequacy and the regulation of financial intermediaries. *Journal of Banking & Finance, 1 (2)*, 207-218.

Kammlott, C. and Schiereck, D. (2000). Wachstum, Förderungsauftrag und Markterfolg von deutschen Kreditgenossenschaften. *Zeitschrift für das gesamte Genossenschaftswesen, 50*, 265-281.

Kaplan, S. N. (1994). Top Executives, Turnover, and Firm Performance in Germany. *Journal of Law, Economics, & Organization, 10 (1)*, 142-159.

Kareken, J. H. and Wallace, N. (1978). Deposit Insurance and Bank Regulation: A Partial-Equilibrium Exposition. *The Journal of Business, 51 (3)*, 413-438.

Kaufman, G. G. (2002). Too big to fail in banking: What remains? *The Quarterly Review of Economics and Finance, 42 (3)*, 423-436.

Kaufmann, D., Kraay, A., and Mastruzzi, M. (2009). Governance Matters VIII: Governance Indicators for 1996-2008 *World Bank Policy Research, Working Paper Series, no. 4978*. Washington D.C.: The World Bank.

Keeley, M. C. (1990). Deposit Insurance, Risk, and Market Power in Banking. *American Economic Review, 80 (5)*, 1183-1200.

Kim, D. and Santomero, A. M. (1988). Risk in Banking and Capital Regulation. *The Journal of Finance, 43 (5)*, 1219-1233.

Kirkpatrick, G. (2009). The Corporate Governance Lessons from the Financial Crisis, *Financial Market Trends*. Paris: OECD.

Kleff, V. and Weber, M. (2005). Payout Policy and Owners' Interests – Evidence from German Savings Banks, *ZEW Discussion Paper No. 05-59*. Mannheim: ZEW.

Klein, A. (1998). Firm Performance and Board Committee Structure. *Journal of Law and Economics, 41 (1)*, 275-304.

Koehn, M. and Santomero, A. M. (1980). Regulation of Bank Capital and Portfolio Risk. *The Journal of Finance, 35 (5)*, 1235-1244.

Koetter, M., Nestmann, T., Stolz, S., and Wedow, M. (2004). Structures and Trends in German Banking, *Working Paper No. 1225*. Kiel: Kiel Institute for the World Economy.

Köhler, M. (2010). Corporate Governance and Current Regulation in the German Banking Sector: An Overview and Assessment, *ZEW Discussion Paper No. 10-002*. Mannheim: ZEW.

Kroszner, R. S., Laeven, L., and Klingebiel, D. (2007). Banking crises, financial dependence, and growth. *Journal of Financial Economics, 84 (1)*, 187-228.

La Porta, R., Lopez-de-Silanes, F., Shleifer, A., and Vishny, R., W. (1998). Law and Finance. *Journal of Political Economy, 106 (6)*, 1113-1155.

Laeven, L. and Levine, R. (2009). Bank governance, regulation and risk taking. *Journal of Financial Economics, 93 (2)*, 259-275.

Lee, Y. S., Rosenstein, S., and Wyatt, J. G. (1999). The value of financial outside directors on corporate boards. *International Review of Economics & Finance, 8 (4)*, 421-431.

Levine, R. (1997). Financial Development and Economic Growth: Views and Agenda. *Journal of Economic Literature, 35 (2)*, 688-726.

Levine, R. (2004). *The Corporate Governance of Banks - a concise discussion of concepts and evidence.* Washington D.C.: The World Bank.

Levine, R. (2006). *Finance and Growth: Theory and Evidence.* Amsterdam: Elsevier.

Luttmer, N. (2010). Bank-Aufsichtsräte müssen nachsitzen. Retrieved from http://www.ftd.de/unternehmen/finanzdienstleister/:machtdemonstration-ba-fin-sortiert-aufsichtsraete-von-banken-aus/50163321.html

Magalhaes, R., Gutiérrez, M., and Tribó, J. A. (2008). *Banks' ownership structure, risk and performance.* Paper presented at the The European Financial Management Association 2008 Meeting. Retrieved from http://www.efmaefm.org/0EFMAMEETINGS/EFMA%20ANNUAL%20MEETINGS/2008-athens/2008.shtml#m

Manne, H. G. (1965). Mergers and the Market for Corporate Control. *Journal of Political Economy, 73 (2)*, 110-120.

Marcus, A. J. (1984). Deregulation and bank financial policy. *Journal of Banking & Finance, 8 (4)*, 557-565.

Mehran, H. (1995). Executive compensation structure, ownership, and firm performance. *Journal of Financial Economics, 38 (2)*, 163-184.

Mehran, H., Morrison, A., and Shapiro, J. (2011). Corporate Governance and Banks: What Have We Learned from the Financial Crisis?, *Staff Reports, no. 502.* New York: Federal Reserve Bank of New York.

Merton, R. C. (1977). An analytic derivation of the cost of deposit insurance and loan guarantees An application of modern option pricing theory. *Journal of Banking & Finance, 1 (1)*, 3-11.

Minton, B. A., Taillard, J. P. A., and Williamson, R. (2010). Do Independence and Financial Expertise of the Board Matter for Risk Taking and Performance?, *Fisher College of Business Working Paper Series, 2010-03-014.* Columbus: Ohio State University.

Moore, D. A. and Healy, P. J. (2007). The Trouble with Overconfidence, *Working paper, Carnegie Mellon University, David A. Tepper School of Business and Ohio State University, Department of Economics.* Pittsburgh: Carnegie Mellon University.

Moshirian, F. (2011). The global financial crisis and the evolution of markets, institutions and regulation. *Journal of Banking & Finance, 35 (3)*, 502-511.

Mullineux, A. (2006). The corporate governance of banks. *Journal of Financial Regulation and Compliance 14 (4)*, 375-382.

Naßmacher, H. and Naßmacher, K.-H. (2007). *Kommunalpolitik in Deutschland* (Vol. 2). Wiesbaden: Verlag für Sozialwissenschaften.

O'Hara, M. and Shaw, W. (1990). Deposit Insurance and Wealth Effects: The Value of Being "Too Big to Fail". *The Journal of Finance, 45 (5)*, 1587-1600.

Odean, T. (1998). Volume, Volatility, Price, and Profit When All Traders Are Above Average. *The Journal of Finance, 53 (6)*, 1887-1934.

Pang, J. and Wu, H. (2009). Financial markets, financial dependence, and the allocation of capital. *Journal of Banking & Finance, 33 (5)*, 810-818.

Pfingsten, A. (2010). Stakeholdermanagement bei Sparkassen. In Wissenschaftsförderung der Sparkassen-Finanzgruppe e.V. (Ed.), *Geschäftspolitische Steuerung, Die Sparkassen zwischen Renditeorientierung und Gemeinwohl* (Vol. 1). Bonn: Deutscher Sparkassenverlag.

Rajan, R. G. (1992). Insiders and Outsiders: The Choice between Informed and Arm's-Length Debt. *The Journal of Finance, 47 (4)*, 1367-1400.

Rajan, R. G. and Zingales, L. (1998). Financial Dependence and Growth. *The American Economic Review, 88 (3)*, 559-586.

Rosenstein, S. and Wyatt, J. G. (1990). Outside directors, board independence, and shareholder wealth. *Journal of Financial Economics, 26 (2)*, 175-191.

Ross, S. A., Westefield, R. W., and Jaffe, J. F. (2003). *Corporate Finance* (Vol. 6). New York: McGraw-Hill.

Roy, A. D. (1952). Safety First and the Holding of Assets. *Econometrica, 20 (3)*, 431-449.

Sapienza, P. (2004). The effects of government ownership on bank lending. *Journal of Financial Economics, 72 (2)*, 357-384.

Saunders, A., Strock, E., and Travlos, N. G. (1990). Ownership Structure, Deregulation, and Bank Risk Taking. *Journal of Finance, 45 (2)*, 643-654.

Schiereck, D. and Timmreck, C. (2001). Unternehmenszusammenschlüsse von Kreditgenossenschaften. In Ernst & Young (Ed.), *Mergers & Acquisitions in der Praxis* (pp. 167-188). Frankfurt am Main: FAZ-Institut.

Schmidt, R. H. (2009). The Political Debate about Savings Banks. *Schmalenbach Business Review (sbr), 61 (4)*, 366-392.

Schöndube-Pirchegger, B. and Schöndube, J. R. (2011). Reputation concerns and herd behavior of audit committees - A corporate governance problem. *Journal of Accounting and Public Policy, 30 (4)*, 327–347.

Schröder, A. (2007). Prinzipien der Panelanalyse. In S. Albers, D. Klapper, U. Konradt, A. Walter and J. Wolf (Eds.), *Methodik der empirischen Forschung* (pp. 261-276). Wiesbaden: Gabler.

Sharpe, W., F. (1977). Bank Capital Adequacy, Deposit Insurance and Security Values, Part I, *NBER Working Paper no. 209*. Stanford: National Bureau of Economic Research.

Shehzad, C. T., de Haan, J., and Scholtens, B. (2010). The impact of bank ownership concentration on impaired loans and capital adequacy. *Journal of Banking & Finance, 34 (2)*, 399-408.

Shleifer, A. and Vishny, R. W. (1986). Large Shareholders and Corporate Control. *Journal of Political Economy, 94 (3)*, 461-488.

Stein, J. C. (2002). Information Production and Capital Allocation: Decentralized versus Hierarchical Firms. *The Journal of Finance, 57 (5)*, 1891-1921.

Sullivan, R. J. and Spong, K. R. (2007). Manager wealth concentration, ownership structure, and risk in commercial banks. *Journal of Financial Intermediation, 16 (2)*, 229-248.

Theurl, T. (2002). Shareholder Value und genossenschaftlicher Förderauftrag - Zwei unvereinbare strategische Ausrichtungen? In T. Theurl and R. Greve (Eds.), *Vom Modell zur Umsetzung - Strategische Herausforderungen für Genossenschaften, Münstersche Schriften zur Kooperation* (Vol. 54). Aachen: Shaker.

Vins, O. (2008). How Politics Influence State-owned Banks - the Case of German Savings Banks, *Working Paper Series, Finance & Accounting no. 191*. Frankfurt am Main: Johann-Wofgang Goethe University.

Walker, D. (2009). *A Review of Corporate Governance in UK banks and other Financial Industry Entities: Final Recommendations.* London: The Walker Review Secretariat.

Westman, H. (2010). Comparison of profitability and risk in commercial, savings and cooperative banks, *Working Paper*. Helsinki: HANKEN School of Economics.

Wheelock, D. C. and Wilson, P. W. (2000). Why Do Banks Disappear? The Determinants of U.S. Bank Failures and Acquisitions. *The Review of Economics and Statistics, 82 (1)*, 127-138.

Wingendorf, C. (2005). Corporate Governance für Sparkassen - Gesellschaftsrechtliche und aufsichtsrechtliche Entwicklungen. In S. Müller, T. Jöhnk and A. Bruns (Eds.), *Beiträge zum Finanz-, Rechnungs- und Bankwesen* (pp. 287-301). Wiesbaden: DUV/GWV Fachverlage.

World Bank. (2010). World Development Indicators (WDI). Retrieved 01.02.2011, from The World Bank: http://data.worldbank.org/indicator

Yermack, D. (1996). Higher market valuation of companies with a small board of directors. *Journal of Financial Economics, 40 (2)*, 185-211.

Corporate Finance and Governance

Herausgegeben von Dirk Schiereck

Band 1 Sebastian Michael Gläsner: Return Patterns of German Open-End Real Estate Funds. An Empirical Explanation of Smooth Fund Returns. 2010.

Band 2 Patrick Ams: Directors' Dealings and Insider Trading in Germany. An Empirical Analysis. 2010.

Band 3 Joachim Vogt: Value Creation within the Construction Industry. A Study of Strategic Takeovers. 2011.

Band 4 Fabian Braemisch: Underpricing, Long-Run Performance, and Valuation of Initial Public Offerings. 2011.

Band 5 Matthäus Markus Sielecki: Creating and Governing an Integrated Market for Retail Banking Services in Europe. A Conceptual-Empirical Study of the Role of Regulation in Promoting a Single Euro Payments Area. 2011.

Band 6 Arne Wilkes: Determinants of Credit Spreads. An Empirical Analysis for the European Corporate Bond Market. 2011.

Band 7 Dirk Schiereck / Martin Setzer (Hrsg.): Bankerfolg und Akquisitionen. Aktuelle Erkenntnisse zur Konsolidierung und Restrukturierung der Finanzindustrie. 2011.

Band 8 Steffen Meinshausen: M&A Activity, Divestitures and Initial Public Offerings in the Fashion Industry. 2012.

Band 9 Malte Helmut Raudszus: Financial Return Risk and the Effect on Shareholder Wealth. 2012.

Band 10 Ramit Mehta: Mergers and Acquisitions in the Global Brewing Industry. A Capital Market Perspective. 2012.

Band 11 Marcel Normann: The Influence of German Top Executives on Corporate Policy and Firm Performance. 2012.

Band 12 Christoph Böhm: Risk-Adjusted Performance and Bank Governance Structures. 2013.

www.peterlang.de